Dining at the Lineman's Shack

Dining at the Lineman's Shack

John Weston

THE UNIVERSITY OF ARIZONA PRESS   TUCSON

The University of Arizona Press
© 2003 John Weston
First Printing
All rights reserved

08   07   06   05   04   03   6   5   4   3   2   1

"The Goat Picnic" and "Hunger" were previously published in the novella
Goat Songs. "Two Ways of Leaving Athens" was published in *Rara Avis.*

Library of Congress Cataloging-in-Publication Data

Weston, John, 1932–
Dining at the lineman's shack / John Weston.
p. cm.
ISBN 0-8165-2282-0 (acid-free paper) — ISBN 0-8165-2283-9
(pbk. : acid-free paper)
1. Weston, John, 1932—Childhood and youth. 2. Weston, John,
1932—Homes and haunts—Arizona. 3. Novelists, American—
20th century—Family relationships. 4. Novelists, American—
20th century—Biography. 5. Arizona—Social life and customs—
Fiction. 6. Arizona—Social life and customs. 7. Depressions—
1929—Arizona. 8. Cookery, American—Arizona. 9. Poor
families—Arizona. I. Title.
PS3573.E924 Z464 2003
813'.54—dc21
2002014100

British Library Cataloguing-in-Publication Data
A catalogue record for this book is available from the British Library.

for Jim McBroom
and in memory of Eloine

Contents

Acknowledgments

No one suggested I write this book, nor did anyone say I should not, so I have all of them to thank. No one read it before it landed on the publisher's desk; therefore, I have no list of people to blame for its inadequacies. However, I should especially acknowledge Jim, my companion of more than thirty years and to whom the book is dedicated, for showing no interest in reading the manuscript, thus avoiding a family squabble.

I do heartily thank Richard Shelton, whom the University of Arizona Press engaged as a reader, for his warm, enthusiastic endorsement before publication, and Ginny Croft, whose patient editing helped make the book much better than it started out to be.

Dining at the Lineman's Shack

A Goat in the Oven

*W*hen The Palace reopened on Montezuma Street, the new owner served mountain lion *barbacoa*. Baked all night in an underground pit, the cat slid around, as all meat will when so treated, between two slices of white bread—either Rainbow or Holsum, Arizona's only bakeries of reach. Chicken white if you sucked the sauce off a piece, it tasted like nothing so much as its dressing. But in the glow of illegal beers and daring friends, I devoured my sandwich and swaggered on into a life of experimental gastronomy.

Mountain lions became a protected species soon after and have, over the years, returned to at least a fraction of their former count, roaming solitarily over a boundless range in the West on great padded feet, "Walking silently over the rocks," as the Navajo say, despite the unambivalent attitude of ranchers who resent providing them with lamb, mutton, or veal, and hunters who resent the natural fact that, to a lion, it's deer season all year. A grown lion will kill every four or five days, with luck, accused by hunters of eating only the choicest parts, such as the heart and liver, leaving the carcass for the coyotes and buzzards to pick. This senseless depopulation of game infuriates riflemen. Actually, the lion probably hasn't abandoned its kill but is lying up in some bushes a hundred yards off—farther if a female with kittens—waiting until evening to return for another meal. Not a healthy spot for a disgruntled hunter to hang about kicking dirt.

Elusive wanderers, mountain lions are rarely seen. The only live one I've ever spotted was standing in a pasture in Laguna Canyon, of all places, contemplatively viewing the traffic. A lion will carry off a dog if hungry enough, as a coyote will a house cat, because between the earth and its creatures he makes little distinction.

The barbecue sauce in which the lion was slathered at The Palace was about the same as it has been forever, the ubiquitous cerement for male outdoor cookery. It takes no pained imagination to see the Neanderthal, slouching at the smoky entrance of his cave with the foreleg of a small quadruped, ripping off chunks of charred flesh, ruminating on the middle distance, and occasionally dipping the joint in a rock depression where he has collected a sauce of blood, honey, and flies. If it's true our responses to things in the present are but a kind of biological remembrance of things past, then we can better understand man's need for barbecue sauce. Charcoal searing, or the open fire, is the most primitive form of cooking, hardly advanced in a hundred centuries except for the convenience of lighter fluid and gas.

We connect backward in a collective unconscious, after all, as Loren Eisley said in an essay about his dog growling over a ten-thousand-year-old fossilized femur. Sometimes we pause to think, this is a terrifying passage we're making, this fragment in time we occupy, this gnat of significance we call me, over which religious fundamentalists have so long fumed and railed, trying to get a purchase on its meaning.

Not so long, really. Maybe five thousand years. And they're going to die too, and be put away in an expensive and hilarious way, like the rest of us.

Which takes me back not quite so far, down into Skull Valley, the Goat Picnic, life in a lineman's shack, disquisitions on swamp life, rotting water, and the complex experience of finding enough to eat during the Great Depression.

Mother's name was Eloine, a moniker she regretted because no one knew how to pronounce it without instruction. Spelled like *Elaine* but with an *o,* it is Ehlówyn or, alternately, Eloweén, in the South 'Lowyn or, finally, Connie, a nickname she adopted with relief when reentering the workforce as a cook late in life.

Modestly educated at Peabody College in Nashville, she became a teacher before marriage to a man thirteen years older, the brother of her sister's husband, and began following his drift throughout North America, a bird of passage seeking the rainbow's gilded bucket. She got high marks in organic chemistry, and in a surviving notebook I read: "Art is the lasting interpretation of life through fit symbols; literature by means of language," and the startling observation that Shakespeare deliberately walked into gloom so he might experience its weight.

At ten, when her mother died on the Old Homeplace in Mount Juliet, Eloine became cook for twelve people, counting her father, her siblings, and the farmhands. It is no wonder, then, by the time I came along thirty years later, she was a master with a small repertoire from which she could coax ideas surprising even to herself. Necessity wedded to goods driven by invention in order to keep from starving or going nuts.

Books were mainly unavailable in our house, but Eloine procured them occasionally, and though with time seldom on her hands exclusively for reading, she kept one propped open near her breadboard, snatching a paragraph as she could, nearly blinding herself with *Gone With the Wind*. Illiterate masochist at four or five, I repeatedly begged her to read *Bambi* aloud as the flour flew at her board. She never failed to cry. "Po' Bambi," she would invariably say, wiping her eyes on her apron. "Po' little deer."

"There are big jackrabbits back up there on Old Baldy," the Dad told us. "Giant rabbits, big as a burro." From time to time he brought home chunks of these illusive beasts, butchered and headless. Slow to understand the obvious signs, it wasn't until I turned twenty-five I realized with a jolt he was poaching deer out of season for a family always on the brink of starvation.

Without refrigeration or any other means of keeping the meat in its raw state, we gorged on this fabulous hare, and Eloine put up some in Mason jars, even in blistering hot weather when the woodstove made an inferno of the indoors, or crafted jerky of it on the hot tin roof. The thoughts below apply equally for legal or poached animals.

Wild venison, leaner, with a gamier taste than ranch-raised varieties, needs a beneficent soak. A marinade of red wine, onions, bay leaves, and juniper berries or whatnot, in which the loin saturates overnight, will do much to temper its rank taste, a method the French use to treat wild boar. Eloine, knowing nothing of wine, used vinegar, onions, juniper berries available in the hills, lots of salt and pepper, sugar, a smear of lard. After roasting the venison, she would add a cup or two of this mix, along with some red currant jelly, to the pan drippings to make a lusty-looking gravy. Modern chefs say venison should be cooked somewhat rare: not in Eloine's kitchen. There meat invariably roasted until it fell from the bone, in part because her boys would not eat it if they could discern the slightest blush of pink, like the serving girls in *Death Comes for the Archbishop,* who looked with horror at the delicate stream of pink juice that followed Father Joseph's knife (he was French), and in part because any living organism would be crisped beyond harm.

Venison, from the Latin *venatio,* or "hunt," adapts naturally and etymologically to sauce *à la Diane,* named for the huntress. Lots of pepper, cream, and red jelly, reduced and strained.

Roasted Wild Venison

First, concoct a marinade, enough to cover at least half of the meat you've chosen. For a 3- to 5-pound roast, combine:

1 bottle (750 ml) red wine or port
2 to 3 cups water, as needed
2 to 3 onions, chopped
2 to 3 bay leaves
10 juniper berries, crushed
10 peppercorns, crushed
1 tablespoon kosher salt
1 to 2 tablespoons balsamic vinegar

Add anything else you think might be good, such as charred, seeded, and peeled chiles.

At least 6 hours before you start cooking the roast, place the meat in a roasting pan, cover with the marinade, and refrigerate, turning occasionally.

When ready to cook, preheat the oven to 425°F.

Drain the roast, saving 3 cups of the marinade. Pat the venison dry, season it with salt and pepper, and rub it all over with cooking oil or lard, even going so far as to wrap it with bacon (venison has so little natural fat), fresh garlic, and dried herbs. Insert a meat thermometer into it as you would for beef and cook to the desired doneness. It should be no more well done than medium-rare, 7 or 8 minutes per pound.

If you roast the meat on a bed of chopped carrots, shallots, and fennel with 1 cup of the marinade, you'll then have a base for a sauce. Take the cooked roast out of the pan, cover it, and let it rest for 10 minutes while you make the sauce: deglaze the pan, adding 1 to 2 cups of the marinade. Reduce this by half, then strain, discarding the vegetables. Return the sauce to the pan; add 2 to 3 tablespoons of cream and 2 to 3 tablespoons of red currant jelly. Stir and taste, adding more salt and pepper as needed. At the last moment, add ⅓ cup sherry.

Prime cuts of venison, such as back strap and tender-loin, are merely seasoned and—yes—barbecued. They need no marinating or long cooking.

The currant jelly mentioned above is generic. You can make a substitute from prickly pear cactus fruit, a hazardous undertaking Eloine tried once or twice but never comfortably. Like gathering pi-ñon nuts, despite their being free for the taking, she found the task both labor-intensive and degrading, something associated vaguely in her mind with Indian food. If you insist on making cactus syrup, I refer you to Janos Wilder, who seems to take joy from it in his extraordinary Tucson restaurant (see his book, *Janos,* page 27). Incidental old Oaxa-can trick: If you're going to cook cactus paddles, *nopales,* boil them up in water with two copper pennies dropped into the pot to prevent sliminess. This might work for okra too.

Eloine had a formidable silvery metal grinder she attached to the table, through which, with a wooden tool, she pushed chunks of meat otherwise too tough to digest, that is, most of the giant jackrabbit.

To make venison jerky, which will keep virtually forever without refrigeration, Eloine cut slices of meat about the size of thick bacon strips, rubbed them with cayenne, salt, lots of black pepper (alleged to keep off the flies or be confused with them), and a souse of bottled sauce if she had some, a touch of molasses. These she laid out on anything flat she could find—cookie sheets, boards—and inveigled some boy to climb up the lean-to ladder that she, with good reason, greatly distrusted, and place the flats of meat on the tin roof, covered over, more or less, with wire screen. Left there several days in sizzling temperatures, the meat dried out and became indestructible.

Meat desiccated in the sun like this, social historian Fernand Braudel tells us, goes back at least to colonial American times, the *carne do sol* of Brazil, the *charque* of Argentina, all produced mainly for the consumption of slaves and for export to the European poor. Travelers on long sea journeys sometimes had to eat slices of sun-dried beef and buffalo in lieu of starvation, though they likened it to pieces of wood swarming with worms.

Restaurateur George Lang, writing of Hungarian cooking during the times of the Magyars, tells of a jerky variant. Shepherds cut their meat into cubes, stewed it in its own juices with onions until the pot went dry, laid it out in the sun to parch, and thereafter put it in bags made of the sheep's stomach, easy to store or carry into battle, though redolent. When they felt like *gulyás,* they had but to take out a piece or two, add to a pot of water, and reheat. For an army on the move, this was a much more practical solution than driving along a herd of cattle, precursor to the ‍K rations of World War II.

These days, jerky is usually made in an electric food dehydrator, the same kind used for drying herbs, or a low oven. There is a depraved agglomeration of possibilities into which the strips may be dipped, dredged, brushed, squashed, masked, and massaged: teriyaki, sweet-and-sour, barbecue, Worcestershire, A-1, Louisiana hot, Tabasco, lime-and-tequila, chili powder, on and on.

Because goats, *chivos,* along with cattle, formed the economic basis of the landowners of Skull Valley, there were far more of them than people, as I have been told is the case with pigs in Iowa. Some were specialized, such as the Angoras, raised for their long, satiny hair used to make Angora wool or mohair, a popular upholstery fabric in those days. The breed apparently originated in Turkey, where it was—perhaps still is—used when butchered to make *pastourma,* something like our jerky. Other goats were raised for meat, milk, cheese, hides, and, I suppose, to create more baby goats. Thus there was a certain logic, actually more Dionysian than Apollonian, to our annual Goat Picnic of Skull Valley, celebrated in midsummer.

Our word *tragedy* comes from the Greek *tragodos,* "goat singer," that is, a tragic poet and singer, which in turn is from *tragos,* "he-goat," and *oide,* "song," like our *ode.* From Aeschylus, Sophocles, and Euripides we know most of what there is to know about extant Greek tragedy, but before them, in the mists of a more primitive time, singers dressed up in goatskins, and we think goat sacrifices occurred (even sacrifice of the singer in his mohair). Something to do with fertility and spring. With sex and fecundity and newly planted seed. Ritual of blood, eating and drinking, ejaculation, admonitory songs to the gods. Mesolithic man beginning to hum.

In the Renaissance, gluttony was paired with lechery, the one following upon the other, thus the overdeveloped banquets of the rich coupled with scenes of sexual debauchery, the simple vineyard lunch with illicit dalliance—or with a couple who hoped to make it illicit before the afternoon waned. These blowouts weren't exclusively the privilege of nobles or materialistic monks. Daily food for most was boringly farinaceous, most often a chunk of bread in thin vegetable soup. Only at the tables of the rich was meat or fish seen with frequency, or milk, butter, eggs, and cheese, according to Braudel, though the Italian scholar Giovanni Rebora disagrees, claiming there was more meat available than we might think, horse, mule, and donkey, for instance, especially in cities along the vast European pack train routes. But the peasants, too, when they had excuse, such as a wedding or funeral or religious holiday, broke loose from daily misery, ate everything they could get their hands on—even though much less than their masters—got as drunk as possible, and lay about in the stubble rapidly producing bastards, to the dismay of clerical moralists. Some legislation went so far as to limit the number and types of dishes, as well as musicians, on big occasions, partly, thus ran a weak argument, so as not to ruffle the jealousies or imagination of the lower classes.

By the sixteenth century, English banquet chefs were dazzling their patrons with descants on nearly all living flesh except cats, rats, dogs, and slithering things. Goats, boars, deer, sheep, dormice, hedgehogs, dolphins, sparrows, robins, storks, and gulls—on and on the list rambles, as if gluttony, like sexual longing, could be satiated only by finding yet newer flesh to devour. For the noble pleasure seeker, a hedgehog, skinned, boned, stewed, then reinserted into its hide and presented on a platter surrounded by whole roasted, truffled, week-old goslings, may have been a thing of carnal joy. For the peasant, the hedgehog snuffled along between life and starvation. Like the extravagantly bored Elizabethan omnivores sated by ordinary viands, Eloine had momentary mad flashes about unusual food possibilities, except for an opposing reason, as we read that a starving person will hallucinate over eating anything available—shoe leather, goggles, weeds, gophers taken raw with beating heart.

In any case, by stretching historic imagination, we might deduce that the Skull Valley Goat Picnic, our local rite of excess, came down in a direct line from the Renaissance summer binge.

As in the Mexican *barbacoa,* the sacrificed animals were cooked overnight in pits. First the cooks (men, of course) set a deep layer of charcoal afire. They placed the butchered *cabrito* in large, deep, rectangular pans with handles for lifting, soused the meat with barbecue sauce, and covered it with wet gunnysacks, a lid of corrugated tin, more hot coals. Then they shoveled over a foot or two of earth and left the meat to bake for ten or twelve hours in its shallow, smoking grave.

The next afternoon women brought picnic dishes, the groaning boards were laid out on trestles, the goat pans were dug up, and the feast began. In memory, there isn't much difference in taste between this goat meat and the mountain lion engorged a few years later, due to the approximately synonymous barbecue sauce.

Everyone showed up at the Goat Picnic except the cowboys who, if they had a Saturday afternoon off, sure as heck wouldn't spend it with a bunch of families and their howling, puking kids. They'd take off for Whiskey Row, up in town, and get started on a good drunk early. There wouldn't be any footloose women there till dark, but no matter; they could lean on a bar, push their straw hats back, cock their butts, and jaw (slowly, almost silently) about horses, the price of beef, some-body's rodeo, a broke leg. Show off, without thinking to, their tight flowered shirts, their tooled belts and silver buckles. Their dress boots with colored butterflies on them, or steer horns or turquoise thunder-birds. Some, the sharp ones, wore spurs with fancy shanks inlaid with another metal or turquoise, star-shaped spokes on the rowels. They'd jangle along wearing these at rodeos, even if they were only riding up on their own horse to observe, but not in the bars. There spurs would be a hazard. People tripping over them, getting tangled up with the guy next to you, fall on your ass.

The Goat Picnic

MIDSUMMER. Under an overhanging cut in the high creek bank where the swallows nested, we shared the stolen wine and listened to the actor tell us of tragedy, the celebrating in temple and field. He leaped to his feet and, crouching like a baboon or a human pretending to be a goat, shook his curly hair and acted out the parts of his drama. We fell back laughing and howled at him and tried to tie horns made of sticks on each other's head.

Over his bare shoulders he wore one of the silken-haired goat-skins taken from his father's fence, where they had been hung the day before to dry. He pranced and crouched in the sand, accompanied everywhere by an escort of shiny flies, and coming close to us, holding us with his reddening eyes and his hands, told us of the death of Osiris. His telling of it and the wine together brought tremors to our own shoulders, as if we could feel the cold fresh flesh.

Above us and away from the creek fifty yards in the grassy area enclosed by the nine huge cottonwoods, the others, the adults and the children, were getting up games of softball or horseshoes or sack races, or drowsing on blankets or suckling their infants or discussing the academic question of when the custom of the Goat Picnic began in the valley. However important the question, the answer was not. Earlier in the afternoon we had all eaten from the tables, particularly from the red gelatin with banana slices in it and the pale goat meat in red sauce that the actor's father and other men had begun cooking the day before in the underground pit. As they were needed, the pans, years ago fashioned for the annual occasion, were uncovered and lifted smoking from the pit. Beneath, the foot-deep mesquite coals burned red and white when the air reached them. The buried meat had bubbled in the sauce all night from the heat of the coals, covered with wet burlap and thick leaves and earth.

The Goat Picnic brought everyone together, even the cattle ranchers with the goat men, the recluses and the derelicts, like the old white-stubbled man who lived in the stable behind the store, subsisting on rotted produce tossed out the back door, fruit from the orchards, the offspring of small birds and animals, and anything alcoholic he could acquire with a tiny check sent each month because of his participation in a war. It was through him we had wine, taken from his hoard under the stable straw where he thought it safe. He had stood by the pit smiling, displaying his few yellow teeth, holding his plate and lilting faintly.

And it brought out people like Margery Hanrum, tough and mannish, reticent, and her slender hired man, who, according to common knowledge, was hired to do nothing more than operate her ranch; and the night stationmaster, who ordinarily devoted days to his ducks and dahlias; and the preacher with his drove of children and the wife with black hairs on her legs. He pronounced a lengthy blessing over the tables, his arms crucified in the air as the gelatins melted.

In the creek, under the cut of the bank, we broke open Mexican pomegranates and sucked out the seeds and the painter made panic designs on our faces with the juice. One of us ran a few steps away and, bending with his hands on his stomach, vomited violently while we followed and moved around him. We put him down kicking in the cold water. Because he shivered we got in with him, and the poet pronounced words over us all.

Above, near the nine trees, the games dwindled with the afternoon. I could imagine the whining children wiping their fingers through leftover cake and meringue. Certain families who had a long drive ahead or stock at home to be tended before dark drove away waving. Women moved slowly among the tables, searching for their Pyrex dishes and their forks, packing them in boxes. The men began to sit on the fenders of pickups to talk and drink politely from one another's bottles of whiskey.

We came howling up from the creek with the red sun behind us, the actor leading in his goatskin, the musician next, piping three notes from a fresh willow whistle. We wove among the remaining people, causing them at first to draw back and then to laugh and salute us with long drinks from their bottles. We circled one pretty girl until she held her hands over her breasts and her father looked worried. Then we found the old derelict veteran standing opposite the pit as if to warm himself, showing his yellow teeth. We gave him a cup of his own wine.

The men brought more whiskey from under their pickup seats. Two young cowboys joined our snaking line, then several other men and girls. The women clapped their hands and laughed and we believed ourselves extraordinary as the day ended. Someone uncased a guitar and the musician gave away his whistle for a borrowed harmonica. We had real music to dance to and call down the night by. The poet began reciting songs to gods, lifting his voice above the music. A man turned on the headlights of his pickup. The actor pranced into the light with his goatskin and his face red from the pomegranates and pantomimed the poet's stories. The rest of us danced in circles like Navajos, pulled and plucked at by the people. Little girls giggled and lifted their innocent skirts.

As the actor and the poet sank in each other's arms, suddenly the wife of one of the goat ranchers, an ordinary, middle-aged woman, hurried into the center of light, holding in her hand a single piece of her garments. She lifted up her arms and, with her head back, danced clumsily and naked before us all until the guitar and the harmonica stopped as if stunned. For a moment nobody moved, then another woman screamed inside the darkness, and then the woman's husband ran to her, trying to hide all of her with his outstretched hands, and someone switched off the lights.

People began moving quietly in the dark. Car doors opened and shut, letting light briefly onto the occupants. A man said, We'd better fill up the pit. That gave us something to do, gathered around it taking turns with the shovels until the pit was filled in and the ground made level when we walked on it. Even that, we did in the dark.

Someone said, I promised the old man a ride, have you seen him?

The cars and the pickups moved away from the nine trees. We sat together on a fallen limb and watched their headlights work over the winding dusty road. After a while we began talking again of what we wanted to become because, I think, none of us knew the words to explain the knowledge of power.

Mexican Birria
Goat in the Ordinary Kitchen

2 kid or lamb legs, 8 pounds total
8 dried guajillo chiles
4 dried ancho chiles
3 to 4 cups beef broth
3 tomatoes
10 cloves garlic
1 tablespoon black peppercorns
5 to 10 whole cloves
2 teaspoons cumin powder
2 sprigs thyme
2 sprigs oregano
3 to 4 bay leaves
5 tablespoons oil
⅓ cup vinegar
1 teaspoon salt (or more)
½ cup mezcal or tequila

A day ahead, cut as much meat as possible from the bones into large chunks; keep the bones. Prick the meat all over to let the marinade enter. Place the meat and bones in a roasting pan.

Stem and seed the chiles, then heat them directly over a flame or toast in a hot skillet for a couple of minutes. Put them in a pan with 1 cup of the broth and simmer over low heat 20 minutes. Blacken and somewhat blister the tomatoes; peel. Peel the garlic.

Puree the chiles, tomatoes, and garlic in a food processor with the peppercorns, cloves, cumin, herbs, and broth used for simmering.

Heat the oil in a deep pot, add the chile puree, and cook 1 minute. Reduce the heat and simmer for 15 to 20 minutes. Add 1 tablespoon vinegar and 1 teaspoon salt. Stir to blend, then add the rest of the vinegar and the mezcal or tequila. Pour all the mixture over the meat and rub it in. Add the remaining broth and let the meat marinate, covered, for 24 hours in the refrigerator.

Note: This is only a marinade and baking sauce, so the ingredients don't have to be exact. Improvise.

The next day, preheat the oven to 375°F.

Bake the birria, tightly covered, for 2½ hours. When it comes out, sprinkle with good salt and stir. Serve in bowls with cut limes and the sauce from the pan. Drop something green on top, like chopped cilantro or scallions or a couple of slices of green chiles quickly toasted in a skillet.

Instead of a modern oven, Rick Bayless, authority on Mexican cooking, prefers a closed-top kettle grill, complete with a pot of watery soup, for steaming the barbacoa, since he, like most of us, can't dig a pit in his backyard.

Eloine would have liked, when the thought struck her, to run not only a clean but a proper house. Though moral, in the quite strict, old-fashioned sense built upon the notion that it mattered what others thought of you, and though quoting a Bible verse from memory now and then, whether in context or not, she had better innate sense than to take religion seriously. The kind of preachers we had on Sundays at the Community Hall were fully developed raving maniacs of whose message I understood not a particle, and neither, I think, did anyone else. The main reason for gathering was social, anyway, and to try to outsing Grandma D'Armand, who could be heard clear to the depot in hot weather with the windows open, and her daughters, Gladys and Ala-bama. These three ladies took Christian clamor to Himalayan heights. In Grandma, breath support originated in a tight, round, corseted body with an uplifted mammary sounding board. You'd think such an exuberant voice, though untrained, could have been channeled into some wartime endeavor, such as the shipbuilding industry of Portland, emanating from a quite unprepossessing mouth in a pink face centered with silver wire glasses and topped by a meringue of white hair. The daughters deferred to the old woman, though 'Bama once sang "You Are My Sunshine" over the radio in Prescott. We all went to hear her on the store wireless. For the event, Mrs. Warren set out extra folding chairs and served coffee.

Despite her lightly worn religious mantle, occasionally Eloine was stuck in her turn feeding some wandering minstrel after church, if the Dad was home. Garrulous windbags needed to be protected from themselves, she believed; in addition, their habits might be catching, and the best way she knew how to prevent this was to fill their mouths with something other than wind. Food was her weapon of choice and her defense, her argument, her democracy and pacific.

But "Lord, what am I going to feed them?" was her first cry when unexpected visitors turned up near mealtime, even as she heard the car rattling along the road, not yet in sight. Often, fortunately, this would be a lone man the Dad brought home, some sidekick from the mine, or someone he'd run into—or made first acquaintance of—an hour earlier at the store. The man would not go away hungry.

Because her cupboard was so often bare, accommodating another appetite threw Eloine into a frenzy, though she recollected herself, for the sake of appearances, and tried to sit calmly and participate in the conversation for a while, starting things off with an un-iced glass of mint tea. "And is there a Mrs. Harris?" she might ask, holding her hands together in her lap, but you could see behind her spectacles her racing mind, the wild doe's eyes of panic.

"Just call me Frank," the man might reply, not knowing to her this was much too forward. She would no more call a man by his given name on first meeting than she would fly to the moon.

"Well, there doesn't seem to be any sign of a letup in this weather."

"No, ma'm, there don't. I was saying anower ago, wasn't I, Homer—"

"Omer—"

"Yes, I was saying this hot spell gone on long enough and beyond. If it don't break soon, we're all agoin a dry up and blow away. Weather like this, a man loses his appetite and can't hardly keep a thing on his stomach. . . . "

Um-hum, you could hear Eloine's inner voice, *it doesn't look like to me you've missed many free meals.*

In the kitchen, sotto voce: "Now, you can come to the table but don't ask for seconds or there won't be enough to go around." If there really wasn't enough to go around, we boys ate in the kitchen, where company wouldn't notice and be embarrassed by the slight but distinctive difference between what we had and he had. As in the hillbilly song, "Take an old cold tater and wait," our kitchen meal might be made up of, communally, one cold fried chicken wing, a gizzard, a spoon of graying potatoes, a biscuit going hard from breakfast, a glob of applesauce. There'd be dessert, unfailingly, because supper couldn't close down the day without it. An advantage to this segregated dining was we could slip out the back door and be gone.

And I find "Lord, what am I going to feed them?" my first thought too when people show up in the early evening and seem quite prepared to stay. One can feign indifference only so long. There's a point after which one *must* invite them to stay, usually when they accept the second drink. As the moment approaches, one mentally searches the kitchen cupboards and the refrigerator. After the invitation is accepted, with a wide-eyed expression of surprise and salivary movements of the lower jaw, then one is free to abandon any semblance of deep conversation and head for the kitchen to, as Eloine put it, "shake up the icebox."

Seeing to it we had a howling Saturday night bath in a tin tub, having us don shoes on Sunday morning and the clean homemade shirt, socks, and underwear we'd wear the rest of the week to school—which by Friday must have overwhelmed Miss Gerrish with a sfumato haze of attar of child—was Eloine's nod to the cleanliness/godliness dictum. That and making three dozen Miss Ruby cupcakes for the annual church picnic or the Goat Picnic. Then she could bask, "Oh shaw, I don't think they were up to snuff," in the compliments of her counterparts, goatherders' and ranchers' wives, cowboys' blowzy women, and an itinerant preacher's widowed, illiterate daughter, Mrs. Cantrell, whose whole passel had the look and mentality of an Ozark movie cast. "Well," Eloine said, lowering her gaze into her lap where her hands lay, "at least they got a square meal. That little bitty one, the towhead, *tsk*. Po' thing." To her, the most awful story lay in Dante's thirty-third canto, the death of Count Ugolino and his sons by starvation in the Pisan Tower of Famine.

She'd sigh, look at the blue-gray dragon's back of mountains beyond which Prescott nestled so far away and toward which our front porch tilted, reach for a corner of her apron to wipe her eyes, and being without it, resort to fingertips and a change of subject. "I just think something went wrong with those cupcakes." In the ordered world of her imagination, children would never go without food or a proper allotment of brains, though she knew good and well recipes, no matter how much "in the hands," as André Watts might say of a Schubert scherzo, will sometimes go awry.

Miss Ruby Cupcakes

⅓ cup shortening
1 cup light brown sugar
2 eggs, separated
2 teaspoons baking powder
pinch of salt
1 cup all-purpose flour
½ cup milk
1 cup chopped walnuts
1 teaspoon vanilla

Preheat the oven to 350°F. Grease and flour a 12-cup muffin pan.

Cream the shortening and sugar, then beat in the egg yolks. Sift the baking powder and salt with the flour, adding milk to make a batter. Beat the egg whites until stiff, then fold in the chopped nuts and vanilla. Mix the whites with the batter. Spoon the batter into the muffin pan.

Bake the cupcakes for 20 minutes or until a broomstraw stuck into one comes out clean.

Icing

Heat 3 tablespoons milk with 1 tablespoon butter and 1 teaspoon maple flavoring. Beat in 2 cups confectioners' sugar. Let cool a while, then ice the cooled cupcakes. Top each with a walnut half in the center.

At these picnics one could indulge one's natural bent for gluttony. Exotic green or red Jell-O, the former with pineapple, the latter with peach halves or banana, impossible to make at home without refrigeration, offset by chocolate pie, white or yellow or chocolate cake, lemon meringue tart, pecan pie, peach cobbler, apple brown betty, mulberry crumble, cookies and fudge and taffy, as much as you wanted because no one was counting. All this followed by a softball game or a sack race and, for me, vomiting.

Eloine liked to see people eat at her table, her skinny boys especially, so when certain glorious dishes, such as creamed peas, came onto my plate, I ate and ate and ate. She forgot, as did I, sickness would follow at about bedtime, as surely as night follows day, illustrating French philosopher Gaston Bachelard's observation "Man is a creature of desire and not a creature of need." Insofar as this may be true, it helps us comprehend the distance between the puma and ourselves, to read in the depths of its topaz eyes not contemplation or remembrance of past good meals, but the moment's necessity.

Never Give a Stone

Our lineman's shack, built sometime after the invention of both barbed wire and corrugated sheet metal, was by nature stuck far out at the edge of reachable civilization, its purpose to house the men—with perhaps a woman to cook and clean—who rode the lines, the fences, repairing them as needed, or tended to and reported on the roving, near-wild cattle whose every cut must have been bred for stew. There was little of what one might call archaic design in a lineman's shack, no ancient legacies of tradition. The best that could be expected of it was reasonable shelter from the elements—the blazing Arizona sun, the torrential summer rains, the frosts and snows of winter—not, however, from the flies, mosquitoes, beetles, mice, the occasional misguided tarantula, nor from the two creatures Eloine most dreaded, the mountain lion and the hydrophobic skunk. Because the need for our shack had passed by the time the Dad got to Arizona seeking gold, he talked whoever owned it and the surrounding acres, thousands of them, into letting him settle in with his as-yet-unfinished family, rent-free. We lived there because no one else wanted to or could, far from the hamlet center, beached at the base of Old Baldy, whose fingers of dry hills splayed downward toward Patterson's pasture, the nighttime highways of rattlesnakes, coyotes, bobcats, or who knew what all. Indians. Wasn't Skull Valley named for the prodigious number of human bones uncovered by the railroad crews? Didn't Elizabeth Curry, a local woman, find an Indian child mummy in a cave?

Every couple of years if she could afford to, Eloine sent to Montgomery Ward for wallpaper, blue for the living room, pink for the bedroom, always with enormous flower patterns that in their extremity of design were so confusing no one ever noticed the flawed matching. These strips were glued up with flour-water paste, the new slap over the old, a method with distinct advantages in a single-wall-constructed house, not least of which was climate control. Some of the paper came loose in bulges here and there, creating the vertiginous illusion of a garden in motion. Although I never heard her say so outright, being tenderhearted, she probably thought it charming that behind these various layers of wallpaper, whole families of tiny brown mice ran on playful innings, and, of course, stopped to gnaw the pasta.

From time to time she had irrational thoughts. "Plum would be nice," she once said, looking at the tattered walls. "Or a brown grosgrain." The catalog revealed no such choices, so it was back to florals.

Two pictures hung on this enthusiastic background, one, to borrow from Penelope Fitzgerald, a "sepia [painting] of distant prospects and bends in the river with reliably grazing cattle," the other a portrait of Uncle Horace in his World War I uniform, more of an icon than a picture. We never knew him because he lived in Nashville and was a lawyer. It was his check, however, sent west each December year after year, that pulled Eloine through the particulars of Christmas.

Our dishes, or replacements of Eloine's originals, purchased a nickel at a time new (after she got to Arizona with her three extant children), came from cereal and soap boxes. By sticking with a certain brand of laundry flakes or oatmeal, you could over time build up a full set of dishes, in theory. In practice, the new just about balanced the loss of the old, slippery things in the small hands of children.

Country shacks like ours had no municipal garbage pickup service. Seventy-five feet in back of the house, a junk pile respired, a collection of broken dishes, tin cans, ruined buckets, fence wire—anything for which another use had not yet been thought of. An old mattress beloved by nesting mice. A dresser fallen into nine or ten pieces. On most estates heavy mechanical equipment like tractors or engines were given preferential treatment and allowed to return to nature from which they came, up close to the house or barn. In our case, we never had anything that ran except for the Dad's truck, so our immediate surround stayed pretty clear.

I hasten to say I did not have a deprived childhood, despite its slim pickings. An advantage, obvious to anyone, to being a country kid in the days before TV was having little suspicion of the outside world. Another was not being required to wear shoes. I was loved, and loved, though not always reciprocally by the objects of my desire, and claim no resentment or dammed-up repositories of neuroses, no diminution of Authentic Self. If I recall a boiling pig's head now and then, it is not to be read as some Jungian blip from *Lord of the Flies* but simply as a recurring flicker of food memory, before age eleven, that should have dissolved from consciousness long ago with most everything else.

Going to school centered our days during the term, nearly our whole life experience away from the shack, an immense distance of two miles. Learning was high excitement to me, at least insofar as it applied in that white stucco, two-room building with a real rope-operated bell and a pendulum clock you could never see because it resided in the hall. But lest I sound precocious, I ought to note my competition. Besides Edward D'Armand (or Mahurin, I forget which at the moment) and a boy named White, my classmates were not remarkable. There was Bobbie Evans, who set his rubber-tired toy cars on the woodstove until their wheels flattened and then said, "I don't know no better," a refrain he was alert enough to realize brought sympathy and could be used in all foundering circumstances. There was Leroy Scott, who did most of his writing on the outhouse walls, aiming for a career as graffito artist like Jean-Michel Basquiat.

And there was Garland (Garly) Drill, a moron. Through no fault of his own, he never advanced beyond first or second grade, did not enter junior or senior high in town, though I once saw him at about seventeen loping down the sidewalk on Gurley Street like a secretary bird dressed in full army regalia, looking ominous. Perhaps he found a calling in the armed services and is now a retired master sergeant living in Sun City. In Skull Valley his mother tried frantically to push Garly along by organizing social events at their place, a couple of miles farther down the big road, such as wiener roasts and Easter egg hunts. He never got to an egg first but tumbled up as soon as he saw you find one to claim he'd spotted it first. Since it was his party and he'd been known to cry so hard at the frustrations of learning he threw up all over his desk—books, inkwell, papers, nearby classmates—you gave him the egg, then he'd run to someone else with the same claim. Thus at the end his basket was fullest and we were, it is to be assumed, enriched.

There was Kenneth, a hyperactive bully who always brought *rotten* eggs because he knew Garly would end up with most of them. I'm not sure of this, but I think that if you want a rotten Easter egg, you let it spoil first, then boil it. Jim Crace, in *The Devil's Larder*, tells of opening a five-month-forgotten boiled egg and finding the dog would eat it gladly, though it had a subtle and unnerving smell, like (I'm guessing) those years-old eggs you can buy in Chinese markets.

The girls wore pigtails and ribbons and had rickrack sewn on their pinafores. They probably succeeded mostly in acceptable ways. Except for poor Nonie, whose two best words were *cain't* and *ain't*.

Miss Hermione Gerrish presided over this piteous aggregation with authority and long suffering, teaching all eight grades in a single room, four rows on one side to the right of her desk, four rows on the other, to the left. There were advantages to this. When you'd finished your own assignment, you could horn in on another's and, theoretically, move ahead faster than predicted. Or if the lesson was arithmetic, you could gaze out the window. Miss Gerrish was young, not long out of college, and married after a few years. So she had to quit, as the received wisdom of the day certified that no woman should work if she had a husband to support her and, further, if there were jobs to be had they ought to go to men first, in the circular logic that men had families to support but women didn't because they had, or ought to have, husbands to support them. The Dad, member of the school board, supported this view. Eloine herself could have stepped into the role abdicated by Miss Gerrish had the rule been less ironic.

I have made peace with peanut butter, after four decades of casting it out with Levitical venom. In Skull Valley we each had, day after day, three peanut butter sandwiches on white Rainbow bread in our lunch bags. Desperately, I tried to trade for bacon-and-egg, baloney, jelly, or most anything else. I'd even throw a hard-boiled egg into the bargain. To paraphrase Scarlett O'Hara regarding her turnips, I swore I'd never eat peanut butter again once emancipated and, alternatively, would have all the whipped cream I wanted. I leave it to the imagination to picture peanut butter squashed between two slices of white bread, four or five hours after conception, carried to school in a paper bag with, say, an apple for ballast, times three.

My resistance held for thirty years, until I met with the insidious *sa-teh* sauce in Keo Sananikone's hole-in-the-wall restaurant on Kapahulu Street in Honolulu. Since then, over another twenty years, I've tried many others, including a dozen canned interpretations. I needn't have bothered.

KEO'S SA-TEH SAUCE

¼ cup oil
2 cloves garlic, minced
1 onion, chopped
1 teaspoon ground dried Thai chiles
3 kaffir lime leaves
½ teaspoon curry powder
1 tablespoon chopped lemongrass
1 cup coconut milk
½ cup milk
1 2-inch cinnamon stick
3 bay leaves
2 teaspoons tamarind sauce
3 tablespoons fish sauce
3 tablespoons dark brown sugar
3 tablespoons lemon juice
1 cup chunky peanut butter

Heat the oil in a skillet over medium-high and sauté the garlic, onion, chiles, kaffir lime leaves, curry powder, and lemongrass for 2 to 3 minutes. Stir in the coconut milk, milk, cinnamon stick, bay leaves, tamarind sauce, fish sauce, brown sugar, lemon juice, and peanut butter; mix well. Reduce the heat and cook, stirring frequently, until the sauce thickens, about 30 minutes. Be very careful not to let the sauce stick to the pan.

This will keep, refrigerated in a jar, for several weeks before baroque things begin to grow on it.

Of table manners in Skull Valley, there was a presumption of clean hands, and one did not place one's elbows on the table and thus eat like a jackknife, nor splay one's arms out, dog-in-manger style, on either side of one's plate, despite the necessity of defending one's supper from snatching hands, as in that fresco by Signorelli at the Abbey Monteoliveto in Siena, in which the foremost monk, while looking quite innocent, is snitching the bread from his brother's plate. The spoon was to be brought upward to the face, not the opposite—face down to the dish. No sniffing food on the fork, no blowing, and no hats. One kept relatively quiet until spoken to, especially when the Dad was home, and asked with a please for anything desired, and to be excused when finished. There were random admonitions having to do with Eloine's vague sense of health, such as "Chew your food slowly. Don't gulp— it'll lie like a lump in your stomach." The Dad, not to be outdone, claimed that chewing with your mouth open allowed excess air into your insides, causing embarrassing explosions later. Like Anne of Austria, who, it is said, ate her meat with her fingers, we boys would have given up knives and forks if we'd been allowed. As it was, if we were having something unusual I especially liked, such as fried baloney, I'd sneak a slice into my overalls, to be savored later outdoors during a lengthy twilight. A slice of fried baloney can be laid down on, say, a fence post out of the dog's reach while one chases the ball in Red Rover, then later retrieved for a transcendent chomp. Pretty much the same signifies for a slice of tomato in biscuit, if it can be got from the table past the parents' eyes. Alternately, as any child knows, that which cannot be stomached under any sauce may be passed beneath the table to the conspiratorial consortium of dogs and cats.

Unlike what I have since learned is typical in the households of children who go on to become great thinkers, suppertime in our house was not an hour of intellectual rondo resplendent with burning insights or insoluble problems, except insofar as the national wolf of starvation scratched at our door and had to be acknowledged. Politics were discussed somewhat—certainly FDR's name came up regularly—yet I think without heat or analysis or the possibility of an opinion other than the Dad's.

He, an old man by the time I came along, probably did work hard away from home as a miner, and I can pity him laboring on a road gang for the WPA or, through the influence of Senator Ida, as an aged intern at the insane asylum in Phoenix, where, incidentally, he danced with the famous murderess and escape artist Winnie Ruth Judd, who died not very long ago. At home he was more an observer than a participant, sitting on the porch rubbing the knees of his britches and giving opinions about how things ought to be done. Home rule, with the Dad in residence, amounted to patrimonial absolutism with little democratic participation in local government. He did no cooking, not even hotcakes on Sunday morning.

In the softwood floor leading from the main room—"living" at one end, "dining" at the other—into the kitchen, where all traffic eventually funneled, holes wore clear through, letting spooks in from the dark below. The Dad repaired these when he got around to it, using patches of tin flattened out of coffee cans, if he could locate a floorboard still solid enough to hold a nail. The result was a treacherous crossing for bare feet and a floor that sagged when stepped on. Eloine complained about sending snakes an engraved invitation, and that other dire creature, the mad skunk.

Multipliedly, the roof leaked with glee when it rained, especially during the hard storms of July, sounding exactly like the opening eighteen bars of Barber's Piano Concerto, opus 38, and we were all sent scurrying with pots, pans, coffee cans, the bucket, and slop jar from place to place, trying to catch what we could of it. Eloine met the first of these summer rains with a joyous shout and bustle because it signified the end of drought. The well would fill up again; the snakes, gophers, pack rats, and other unwanted creeping or leaping things would return to their normal arenas of life; and she'd have rainwater to wash her hair in.

Proud of her hair, black, glossy, and down to her waist unpinned, she gloried in a rainwater shampoo, a ritual during which she drifted away, gone off to some sensual chamber of privacy where, perhaps, she excused herself from thinking of food, so little of it. Her hairdo, a complication of upswept pompadour, curls made with an iron heated over the lamp, and a flat braided bun in back, was a Birnam Wood of pins. These served not only to hold the pile in place but as adaptable mechanical instruments. For instance, to zip a recipe from a magazine, she had but to reach up into her hair, pull out a pin, and strike, leaving a deckled but efficient edge. Or to test a cupcake, to clean under a fingernail, or with the rounded end, to scratch in an ear.

As the deluge subsided, Eloine reminded us not to discard the last filled pans, set about all over the house like votive waterpots. She would have unbunged the rain barrel at the first sign of the coming storm and stuck in her big kitchen funnel. There being no bathroom, all bathing was done in the kitchen, either bent over the dishpan or, at certain disagreeable times, in a galvanized tub. Collected rainwater supposedly made a purer bath for body and soul.

These floods, two or three a summer, threatened more seriously than they performed. The house, though not built exactly on shifting sand, stood but a few feet higher than the little ravines and the general floodplain surrounding it. You could see the summer storms a-building, black, boiling clouds to the northeast over Big William Mountain gathering ferociously, lightning sulfurously streaking. Before the storm hit us down below, the grasses began to shiver as if something big were breathing across them, and the air turned sweet with the smell of rain. A half mile away, the big creek began to boom with muddy flood, a muffled, ominous, jungle throb. With water pouring down from the mountains, it would soon overcome its banks and spread out across Patterson's pasture, a roiling brown porridge. Rushing to meet it from the other direction, from Old Baldy behind our house, a lesser flood, until surrounded we seemed about to float away, though never did. To me, rolling, murky water was, in balance with white-faced cows, the world's most terrifying element.

Had the flood got too deep, Eloine, stoic in emergencies despite a shriek or two, would have gathered us up like a flock of geese, crossed the back side yard, and begun climbing the hill, then turned, her hand to her face like Ma Joad, to watch the house tumble away.

The torrents left in their wake dead animals. Not so often the nimble creature of the wild, but calves, horses, a donkey, perhaps a dog. And thereafter, a renewed colloquium of buzzards, roosting by late afternoon in the cottonwoods, satiated, like fattened bishops on the lookout for sin.

And they brought out a vast assemblage of toads of all physiques, from tiny, fingernail-sized ones that must have been astonished by this washy entrance into the world, to damp, flabby, cold ones the size of a catcher's mitt. These were alleged to cause warts on those who played with them. Their stock of activity being extremely limited to larger or smaller hops, they didn't occupy our attention for long. The thin, graceful, blue-green lizards that spent their afternoons clutching the sides of the unpainted boards hid in the cracks during storms.

After the lightning, thunder, and storm passed, the light, as if it had been washed, came in low and bright, like a new slick green made by mixing yellow and blue.

Every year, besides two patches of nasturtiums at the front door and the wild rose hedge, which flourished, Eloine planted a vegetable patch, which did not. As a recurring expression of optimism in an otherwise cheerful soul made bleak from counting pennies—"I declare, I don't know where the next meal's coming from"—she found, begged, or borrowed seeds and sowed a few rows of greens after cajoling some male of the family into scratching up the sandy, barren soil. Hers was not an attempt to harness raw nature for the beauty of it. This was not a place to walk in the violet evening, to tread on perfumed thyme. Diverted waste water and some well water trickled into the garden. There were no Genovese fountains here, no artesian springs. Nevertheless, all started out just fine. Until June. In June of each summer, without fail, the well ran dry, body fragments brought up by the windmill the first signal of impending doom. Rodents, particularly gophers and pack rats, and snakes burrowed their way through the well walls or slithered in and drowned, too crazed to travel to the swamp. The Dad dumped in bags of chloride-a-lime, which did nothing to disintegrate the animal parts but allegedly rendered them harmless. As the people of Paris had to tolerate terrible infiltrations of pestilence in their drinking water from the Seine, even in the eighteenth century, we gulped and went on. As far as I know, we never scooped up parts of a human body, as I've heard was sometimes a problem in Sicily years ago. Eloine strained and boiled.

Bathwater was then hauled bucket by bucket from the swamp but was not in great demand. The Dad and his cronies brought drinking water in a metal barrel and we were instructed once again about rationing, as we were continually when it came to food, a Wagnerian leitmotif.

Had the well not gone dry, and the vegetable garden matured, this is what we would have eaten, to the everlasting distress of the boys. In it the mystic ingredient is sugar, Eloine's answer for all greens—that, and cooking them for at least an hour.

GREENS WITH HAM HOCKS

If you don't have ham hocks, the "plain" greens can be cooked with salt pork for flavor.

2 to 3 large smoked ham hocks or 2-inch square salt pork
6 cups water, maybe more
2 to 3 teaspoons red pepper flakes or pinch of cayenne
    pepper
3 tablespoons sugar
seasoned sea salt
2 big bunches mustard greens
2 big bunches turnip greens or collard greens
1 teaspoon baking soda
sea or kosher salt and black pepper
1 tablespoon vinegar

Place the ham in a large pot and cover with water. Bring to a boil, adding the pepper flakes, sugar, and seasoned salt, about 1 tablespoon at first. Reduce the heat and cook slowly for an hour or more, until the meat begins to fall from the bones.

Wash the greens very well and pick over them. Add the greens and soda to the pot and boil over high heat for 30 to 40 minutes, stirring and turning several times. When the greens are cooked, taste the likker to see if it needs more salt; if it does, wait. Lay the greens on a dish and top with the meat, then sprinkle with sea or kosher salt and black pepper, lightly, and the vinegar. If she had some, Eloine added cream to the greens a minute before serving.

Eloine did succeed somewhat longer with spearmint, growing in the damp earth beneath the water tank, but it, too, petered out in the drought. Tough herbs like rosemary and lavender would have survived, and she did like sachets in her dresser drawers. I don't know why she didn't try them.

The list of edible plants we never met was long: alligator pears, artichokes (which Thomas Hill in 1586 wrote not only made your breath and armpits smell better but improved the venereal act and caused more male babies to be born), fennel—the staple of Provençal cooks—mangoes, papayas, limes. Eloine pined for something called a persimmon and sang a little tuneless song about a possum up a paw-paw tree.

She never visited in another home except the Shoups', the chicken rancher. Grandma Shoup, who as an octogenarian had entered into the misty realm of ontology, played unknown songs on a pump organ in the living room. She claimed they were transmitted through her, a kind of latter-day Clara Schumann, from Johannes Brahms, whom she was contemporaneous enough to have known. Further, she collected hundreds of arrowheads and displayed them against cotton batting in picture frames. Her daughter-in-law, Eloine's age, carried about her the resignation and moral grace of James Agee's dust bowl people, but was much better off than they. The Shoups had not only electricity but an indoor toilet. Mrs. Shoup grew a glorious garden because of a good well and a perpetual supply of chicken manure. After a visit she cut for us an armload of flowers—lilacs in spring, snowballs in summer, chrysanthemums in fall—and some degree of barter caused something to be exchanged for a fryer or a dozen eggs. And last Sunday's paper, with its thrilling funnies and other sections from which the Dad would read aloud ominous news of, for example, the invasion of Poland.

For these visits Eloine put on a better, but not best, dress, combed up her hair into a pile, puffed on some face powder, a dab of lipstick, clipped on a pair of tortoiseshell earrings, and carried a purse, though to get there she had to climb ignominiously through three barbed-wire fences and suffer the terrorism of the cows. Among certain things she believed had been sent into the world chiefly to irritate her, white-faced range cattle topped the list. Like dogs, they sense when you are afraid of them and will charge you just for the pleasure of seeing you bolt. Eloine resented this discourteous action of other females, who then stood by and watched her underwear flash as she scrambled under a fence, wallowing in their coprolitic leavings. The steers hung back more timidly, but then you can't blame them for it, considering their loss.

Mr. Shoup, a quiet man, let us climb up into the loft of his chicken barn once in a while to view a nest of owlets, though the sight of a huge owl flying out overhead by day (an alarm they never knew at night) was apt to frighten his chickens out of their wits and cause blood in the yolks of their eggs. The nest smelled of dead rodents. Actually, a lot of the countryside smelled like dead things because, as part of the overall plan of creation, creatures die in their tracks, to be slowly devoured by maggots, buzzards, beetles, foxes, coyotes, bobcats, starving dogs, feral felines, and who knows what all else. It boils down to a matter of food.

We had no ducks in Skull Valley, wild or domestic. No flock of mallards rested on our ponds or V-shaped gaggle of Canada geese ever crossed our white and azure skies. Eloine launched into a free-range turkey scheme one time, though, and concluded from the experience they had just enough brains to come home at night to be penned. On the other hand, giving credit where due, her turkeys learned to range all the way over to Mr. Shoup's ranch, a distance of a mile, fly over the fence, and eat with his chickens, a practice not much given to improved neighbor relations. Why coyotes or the stealthy lion did not eat them as they strolled under the cottonwoods, gabbling and chattering like nineteenth-century English noblewomen, I can't imagine.

The pen Eloine shooed the gobblers into every evening, a wobbly wire structure nailed to four posts, was meant along with the dog to discourage predators. At one side she erected a lean-to of old boards set on upturned discarded buckets and pots, rocks, shelter of a sort, under or on top of which the birds might roost. In architectural type it looked like any of those small wooden structures you see in country yards all over the United States, built for what purpose you can only guess, but invariably trashy. Whether pigeons, rabbits, chickens, or turkeys, the stock petered out before long, gradually consumed at the dinner table, unreplicated.

Yet from time to time we had a few hens, fewer still that made it to Eloine's skillet because of the coyotes. Eschewing the ax as a dangerous, man's implement, she could wring a chicken's head off with one gyroscopic windup and a shriek. The shriek, infallible, helped fend off the flying blood because, as is well known, the body of a decapitated chicken flings itself all over the place, even well up into the air, sending spatters for fifteen or twenty feet. She shrieked the same way when she dropped a dish or when running from airborne snake parts. Our dog, Buster, harbored a monomaniacal love of killing rattlesnakes by shaking them to pieces. Altogether, there was something Mediterranean in these scenes.

Frying chicken is as much an attitude as a task. It takes an hour and cannot be rushed. At the last it must be lightly crusted, nothing like the vulcanized celeriac-looking stuff sold in fast-food drive-throughs or your local grocery's "delicatessen" section, a misnomer if ever there was one: from the Latin, *delicatus,* or "delicate." Fried chicken doesn't have to be served piping hot; it's good hot, warm, or cold. The raw pieces should not be banged around inside a paper bag with flour and elaborate spices under the illusion that to do so is effective, sophisticated, or time-saving. If the bird is cut up correctly, there will be a pulley bone for the kids.

Chicken sold in supermarkets, no matter what it is called—fryer, roaster, broiler—is all the same chicken. For frying, one needs a young bird with small parts; otherwise, it will never get done at the bone.

Eloine's Fried Chicken

1 young chicken, no more than 3 pounds, cut up into
    11 pieces

In a bowl, some milk or buttermilk, 1 teaspoon salt,
      some pepper
On a plate, plain flour, a bit more salt and pepper, a pinch of
      cayenne pepper
In a skillet, a quarter inch of melted lard

Turn each piece of chicken in the milk, then in the flour, shake it lightly, and lay it *gently* down in the medium-hot oil. The oil should not be blistering hot, about 275°F. Instead of smoke and spatter and crackle, there should be a light, chattering sizzle. Don't crowd the pan. Turn the chicken pieces *gently* to brown them on all sides, the object being not to galvanize them but to cook them through. Transfer them to a rack over paper towels to drip.

Then drain off the fat, but don't clean out the skillet.

Make a gravy by mixing 1 cup of milk with 2 tablespoons of flour in a bowl. Beat the mixture until smooth, then pour it into the skillet and heat slowly, stirring all the time and scraping up the brown scabs of whatever has stuck to the skillet. Add more milk if the gravy gets too thick. Taste to see if more salt and pepper are needed. Near the end, you may add a tablespoon of something alcoholic: sherry, port, Madeira. These lose character if added during the cooking.

In all this, one must try to be light in touch, including seasoning, avoiding Mr. Prudhomme's Louisiana firecrackers. We're talking southern fried here, a thing quite different from the gumbo and blackened redfish affliction.

Young rabbits, that is, wild cottontails, are treated the same. Domestic, or hutch-raised, rabbits are another matter, and hares—or jackrabbits in western thought—are to be avoided. "I wouldn't try one of those again if my life depended on it," Eloine said, which was about the same position she took on possum. "The longer you chew it, the bigger it gets."

A writer I once knew, reading a story of mine, said cottontails and jackrabbits could not inhabit the same ecosystem. Obviously she did not grow up in the sticks.

The other fundamental chicken dish on Eloine's table was chicken and dumplings, a way to dispatch an older hen or a rooster. I have never been able to duplicate this dish, but essentially, after boiling the chicken for an hour, until the meat falls from the bones, you thicken and whiten the liquid a bit with flour, then lay in the dumplings. Eloine's dumplings were not the sticky, doughy blobs so often plopped in from a serving spoon; they were rolled out thin, like pie dough, cut into 1-by-3-inch rectangles, and slipped one at a time into the simmering stew to cook for about twenty minutes, as they rose only slightly. They came out slick and light. All this I know. How to do it, I don't.

With pigeons, the older boys—Billy and Omer Jr.—had some luck. The birds flew about in open-air range much of the time, returning in the evening to coops improvised from apple crates. Other people in the valley raised squabs (and sometimes bullfrogs) as delicacies. We ate the full-grown bird, brought down with a shotgun, Eloine having followed the logic that a mature bird, fending for itself, thus costing nothing to feed, would help feed, in turn, more hungry mouths than a squab could.

I was never too clear why Marlon Brando, in *On the Waterfront*, raised pigeons on his rooftop, but think they were not intended for the table. A young writer I know who grew up in the Brooks Range and therefore has unique survival skills claims to have eaten nicely for a week in Tucson by consuming the pigeons strutting torpidly about him in the downtown library park. After shooting them with a Y-shaped homemade slingshot, the name by which we knew it in Skull Valley no longer politically correct, he roasted them after dark in a nearby wash west of town. To him, reared north of the Arctic Circle, anything walking, running, swimming, or flying was seen as food, and he would have been appalled should someone have complained, as he was when "caught" washing himself, naked, in the public restroom of the courthouse.

It is a sign of economic collapse when a city's public spaces become devoid of pigeons. I doubt there were many left in St. Mark's Square or Trafalgar at the end of World War II, though clearly enough pairs lived to generate thousands to follow. I've never actually found pigeons on a menu, not even at Les Pigeons in Tunis.

The flesh of a grown pigeon is dark and tough and could probably be put to some indestructibly reduced form during wartime, such as K rations. However, to country people in need, pigeons are classified as ordinary food, though I realize to city dwellers they are but flying rats. If, say, you are a Boy Scout and eat them out on the range, skewered on green willow sticks and cooked over a campfire, where gnawing and tearing are allowed, they taste pretty good, but a long dip in marinade is recommended before the hike.

It is just as well Eloine never learned to fire a gun, what with her equivocal eyesight and her natural terror, however subdued, of living deep in the Arizona wilderness. But, as with cottontails, if she could get the Dad or the older boys to bring down a covey of quail or doves, she'd dress them out and cook them. With hunt in the fall air, she stoked the great black cookstove and rattled her pans even before the first shot was fired, as if by showing confidence from her quarter, she might inspire the menfolk in theirs. Though at other times, when the Dad and Billy, like many hunters, killed for sport the pretty birds raiding the apricot tree—finches, orioles, cardinals, sparrows—she would fling up the kitchen window near the massacre and mourn, "Po' birds, po' little birds."

Occasionally, and each time briefly, Omer and Billy and Donald Shoup, the chicken rancher's son, slipped into their "springs to catch woodcocks" fantasy, wherein they believed they could trap edible birds by the hoary method of propping up a wooden apple box on one end with a stick attached to a long string, seeds or bread crumbs scattered about the box and under it. The trapper, invisible behind a bush, holds the string and waits in breathless anticipation for the birds to peck their way beneath the box, at which instant he yanks on the string, thus pulling out the prop, and down falls the box, trapping a half-dozen quail. The logistical detail of how to get the winged creatures out from under the sprung trap was never mastered, but neither was it ever called into need. The hunters soon learned each season that sitting as goalie, string in hand, behind a bush was a hopelessly boring occupation, so guess who was assigned the task.

Squatting in a dry wash at age six or seven, holding a length of twine all afternoon into evening, until someone looked around and realized I was missing from the supper table, a similar inactivity to snipe hunting, got me a certain degree of sympathy and Omer and Billy trouble. From it all, I caught not even a sparrow, yet I was taught that in Exodus, the fleeing, wandering, disgruntled Hebrews are visited by flocks of quail that, exhausted and blown off course from their migratory pattern, fall to the ground for the picking, or as Psalm 78 so poetically has it: "he rained meat like a dust-storm upon them, flying birds like the sand of the sea-shore, which he made settle all over the camp round the tents where they lived." There would have been enough left over for jerky, I should think, if the chosen had had their wits about them, plenty of blazing sun, and dry air.

Farm-raised quail, in vogue from time to time, probably taste about the same as their wilder brethren, are a bit more tender thanks to a less panic-stricken existence, and have no buckshot buried in them. America's best food writer, Molly O'Neill, has even suggested quail as a substitute for Thanksgiving turkey, largely because, there being so little of it to chew, the family can do more talking. Both she and Mark Miller, of Santa Fe's Coyote Café, use honey in the marinade, his infused, of course, with red chili sauce.

The first tendency of men cooks, once again, is to light an outdoor fire. Eloine, having no grill or barbecue, pan-sautéed quail in drippings, a jar of which always resided on a wing of the stove or on the drainboard, stratified in layers, white, brown, honey golden, bits of past meals ambered, in suspension for another use. Were this lovely small jar of drippings magnified to an amount required in a successful restaurant, we'd be looking at a giant vat of grease. Many main courses from Eloine's skillet tasted reminiscently of their forebears, an ever-deepening complexity of flavors.

Since small wild game birds have no fat, one must grease them somehow. Quail are often wrapped with bacon, like tiny early term mummies, or—to extend this horrid metaphor—drowned in a Thames of barbecue sauce, thus effectively destroying their identity. Today I'd suggest you brush on an herb-infused olive oil, whether you are sautéing, roasting, or grilling, and add lots of freshly ground pepper. I would also ask that you stop cooking while the quail are still pinkish inside, as further punishment will make the flesh not only look but taste like lead. On the other hand, Alice Waters, of Chez Panisse, marinates quail in wine, duck fat, garlic, shallots, and juniper berries before proceeding to do anything else with them, which leaves one with the thought that she'd rather not be faced with them at all.

These birds, unlike their heavier relatives, guinea hen or reclusive pheasant, being too small to slice, beg for a relaxation in manners. They are best eaten at the picnic table of a Sonoma winery, where etiquette becomes something quite secondary. One may try to dissect a quail on the plate with knife and fork.

Babette, she of the famous feast, began her meal—after the turtle soup—with what Molly O'Neill calls "Cailles en Sarcophagi." This is an unparalleled treatment for the simple quail, involving as it does puff pastry shells (the sarcophagi), truffles and foie gras, figs, white wine, and demi-glacé. Babette, you will recall, served the roasted heads and feet too, stuffed realistically back in with the birds, providing a chance for the visiting general to take up a small cranium and snap right into it with his front teeth, further astounding the other guests, those kind of narrow people who said, "Never would you give a stone to a child begging for bread."

Or a Snake When He Asks for Fish

*T*o "fritter away the time" defines, I suppose, chopping up or squandering foolishly an irreplaceable gift. In any case, we boys were regularly accused of doing it.

It is arguable that spending an afternoon sloshing around in a mucky pond you yourself have created by damming up a rivulet of swamp runoff can be called time frittering. While in the swamp, our own private Giverny, covered from head to toe in primordial slime, we were ardently alive, squelching in the ordinary clay from which we are all evolved and to which we are aboriginally attached. This was a perfectly intelligible wilderness. Muddying the waters also helps to keep down mosquitoes, it could be argued, though not very forcefully. As is well known, malarial mosquitoes like a calm, stagnant dunk. When you create a pond, things come to it—not fish, of course, but frogs and their lovely long, slimy, pearl ropes of eggs, skating bugs, beetles able, as Annie Dillard taught us, to slurp a frog right out of its bones. Crawdads. Water snakes. We hoped for a crocodile or alligator but none came.

The most exotic creatures to visit our pond were the dragonflies, blue-green, lazurite blue, tan, red, zooming with their double sets of leaf-vein dry wings like biplanes but attached somewhat differently. They looked at you, or appeared to—how could they not?—with bulbous, quiet eyes from a face made of a layer of chitinous flesh or whatever insects are constructed from, and bit at your fingertip, a mere touch, with a mouth that, if blown up with an electron microscope, would give the bug movie guys bad dreams. Feet of tiny grasping claws at the ends of needle legs. Their tails were long and sectioned like miniature loin roasts tied for the oven, and while we were not certain in what they terminated—anus or sexual organs—they could bend down and forward. In any case, together two could fly about over the water in what appeared to be erotic attachment.

And in the susurrating grass, nesting larks and field mice; in the reeds, red-wing blackbirds, compared to which no bird sings better. Farther out from the epicenter, in drier, rockier earth, whippoorwills, those fabled birds invisible by day, and toward the sandy creek beds, killdees with their teasing flight, and doves in their primitive nests. Woodpeckers knocking in the trees. Sometimes even a small flock of brilliant green-and-yellow parakeets, escaped from Mrs. Lucille Ida's cages. And who knows what appeared at dark or dawn: that same index of coyote, bobcat, deer, the silent lion?

While acquainted with ghosts, boogeymen, and witches, there were other night gatherers we had no certainty of, such as werewolves, banshees, phantoms and goblins, until Jimmy had an experience from which he could assure me they did indeed exist because he'd seen them one moonish midnight in our front yard when he got up to piss out the door.

"What were they doing?" I whispered.

"Sort of gibbering under the heavenly tree."

"How did they walk?"

"Like they didn't have real feet. Like clouds. Then they dissolved. They were having a coven." *Coven* was one of his new words.

I knew about billy goats gruff and, as noted, ate of them sometimes, and believed if a wooden bridge could be located, beneath it would be living a family of ill-tempered trolls, something I very much longed to see. I wondered why their kids didn't have to go to school.

Somewhere in the world, someone probably eats frog-egg caviar and tadpoles, but I'd as soon not know of it. Eloine eyed, in her mind—not in actual fact—the frogs as potential food, if worse came to worse, but these small and bony creatures compared only in name with the fat, heavy, evil-tempered beasts Mr. Edge grew in a hole in his backyard.

Well, you might say, you'd be evil-tempered too if someone were trying to pry you out of the mud and cut off your legs. I participated in this not altogether gratifying hunt many years later, in a back slough of the Colorado River, an eerie nighttime chase with flashlights and harpoons in black water up to the testicles. It is at times like these you begin to suspect the river of harboring as-yet-unclassified reptiles. While frogs' legs may be treated in all manner of ways with indigenous names—for instance, the *rane in guazzetto* of Lombardy—the best is to sauté them, lightly floured, in butter with black pepper. A touch of garlic. A glass of Muscadet. Minced basil leaves and lemon. A sprinkle of sea salt at the very last. Or a Thai *ping* of minced lemongrass and kaffir lime leaves, a light rain of red pepper flakes.

Frittered time or not, bringing Eloine home a big batch of watercress or a bucket of mulberries and promising to wash our feet got us back in her graceland. By then, anyway, late in the afternoon, she'd be occupied with supper, rolling out the biscuit dough. Homemade hot biscuits with butter (Nucoa) and a thick slice of ripe tomato remains for me the cardinal meal when simplicity, not necessarily health, is concerned.

Fritter as a food comes to us from the French *frire*, "to fry." In common sense, it implies chopped-up things, meat, vegetables, or fruit, mixed into a batter and frizzled as little cakes, often deep-fried into dark sienna crispiness. In the Northwest one finds fritters coated with not-too-finely ground hazelnuts, with crab on the inside; in that case called crab cakes, spiked with chopped scallion and bell or hot red pepper, served with rouilles of mustard and racy mayonnaise. In restaurants these go up in price relative to the decline in taste. In Pacific Rim dining, additions of minced kaffir lime leaves and lemongrass, with perhaps a hint of coconut cream, and shrimp instead of crab cock the tongue. A sparkle of Keo's peanut butter *sa-teh* on the side (see page 25).

Croquette, also from the French but this time imitative of the sound it makes when bitten into, *croquer,* was Eloine's nomenclature of choice, and canned salmon the ingredient. Eloine's shaped croquettes August Schlegel might have called "mechanical" rather than "organic" in form, that is, a shape which improves upon a mass without reference to its quality. Except in presentation, they were not essentially different from her salmon loaf. She concocted the croquettes by mashing—not too thoroughly—the salmon and mixing it with whatever was on hand—milk, an egg separated, the white whipped, bits of this and that, such as bell pepper and onion—until the whole could be formed into pyramids about two inches high. Rolled in crushed saltine cracker crumbs, they were then set down in hot lard to fry. She spooned the oil up onto the sides of the pyramids until they crusted enough to be laid down without falling apart. These are delicate and collapse easily. She stood them, two or three per serving, in puddles of hollandaise, that is, her white flour gravy enriched with an egg yolk and a drop of yellow food coloring. Billy preferred his with ketchup, a brutish choice only a small remove from barbecue sauce.

The idea of fresh fish had not penetrated the continent as far as Arizona in the days before refrigerated trucks and planes, yet I recall one black catfish swimming in the kitchen sink. Caught by Billy in some local hog wallow, it languished there one whole afternoon and did inflict on my hand, as I had been forewarned, a painful jab. While I don't remember eating of him, he returns to mind when I think of Vardaman and his huge fish (in *As I Lay Dying*), the one he confused with his dying mother, and Dewey Dell, who had to cook it while her mind was on another of life's more serious predicaments.

We had, instead, canned tuna and salmon, one of which came in a tin with a glorious electric green-gold iridescent interior, one of the only unnaturally beautiful things I had seen up to that point. How could they make anything so stunning, I wondered, and why hide it inside a can of fish? Most modern tuna, packed in water, is a pointless exercise in tastelessness, as confused as cooks who try to make *salade Niçoise* with fresh albacore. If it's not packed in its guileless oil or olive oil, it ought to be given to the cat.

In a publicity stunt for *A Tuna Christmas,* I once won a prize for tuna-noodle casserole, leaping off from Eloine's version but using four varieties of cheese; hers would have been either Velveeta or longhorn. The point in such a case is to try to avoid eloquence in favor of gluttonous indulgence. If one is the sort who through some weight of puritanical guilt believes sex reprehensible in the nostrils of God, no matter how necessary to the species or how much fun there is in the doing, then casseroles such as these are to be avoided. And cornflakes or potato chips on top are treasonous. Would you do that to a cassoulet?

One time while living in Marseilles, I determined to run down all the cafés M.F.K. Fisher wrote about in her book on Provence, though forty years later. Among my successes was Les Deux Soeurs and an incomparable *salade Niçoise* composed, of course, with canned tuna packed in oil. Such a simple dish, you'd think, how were they able to make it so much better? Or the whole fried *loup* on the other side of the Quai de Belges or, for that matter, the whole fried rockfish at the Ai Cagnai in Venice in a back street on the way to the Peggy Guggenheim museum, a friendly, scatter-brained café, following a cold salad of calamari, scallops, shrimp in olive oil with parsley. At Ai Cagnai you eat what they decide you shall have. Or the enormous platters of deep-fried sardines, heads on and not dressed out, in a two-man café I'll never be able to find again, on the outskirts of Athens. We become so enamored of innovation, the psychoactive hit, the most megahertz, we lose the direct pleasures. We can't seem to dance without strobe lights and crystal meth.

The Quality of Life

STANDING IN THE SIDE DOORWAY of the café opening to the outside tables on the pedestrian alley, the two waiters talked about the younger one's current problems. He, the younger waiter, was also the taller, with vigorous black hair and black eyes that occasionally flicked over the four occupied tables. They were dressed alike in white shirts and black pants with white aprons, except the younger one wore his collar open, revealing more black hair and a thin gold chain, and his cuffs turned back to display a Rolex on one wrist and a gold link bracelet on the other.

They were cousins, each a grandson of the original two sisters for whom the place was named, Les Deux Soeurs. It was hot, even for Marseille the first of September, and few people had ventured out for lunch. Those who did ordered *salade Niçoise* or shellfish on ice with wine and bread, and lingered at the shaded tables. No one wanted bouillabaisse on day like this, or paella, for which the restaurant was well known. The tables in the sun remained empty, the light reflecting brilliantly from the cloths and silver and goblets. The two waiters turned to watch a white sloop leaving the port under power, sliding among the smaller boats. "Is that the one?" the older waiter asked.

"Yes," the other said. "They go to Cannes, now with the new generator. Three days, so much trouble."

"How did Helêne discover you?"

"*Ai.* She follows me. Passed over the receipts to Tante Joelle and followed me. How was I to know?" He shrugged and looked hopelessly at his cousin, then glanced at the table where the American ate alone.

When he lifted the bottle from the ice and bent to refill her glass, the young waiter touched the American with his thigh, the way he always did to women, even ugly ones, which this one was not, because it calmed them, like eating bivalves and drinking wine. Today she did not move her arm. Her hair shone with gold lights and she looked sad. Four times before she had dined here but with a man, an American also. Then she had not seemed melancholy. "Everything is okay?" he asked and she smiled, answered in French. Her accent was not bad for an American. Not Provençal but not bad.

Elaine Phillipson had worked hard on her French pronunciation for the past six weeks, driving five days a week into Aix to attend the intensive course for foreigners. Now she hoped they'd at least be able to understand her when she began her lectures to the faculty and fourth-year students at the medical university.

The sixth, and last, lecture was almost written, lying beside her plate in a green plastic folder; she could finish it in a couple of hours. Now she had two weeks to kill before beginning the series, maybe three.

It was during this gap she and Jim had planned to knock around Nice and Cannes or maybe the other way, to Biarritz and down to see the new museum in Bilbao. She had watched him grow restless and irritable the past weeks, leaving a trail of unfinished books and papers all over the apartment, buying huge stores of food and wine they'd never be able to consume, and declaring that if he had to visit another goddamned medieval French town, he'd go berserk.

Five mornings ago he left.

"I'll be back," he said. "Don't worry." He was just flying to L.A. to check on things, he'd let his business go to hell this summer, he couldn't get any straight answers on the phone, no e-mail or fax, the fucking mail strike made it next to impossible to keep up. Descending into the Metro from the Prado, he'd seemed jaunty, already recovering, ready to hurl himself back onto Wilshire Boulevard reinvigorated, his mind like his tanned skin glimmering.

After his departure Elaine wandered a long time in the street market, buying only two tomatoes, huge and luminescent, from a loud, funny woman with peasant hands. When it began to get really hot, she crossed the Prado and selected a dozen peach-colored gladioli on five-foot stems and tried to understand the seller's fast, tough Marseilles. It was like visiting in Georgia or Alabama—the language in the South was not what you heard in school, but nearly. In the huge old apartment on Rue Paradis, the glads seemed gentler than they had in the sun, a softer flush, not as cheerful as she'd expected them to be.

That was going to be the problem. How to keep up her spirits until she could walk into the amphitheater and begin her lectures. In the meantime, what? She knew no one in Marseilles, not a soul. They had been out to the Île d'If, up to Notre Dame de la Garde, to the harbor museum—and all those medieval towns. She picked at her salad and watched a long white boat glide out of the harbor so silently it might have been trying to slip away all by itself, self-propelled and unnoticed.

"*Dunc,*" the younger waiter said, leaning over her shoulder, wiping the wet wine bottle. "Everything is okay?" She felt his thigh press against her arm. His leg, she imagined, would be white but heavily overlaid with black hairs, long, muscled because he rode a bicycle to work. She had seen him weaving suicidally in the morning traffic. She caught the quick burst of sweat as he fussed around her, a French odor, not unpleasant. Some waiters could kill with an uplifted arm.

"You have begun to teaching?"

"No," she said, and watched his eyes glance at her hair. "In two weeks. Or maybe three, no one seems to be certain."

The waiter shrugged, the big southern gesture of shoulders, arms, face that said, *This is the way of things, it is fate.* Setting the bottle back in its bucket, he tinkered with the extra plate and silverware, making them clink together, a small, deliberate racket. "It is hot like this in Hollywood?"

She smiled and felt lightened. This waiter, Nicolas, had only the blurriest idea of America, centered in Las Vegas, where he believed all the Bunnies lived in some sort of constant centerfold orgy, and in Hollywood, where the streets glittered with starlets. "No," she said. "Not so much."

"And monsieur?" He lifted his gaze from the cloth, glanced at the empty chair.

"Gone home."

"Ah," he said, "the starlets." He took out a pair of dark glasses with lenses made of blue and green and red plastic and set them on his face, snapped his fingers, struck a pose. The gold at his neck and wrists shone wetly, like his skin.

She opened her manuscript and read the first sentences to herself in French. They seemed overargued and scorched, as if the sun could do something to syntax, but she relished the language. Foreign words meant just what they meant; they didn't slip and fizz away to say what was neither adequate nor intended. Always too much, too rich, and too little. Their language, hers and Jim's, was never pure enough, it seemed to her. It grew out from under their design and puffed itself up, too much nuance.

"How was I to know?" Nicolas said again to his cousin, standing in the shade of the doorway. "They surprise you."

"*Ai.* That is the truth."

"So much trouble, you wouldn't believe it. And for what?"

"Helêne is jealous. They all are."

Nicolas took off his dark glasses, turned them backward, and tried to look at the boats. "She lives on Rue Paradis."

"Who does?"

"The American."

"How do you know that?"

He shrugged. "Near the corner of the night market."

The older waiter left the doorway for a minute, attended to a pair of women who were feeding most of their *loup* to a dog under the table. When he returned, wiping his face with his white cloth, he said, "That place is dangerous."

"Do you need anything? Prices have dropped a little, not much."

"It came in on the sloop?"

"Maybe. That I don't know. My business in the boat was not mercantile." The cousins laughed and the older one offered his pack. The other took a cigarette but did not light it, slipped it instead into his shirt pocket. Inside the café he ordered a cup of coffee for the American woman and, while it was being made, joked with Tante Joelle about the tourists.

This time when he approached her table, he reached across it so she could see his eyes. She looked up from the papers in the green folder. "You read late at night," he said.

She sipped the last of her wine, becalmed like the air, and watched the two French women gorging a dog under their table, a terrier-sized creature with pointed, hairy ears. The women had not spoken to each other at all, but fed their fish to the dog alternately, letting it swallow and then lick their hands, as if they could communicate only through its mouth, with its tongue. Anger or hunger or despair—something—hung over their table like another shade.

She wondered how Nicolas knew she read late at night. The apartment, on the southwest corner of the building, although spacious and white and aired with old-fashioned ceiling fans, stayed too hot for sleep until after midnight. With the windows open, she lay on the bed listening to the pigeons scuffle on the ledge, and the low talk of the people who drove up and double-parked briefly in the *place* below, and the occasional sudden crystal laugh of the prostitutes who sat on the fenders of parked cars. Nearly every night she heard the Pathétique

Adagio floating out the open window of some nearby building, just the morbid opening bars played on a piano, never finished.

"I'll be back," Jim said.

"I have plenty to do," Elaine answered. "One lecture to finish, all those books to read. Tell your mother I have been sending cards. Explain the strike."

"*La grève.* Shit. Fucking socialists. I don't know what keeps this country from going down the tubes."

"They see it as a right, something they're born with. I do wish someone could tell me when the term starts, though."

"Maybe we're too tied to calendars. Not laid back enough. Do we die of heart attacks more than the French, doctor?"

"Their medicine's archaic, they gorge on carbohydrates and calories and red wine, they smoke, but yes, we do. They say it's the quality of life."

"Whatever that means. Don't worry."

"I don't worry much."

"And I'll call you."

He kissed her lightly on the cheeks, three times as the French do, then laughed and kissed her mouth. She watched him disappear, trotting down the escalator, carrying his bag over his shoulder, in faded jeans and court shoes looking young, probably already seeing the slick mirrored buildings of L.A. and the whizzing racquetball.

The language course at Aix finished, she had nowhere in particular to go in the mornings. In the market she bought tomatoes to have for her lunch with olive oil and basil and garlic, and as she was waiting to cross the Prado to the flower side, she saw a waiter they knew, Nicolas from Les Deux Soeurs, pedaling like a lunatic through the traffic whirling around the rotunda with the fabulous fountain. She bought gladioli on long stems and climbed back up the street to the big white apartment.

Jim had called, as promised, after three days, at 2:30 A.M. her time, confused by the spin of the globe. The connection was so good she could hear him breathe, the clink of ice in his highball, the low gurgle of the hot tub, and imagine his skin glowing like the enthusiasm in his voice. He'd been sailing all day, out from Balboa with a new client he was circling.

"Finish the sixth lecture?" he asked.

"Not yet."

"You're stalling."

"Yes. I do that."

"You believe you'll run out of things to occupy your mind. You won't."

It was true. She clung to nearly finished projects, left the last chapter drifting, afraid of closing up. She had, Jim believed, an endemic revisionist disease. "You must have played in your food when you were a kid," he said. Maybe that was why she preferred research to practice; it was easier to revise a theory than a patient.

She regretted now having agreed to the visiting professorship in Marseilles. Already, well before it had even started, not only had Jim begun to pace and fume about the incompetent French and the nincompoops he'd left in charge back home, but the romance of the whole idea had dissipated. When she visited the school, no one knew anything about her. The one professor who might would be on holiday until the middle of the month and had left no instructions. But she had signed on and would see it through. Maybe her eccentric accent would keep their attention.

She listened to Jim sing on about California and heard the pigeons adjusting themselves on her window ledge. Below, in the *place,* a woman's laugh climbed and fell in peculiar hollow intervals, like pan pipes. The despondent Adagio began, played on a piano somewhere in the neighborhood.

He'd be gone a while longer than he'd hoped, it looked like, Jim said. Things were in a tangle, just as he'd known they would be.

"I'll have plenty to keep me going," Elaine said.

"You've been wanting to get at those books you bought in Paris."

"Yes."

"Finish that last goddamn lecture and you'll have the time."

After Jim's call, wide awake again, she pushed open a pair of dilapidated shutters and stood at the tall window. In the street a car pulled out of a space, turned, and headed toward downtown. Beside another, three figures stood close together, talking. She heard wisps of their laughter and smelled the smoke of their cigarettes. It used to be, when she was younger, she regretted every bedtime in any city because other people would still be up doing things she'd never know about, going places she'd never see, tasting food created only late at night while her senses lay obliterated. She wasn't sure but what she felt half that way still.

Despite her accomplishments, she guessed she'd always be nagged by the suspicion that whatever her choices, they fell short or wide of some invisible mark, that she was, after all, only a professional.

The two women at the other table had still not spoken and one of them was crying. She had put on dark mirroring glasses and folded her hands in her lap, but the tears ran down from behind the lenses. At their feet the dog looked expectantly back and forth. The other handed her a tissue and nodded to the waiter standing in the doorway. He, the older waiter, brought their check, laid it down on a plate, and backed away, slapped his white cloth at the seat of a chair.

"I know you prefer it," Nicolas said, approaching with a small tray balanced on his fingertips, "but flan is too [a word she didn't know] on so hot an afternoon." He set before her a bowl of raspberries in light cream. What were they called—*framboises*. He tinkered with the extra setting again, held up a goblet to the light. "You have taken the boat out to the island?"

"Yes. The breeze was cool, but I was disappointed because the boat didn't really go to Île d'If, like they promised."

"So you did not meet our Count of Monte Cristo. Do you like old romances?"

"I don't have time anymore to read fiction."

"You read late at night. One o'clock sometimes. Two." His black Mediterranean eyes played, full of pranks and license, of surface. His skin, undressed, would not be as white as she first imagined, but darker, more like his exposed face and neck. Marseilles was an old, old port, the guidebooks said, the oldest town in France. The ships had been coming and going for twenty-six hundred years.

The glads lasted five days, shriveling blossom by blossom from the bottom up until she lifted them out of the jar, snapped them in two, and stuffed them into a plastic bag, carried it down to the street door.

Every day the collectors came in their loud, odorous, speeding truck to gather the discrete gray sacks.

She had set aside the morning to walk down to the port along Rue Paradis or Roma, before the heat struck, and see the fabled fishwives selling the night's catch at the Quai de Belges. Later it would be a simple thing to drift over to Les Deux Soeurs, where she and Jim had eaten three or four times and she could feel easy alone with the two waiters—Nicolas, the brash one, and his cousin. She'd take the unfinished sixth lecture with her in its green folder, in case she had a thought.

Standing in the doorway of the café, shaded by the blue awning, the cousins watched the two women who had not spoken to each other walk away, separated by the width of the little hairy dog. "You should avoid the night market," the older said. "Sooner or later they will arrest you."

"What have I done?"

"Think of Helêne."

"Yes. She would be in a tower of rage."

"And Tante Joelle will fire you."

"She reads late, late."

"Who?"

"The American. And leaves her shutters open. Sometimes I have seen her come to the window and look down, wondering, I think."

"Not necessarily about you."

Nicolas shrugged. "Who knows? Who can really tell?"

Elaine laid out francs enough to pay her check, noting the coffee and berries were not listed. So, then, this would have to be her last lunch at Les Deux Soeurs. To return again would be the same as inviting Nicolas to ring her bell at midnight or climb the rococo facade of her building, appear on the ledge among the pigeons, and push open the shutters. Well, there were plenty of restaurants around the port or in her own neighborhood.

Thoughts of the coming days dropped on her shoulders like heavy rats. She felt oppressed by the foreign sun, the impending and ceaseless straight, shallow looks of the dark French men and the darker Arabs. She would take a taxi home, do something or other to the apartment. Tomorrow the market would return to the Prado, she could buy a new bouquet, wander among the tables of cheap clothes, the stalls with vegetables more beautiful than flowers. Tonight, perhaps, she would finish the sixth lecture. Perhaps the pianist would finish the Adagio or attempt the Viennese-sounding Allegro in the next movement. Like the prisoner who must be soothed by the sound of his jailers' footsteps, perhaps she would be comforted by the thought that Nicolas, down in the street late, doing whatever he did among the silent cars and the laughing prostitutes, would glance up at her window and wonder if she were lonely and what she might be reading.

The multitude of little fishes, the anchovies of Venice or Cagnai, may be fixed at home, of course, with the courtesy of simplicity— lightly dusted with flour and black pepper, immersed for a minute in a hot deep-fryer, drained on paper, sprinkled with sea salt, and served quickly with lemon wedges, a confetti of minced parsley and cilantro. Guests will subside into a state of contemplation.

Partly because the fishes haven't been beheaded or gutted.

You could do this if you're fastidious and even-handed, but in Piraeus or Venice no such operation takes place. Like a cat in the sun, you can more or less close your eyes and purr. A cat will start in at the head end of a live fish, I've noticed, perhaps to get that part over with first, certainly to quiet the flailing meal. Think of flavors and crunch, not body parts.

Charles Perry, a food folklorist, writes that batter-fried fish arrived in both Japan, as tempura, and England, as one half of fish 'n' chips, from Portugal in the sixteenth and seventeenth centuries (the other half from Ireland). In the case of Japan, it was the merchants observing temporary Catholic religious seasons (*tempora*) who brought the idea; to England, Jews escaping an ongoing Catholic religious season (Inquisition).

A powdering with salt-and-pepper-flavored flour or cornmeal was quite enough fuss, Eloine believed, on the rare occasions when fresh fish came to her hands, such as the catfish Billy caught. For frying, clean tasteless oil, perhaps combined with butter, would suit me best today; she used a spoonful from her grease jar.

It does not escape me that much of what I tell of Eloine's kitchen swims in lard. One may think of these dishes often but only to resist the urge except occasionally, aware as we must be of Dr. Nuland's dire predictions about every pat of butter we ingest in *How We Die,* an unsentimental account of, as he says, "Life's Final Chapter."

The Silent Ukulele

*J*oy, thought by many to be a difficult emotion, was to Eloine second nature. First nature was, alas, remembering our penniless state. She could giggle, shout, and laugh one minute, and the next, as if a cloud had crossed her brow, turn dark and glum and wring her hands. She didn't *wring* her hands, exactly, in these moments of gloom, but rubbed the right one over the left, wrist to fingertips, down over the gold wedding band, a smoothing gesture, perhaps signifying only a wish to drive away wrinkles, those encroaching signs of mortality, as every night without fail she patted Pond's cold cream onto her face and neck, dabbed out of little white crocks. "I declare," she might say in a black moment, "I think I just ought to give up the ghost, it all seems so hard. Like being alive wasn't the main intent." Phonetically, because she had no final *r*'s and not many interior ones either, those words would be rendered more accurately as "Ah declaya." The glass object into which she gazed to judge the extent of deterioration was a "meera."

She maintained a degree of vanity, hating to be caught in a soiled house dress by unexpected company or on washday without her girdle, her apron and stockings wet, her hair in a tousle ("I look like Medusa," she said, an image lost on me for many years), water on the kitchen floor, and "not a thing in the house to eat."

When a teenager, she was kicked by a mule that smashed her shin, leaving an obvious dent and misset bone. Written in 1918, a letter from Papa to a friend noted, "Eloine is here on a visit and doesn't hobble much on her bad leg"; nevertheless, this, combined with feet crippled by vanity's shoes, made walking difficult. Yet there was seldom any other way of getting around. The Dad's mine truck, quite often in running condition but left finally to rot away in the yard, was not used for frivolous trips, and both of the cars he bought within my memory were soon repossessed.

Therefore, Eloine did not venture abroad as often as her personality would have led her, but liked to get gussied up when she did. Getting "gussied up," I might here note, was not the same as getting "all dolled up," a term of contempt for women of questionable taste. Had circumstances been different, she'd have gone in for inauspicious style, not couture but "good" clothes, perhaps a blue suit with fur trimmings, size 40 to 42. Of black, she said, "It makes my complexion yellow. Promise me you won't bury me in black."

Every now and then the folks of Skull Valley would get their blood up and throw a dance in the Community Hall, the same one-story white wooden building in which Sunday School and Church would be celebrated the next morning. Nearly everybody went, the D'Armands and Cantrells excepted, and took their kids. Miss Nellie Bishop, who could render the tonic, subdominant, and dominant chords in any key on the piano, accompanied a fiddler, sometimes a guitarist, sometimes two or more of each. The dances, a mix of square and round, gave anyone the chance to shine who got the urge.

From an unpublished nineteenth-century family history, I read:

After the country began to get settled so there were enough youngsters, they would have flax pullings. Then the boys would sidle up to their best girls and help them along with their work. Now and then, some would make a party at night, but that soon went out of fashion, as the people on looking around, soon found out that it was a lower class that resorted to such amusement. Some even tried to have dances, but soon got so ashamed and quit when they found out that the devil always attended every dance that was gotten up. Let me say to those that are so far behind the times in this enlightened day and age of the world, who go to dances, to stick your fingers in your ears and stop the sound of the music and you will think you have gotten into a set of fools, just to see them hopping and skipping around over the floor.

If the devil attended the Skull Valley dances, he appeared after we had to go home at about ten. Jim Crace, in *The Devil's Larder,* has solved the vexing question of what else the devil does at night. With his thin white hands he picks into his bag all the best mushrooms growing in the woods, leaving the tasteless ones for us, which explains why only a few early risers can wax poetic over mushrooms while the rest of us, never knowing better, find them in need of deep reconsideration. I think Crace's research also explains why, in Skull Valley, we had only poisonous toadstools, a batch of which, so the story went, killed Ruby Russell's toddling child. But Ruby was *not all there,* "Po' thing," and could not remember how the child came to be in the first place, so her account of its death might or might not have been accurate, the sort of circumstance one didn't look into closely. In any case, the child died and served thereafter as a lesson to us all who might be tempted to pick those pale caps in the meadows or the sepia-colored, thick, frilly growths off the bark of fallen trees. Omer, in later life, claimed, not in Eloine's presence, to be an expert mushroom picker. Apparently, he had worked out some agreement with the devil, and together, each fond of plants or fungi with entertainment value, they romped the midnight woods and high deserts, picking and choosing. I have wondered what the devil wears on occasions like this. Omer was a nudist.

We had no drunks that I was aware of, but how would I have known, far from the center of village knowledge, still in a caul of innocence? The question of drink did come up regularly after there was a dance, especially if held in Kirkland, seven miles down the track, crossroads with a tough reputation, but I seldom knew to whom to attach such a mystery, though Jimmy had nominees I could borrow. About loose women, I sensed only Eloine's displeasure with one or two who fed their kids solely on pickles and wieners. "I have half a mind to send them over some of this roast," she might say. It was the thought that counted.

Of liquor, in Eloine's house there was none. One year, though,

Colonel Fitzhugh, a recent arrival with wife and tubercular son, invited for a Christmas steamed pudding, brought brandy to burn over it, an amazing transpiration. But then, he had been to France. To Eloine, brandy was not aqua vitae, but tasted like medicine, which it was, of course, from the discovery of alcohol in the early twelfth century until it finally got out of the hands of apothecaries into the clutches of the general public in the sixteenth century. That it might taste like medicine was also a way of keeping us boys from lusting after it. In our house, cod liver oil stood for medicine. Or the other way around.

Eloine's syllabub, a thick boiled custard I sickened on every year, had no whiskey in it, though she allowed in the South, Papa and his gentlemen friends put a drop in theirs, a claim I doubt from having read his obituary eulogy, as he was praised as a pillar of the Baptist Church of Mount Juliet.

Ever vigilant for something edible she had overlooked, as evidenced by her passing thoughts on frogs and her interest in what we had seen in the swamp or on our ceaseless forays into the hills and woods, Eloine admonished us, "Now, you boys scratch around while you're out," meaning, keep your eyes open for more than only snakes. Mr. Patterson let her have all the silage corn she wanted in summer, and the fallen apples later, sometimes a neighbor had an extra lug of tomatoes, but these were stopgaps, beads on a long, undecorated string. Jimmy and I foraged as we roamed our *terroir* and knew what was edible—a certain little bulb, for instance, possibly a wild garlic, growing at the foot of a short stalk with purple flower, sweet as a nut. Black walnuts that dropped from the trees in autumn and ruined whatever clothes you were wearing. Wild grapes, no bigger'n a minute, and elderberries from which Eloine made jam, the fruit of a single big mulberry tree still growing, year upon year, beside the burned-out depression of what had been somebody's house long before our time. We knew where all the birds were nesting, except the killdees and whippoorwills, which are invisible, but didn't gather eggs to eat because they might not any longer be yolks and whites but half-formed babies.

The Government, that amorphous squid in Washington run by the chin-up man with the cigarette holder, sometimes pitched in.

Omer (junior), being oldest, was assigned the ignoble task of dragging a wagon, *my* red wagon with the wooden side rails, all the way to Mrs. Warren's store, a two-mile hazard course over paths, byways, and dirt roads, in order to be handed ten pounds of beans, ten of rice, and ten of flour, the allotment to "poor" people, which explains why Eloine would not go herself, nor would have the aloof Dad had he been present, but for a different reason. I thought such an adventure perfectly sane and remarkable, but not so my snarling brother. He still felt humiliated by it, and similar deprecations, sixty years later when we had our last laughs together. Fifty cents he earned as a ranch laborer, in any given fourteen-hour day, and Eloine was glad to have it. Fifteen dollars a month, plus the government beans, flour, and rice, judicious poaching, raids on cornfields and orchards, the lucky shot—and no electricity, gas, rent, or water bills to pay—went a long way toward placating the jaws of the wolf. Angela, of the famous *Ashes,* was no worse off. She may have burned room partitions for heat, but there were times when Eloine eyed the flour-pasted, many-layered wallpaper and mused, in one of her moments of hysteria, on what could be made of it with, for example, some watercress growing wild on the creek banks. On an upward stroke, at least no one shared our outhouse.

Sometimes it seems as if it's the little inhuman misdemeanors we commit, even without malice, that cling to our fur like baby monkeys. One afternoon, long after Skull Valley days, strolling along toward the bridge to Paradise Island in Nassau, I was met by a small boy, maybe five. Neither black nor white, of the more synthesized island brown, he had a nose deformed by accident of birth or genes. He approached carrying a conch shell. In the most polite, child-elegant voice, in precise English, he said, "Please sir, if you will give me five dollars, I will let you have this shell."

When I said no, now passing, he turned and quickly adjusted his plea. "One dollar? Seventy-five cents. Anything." I walked on, looking back once, struck with remorse, to see him examining something in the weeds, as all kids will. It wouldn't have hurt me to give him a dollar. Hell, five dollars and he could have kept the damned shell, his day would have been nicer, and mine, too. He has forgotten. Just another failed attempt to enter into business with the white tourists who would, in his experience, buy the commonest things sometimes.

He was probably the son of one of the conch salad vendors whose booths line the quay under the bridge. For two or three dollars you can buy a made-on-the-spot salad, created from a just-killed conch, beaten, macerated, chopped, whacked, and dipped into a bucket of . . . well, perhaps water, mixed with onions and peppers, "cooked" in fresh lime juice and salt. Consuming this creation, made in conditions that should give pause, is but another gastronomic adventure, not for one who asks, "Do I dare to eat a peach?" but nothing at all to one who grew up on the edge of a swamp.

Conch meat, the consistency of full-grown octopus, is a staple of Bahamian cookery. Besides as the raw salad, above, it's offered in the fritter manner, where mincing and grinding make easier chewing, and as steaks, which despite a good pounding require more thoughtful mastication and sound teeth.

In our swamp, meandering through Patterson's cow meadow, there was a section about a hundred feet long running quicker and clearer between grassy banks a foot apart. In this area there grew, from time to time, families of crawdads. Eloine had known these creatures in Tennessee and welcomed them when Jimmy and I could catch two or three dozen. I believe she used only the tails, shelled, rolled in a mixture of sugar and spices and grease, and baked in the oven next to the biscuits, then squirted with lime or lemon juice. I remember them as crunchy and sweet.

On the other side of the world, in the city of Cairns, from which you take a boat out to see the Great Barrier Reef, they eat an appealing arthropod called a bay bug, an amalgam of small lobster, shrimp, and crawdad that lives in the vast, shallow bay's murky waters. In the kitchen these are treated simply, as you would, with respect, treat a lobster—or a crawdad—at most floating them along with brandade of emperor fish, shaped like quenelles, in a cool gazpacho sauce.

Farther south in the glorious city of Sydney, fish at the Rockpool Restaurant lifts off beyond gravitational attraction, involving coconut milk, kaffir lime leaves, ginger, Thai basil, and a farrago (from the Latin *farrago,* mixed fodder for cattle) of other Asian ingredients, just to demonstrate to what ends one can go as a panic-stricken young Australian chef. A friend says his meal there was among the five best he has had in his life; he was unable to tell me anything about the first four. In my handling, the dish, in visual attractiveness, resembles the mouth of the Río de la Plata.

When a mountain lion yawns, you can see the gap's big enough to stick a year-old baby's head in. At the flash end of the yawn, she pulls back her lips, then you get a good look at the four yellow canines, about an inch-and-a-half long, all those other crunchers, cutters, grinders, and you understand how with all that, plus retractile claws and her weight, she can kill a mule deer in no time. Or just about any beast or brute she comes upon in spare pine forest or rocky mesa.

The lives of deer and mountain lion in the West have always gone together, hoof and claw, when nature is left alone. But "It's a fundamental Christian value to dominate animals" I read with astonishment in a book on lions written by a wildlife scientist who favors "sport harvests," yet another euphemism for eradicating bothersome animals. In the 1920s in the Kaibab Forest, in general an area bordering the Grand Canyon on the north, the government's biological control system, prompted by hunters who like to think killing deer is the exclusive right of man, eliminated all the natural predators. Succeeding beyond their wildest dreams, they raised the deer count from a measly 4,000 to 100,000 in twenty years—then stood by and watched 60,000 starve to death. Great thinking.

All this, following from Teddy Roosevelt's lead, that ambivalent champion of wildlife and manly outdoor rusticity, resulted in the deliberate killing of some 65,000 mountain lions in the first three-quarters of the twentieth century in western North America, the one I tasted in barbecue sauce included. It would take nearly another twenty-five years for Arizona to stop paying bounties for dead lions and regulate their deaths by elevating them from shoot-on-sight varmints to big game animals, which translates: You can still kill them but you have to buy a license, hire a guide, locate a nearby airport and taxidermist.

One Sunday morning at the Community Hall, after the week's raving maniac had finished preaching, word went around that Alf

Rainey had shot him a lion, so there was nothing to do about it but pile into cars wherever there was space and drive up to his place to take a look.

Old Alf Rainey was famous for a number of attributes, an attitude toward bathing and clean clothes among them. A prodigious aptitude with chawin' tobacca and spit, another. A succession of women, each of whom came down with nerves. And a rotting display of varmint hides nailed to his goat sheds—coyote, bobcat, raccoon, porkypine, squirrel, jackrabbit, skunk, mountain lion—and soon to be another. He raised both kinds of goats, the scrawny sort we ate at the Goat Picnic and Angoras.

Standing by the open tailgate of his stake-bed International truck that he kept the side hoods hooked up on all the time so air could circulate in the engine better, where he'd laid the cat—cougar, he called it—he said, "I seen him come slippin' down offa that needle rock right at sunup, through the draw yonder, in a the herd before I could get my rifle out. And sure as heck, he was carryin' off a kid when I shot him." Hawk, spit. "Took me only the one."

The cat's head hung off the truck edge and you could get right up to it. Its eyes were mostly closed, dark-rimmed slits crawling with black flies, but you could see a slice of tawny eyeball, gone dry and dull. It had a wide, flat nose, light and leathery on the end, black nostrils, and a soft-looking white chin under its whiskers. I was fond of Zane Grey at about that time and remembered his description of a trussed, live lion in *Shooting Lions in the Grand Canyon:*

> I wanted to see a wild lion's eyes at close range. They were exquisitely beautiful, their physical properties as wonderful as their expression. Great half globes of tawny amber, streaked with delicate wavy lines of black, surrounding pupils of intense purple fire. Pictures shone and faded in the amber light—the shaggy tipped plateau, the dark pines and smoky canyons, the great dotted downward slopes, the yellow cliffs and crags. Deep in those live pupils changing, quickening with a thousand vibrations, quivered the soul of this savage beast, the wildest of all wild nature, unquenchable love of life and freedom, flame of defiance and hate.

Unquenchable, indeed.

"Brr," Eloine said, "he gives me the heebie-jeebies."

"Can I touch him?" I asked.

"Better not, you might catch something."

"I heard Indians eat them," a woman said—Gladys D'Armand it was, fat and dark, before she got married again and we had to remember to call her Mrs. Knob. "Wonder what it would taste like."

"Like eating your house cat, I imagine," Eloine said, "and I'm sure not hungry enough to try that yet," though you could see her cook's eye taking stock. A hundred pounds of meat going to waste. Stew. Jerky. It wouldn't be until ten years later I could tell her, from first-taste experience, that mountain lion, barbecued, wasn't bad. Pale and slippery but not bad.

"Course I been a-smellin' cougar for a week," Alf was saying, his chaw in his cheek like lump jaw ("How he could smell anything but goat's beyond me," Eloine remarked behind her hand) "and night before last it was, he come right in a the bedroom where me and the missus . . . " ("Ain't they all called missus, though," said Gladys) "was sleepin'. Felt his breath on my face, like to give me a heart attach."

"What'd you do then, Alf?"

"Just laid there not darin' to move a muscle, think if I was to he'd take my hand off or worse, and my rifle clean out in the kitchen over the door, but when the missus broke out in one a her snores, he taken off."

"How'd he get in the house?"

"They're smart as a dog. Lift latches, turn doorknobs, take the screen offa window if they've a mind to. Or come right through the glass."

Alf put one foot up on the running board, spat into a patch of rabbitbrush, crossed his muscular simian arms—he wore singlets two generations before they were considered hot—and said, "Reminds me a the time up in Wyomin' when we used a run a thousand head a sheep in weather so cold it'd fix a brass monkey."

"Here we go again," whispered Mrs. Warren.

It was about then that Jimmy, standing on a rear hubcap looking at the lion from the other end, made the observation that it was a her—not a him—because her teats were full and leaking milk—

" 'Preciate it if you'd climb down offa there, sonny."

—meaning that somewhere in the scrubby brush not too far away one or a pair of kittens too young to wean was rapidly starving to death. Maybe up in that granite-rock canyon near the Dad's mine, The Boston and Arizona, in the Indian caves.

"If you-all have heard enough," Gladys D'Armand said, heaving her body around in its yellow dress with the whole field of red poppies on it, "I believe I have."

"If you'll just drop us off at the lane," Eloine said, "I'd be obliged."

"Be happy to. What you-all having for dinner today?"

"I got up with the chickens and started some dough to rising." Elisions like this might have sidetracked Gladys. We knew she meant there wouldn't be much of anything. A slice of gummy roast and spaghetti and a cloverleaf roll. "But I think I've about lost my appetite," she said.

Mountain lions were another creature Eloine dreaded, and seeing one up close didn't help much. It made them real, whereas before she had, I think, shoved them over into a spiritual realm, a mystic evocation of the Navajo and Hopi, like kachinas and thunderbirds, more symbolic than actual. They don't typically come down into domestic sites, though I have an acquaintance in the hot, forested area of northern California near the Pit River who shot one recently in his chicken and duck yard that had begun making regular early-morning raids. A transient young male probably, not yet with his own range, passing through and finding an easy mark.

It was from this same chicken yard I acquired a truly aged rooster for an authentic coq au vin that required a hacksaw to dismember and three hours to cook. I ought to have served it as a company dinner, rather than family, because then no one, out of politeness, would have dared say what others said. You couldn't blame the lion for passing over this one. I don't know whether any anthropologist or dentition specialist has made a study of pre–World War II French peasants' skulls, but I'll bet they'd find some iron-tough jaws and teeth if indeed, as we're led to believe, coq au vin was a typical solution for dispatching geriatric cocks.

Eloine's spaghetti, served plain with margarine, salt, and pepper— no tomato sauce or cheese—I still prefer to the tyrannical white rice the government issued. I've never liked rice except in puddings or risotto and don't apologize for this confession. Alongside hummus, in a slightly inferior position to pasta salads, rice is a questionable food, that is, if we are talking about any level of gastronomic illusion rather than mere subsistence or "convenience," that hateful term. Mutually, there is something about rice that does not like me. I can't cook it successfully more than three times in ten, even with an electric pot, and each time wonder why, once again, I let myself be talked into trying. It's a paean to the adaptability of mankind that we can cultivate, cook, and consume so many unappetizing things and even wax poetic over them, as in the Cambodian figure of speech when water is brought into the fields of seedlings—they call it the "drowning of partridges and turtledoves." Wouldn't you prefer eating partridges and turtledoves? There must be innumerable Chinese panegyrics on rice. Recently in the *Los Angeles Times,* a Viet-American food writer, aghast, wrote, "I've observed my friends snap these [shrimp] up like crazy, *sometimes even eating them without rice"* (emphasis mine).

Our sister, Martha, who fled this vale of tears with lots of money in the bank, having lived a spinster in symbiosis with Eloine and therefore never learning to cook, discovered late in life she could boil rice and subsist on it, a dolorous existence. I think of her with sadness as all alone she passed her last months in company with an ever-present pot of coffee and another of gluey white rice, standing at the stove with fork in hand—the hand that for forty-five years held, in succession, the 328,500 cigarettes that did her in.

One of the worst food disasters occurred with the death of Bossy, our brown cow. Where and how Eloine got her, I know not, probably about to be discarded by her previous owner because of age, walked home by Billy with a rope behind his horse, itself a crazed animal, as Billy was Eloine's jewel of Faulknerian inclinations.

The cow, housed in the barn, gave milk and grew fatter with calf.

Jimmy, two-and-a-half years older, companion and the facilitator of all my troubles, born with a fabulist's mind, sly as a weasel—a gift that must have helped him enormously in later life—decided one day near Bossy's term that, due to her special condition, she should be fed whatever she wanted. So we gave her buckets full of mash, a rich mixture of some sort meant as a dietary supplement to ordinary hay, something like vitamin pills or steroids.

By the next day she bloated, gave birth, and died. A 50 percent loss of our mature livestock, Billy's loco horse being the other 50. Getting rid of the cadaver of a grown cow is no simple matter, either. It cannot be left, as Antigone might say, "unburied, food for the wild dogs and wheeling vultures." It has to be dragged, by horse, truck, or tractor, somewhere far away. Eloine bemoaned both the death of the cow and the loss of several hundred pounds of meat, but the rule was, you didn't eat an animal that died of its own accord, an example of sensible Deuteronomic wisdom on the one hand—*You shall not eat anything that has died a natural death. You shall give it to aliens . . . and they may eat it, or you may sell it to a foreigner*—and an illustration, on the other hand, of hope for what tomorrow would bring.

The calf, however, thrived, fed first with a twisted rag dipped in Carnation canned milk, then from a baby bottle, once one was located, not an item kept back in Eloine's cupboard because she nursed all five of her children until, as she said, "You bit me, then that was that. You got solid food."

It should go without saying, Jimmy and I never admitted to the murder of Bossy, as neither did Omer ever confess, except to me on his deathbed, the killing of Margaret, Eloine's pet brown hen, by a method too revolting to believe or report.

I wasn't present at the butchering of the calf, or have suppressed the memory, but recall its head bobbing in the big pot on the stove and of being fooled by Eloine, who had sometimes the mind of a medieval trickster, into eating the cerebral cortex, thinking it scrambled eggs, a moment I was reminded of in *Indiana Jones and the Temple of Doom* when they offer chilled monkey brains, in situ, to the heroine who sensibly faints.

A calf's brains with scrambled eggs, the Hungarians say, should be of a creamy texture, like risotto. Add salt to taste.

The other whole head I recall boiling on the range was a pig's. Eloine did not raise pigs in Arizona, though she had in Tennessee, where the smokehouse was still an integral part of the farm, and I presume she knew what could be made of all a hog's parts. This particular head, given, thrown away, or purchased for a quarter, yielded god knows what for the table, but understanding the squeamishness of her boy eaters, Eloine disguised its true nature in scalloped potatoes (or a mess of greens for herself alone), meat loaf, scrambled eggs, a casserole of white beans (her modest take on cassoulet), or wherever unparticularized bits of pig might fold in.

So, though one would not call Eloine's cooking mysterious in any Appalachian way, it contained secrets. A farmer's genteel daughter who rode the train each day from Mount Juliet into Nashville to attend college, large of bosom and hip, with tightly corseted waist, high rolled hair, prominent dark eyes behind round spectacles, as old photos show, Eloine was hardly prepared for exotic recipes. Her strength lay in a practical and poverty-born sense that there must be more edible food in the world than most people realized. She was, I think, quite capable of tossing into the soup pot wild roots and greens or body parts few others, even in the hobo camps, would consider edible. "Get out from under my feet," she would say in a distracted mien when she was about to experiment and wanted no witnesses.

As Alice Waters believes, according to Adam Gopnik (he who said never serve amusing noodles), "in . . . the reformed carrot in the backyard garden insensibly improving the family around the dinner table," Eloine believed in the evening meal. *There, see what I have done, once again, from nothing.* Apogee of the day, to which those gathered ought to pay attention and for which count their blessings. To eat her food was to bless it. That some sanctimonious visitor might wish to offer a prayer to God "for this we are about to receive" set rather hard with her. She wondered (you could see the tight set of her lips) why so many men, especially so many pious ones, credited God and overlooked the forager, scrimper, and cook.

Particularly in the winter light and slight stench of a coal-oil lamp, with a shine of dampness on her face from the stove, her black hair tendrilling alongside her temples, she sat like the polestar, triumphant at the table head, often too tired to eat (but she would have been picking in the kitchen), pleased to be in charge of this concerto. If there was company, she complemented it with a little appoggiatura of doubt: "My biscuits just didn't rise tonight."

This preemptive self-denigration I hear from many cooks and catch in myself also, a kind of apologia before the fact, as students will do when handing in a paper that actually might be brilliant. I don't imagine Alice Waters doing this.

Of music in our household, more might be said, but not a great deal more. The Dad, who claimed he could fix anything mechanical so far devised by the mind of man—if so inclined—and who was praised in an old letter from 1924 by the Porcupine Davidson Gold Mine Ltd., of Broutford, Ontario, as being "a good mine mechanic on all classes of machinery, a good mine blacksmith and a particularly good hoistman and Diesel engine operator" was a musical tinker too.

With a couple of like-minded men gathered in our living room on a summer evening or on the porch, he could play the violin, guitar, harmonica, Jew's harp, and banjo, as well as sing (when not with an instrument in his mouth) old mid-southern songs like "Red River Valley" and "In the Gloaming," "She'll Be Comin' 'Round the Mountain," "Buffalo Girls," and "Old Black Joe." I preferred "The Streets of Laredo," but their repertoire petered out at the Louisiana border.

What the quality of these recitals may have been I cannot with certainty say, nor when they ended, as I always fell asleep, to awaken the next morning with a blank in my night, sure once again the best parts had happened after I was put to bed.

The Fitzhugh boy, the tubercular kid Omer's age who came with his parents, Colonel and Mrs. Fitzhugh, gave me astonishing outgrown gifts, such as lead soldiers, Parcheesi and Monopoly games, but the best of all a ukulele complete except for strings. It came with an instruction book. I sang and accompanied myself, employing all the right frets and fingering, so as to be ready when the day came we might afford new strings, a day that never came. My only other musical instrument was a Sears drum, about ten inches in diameter, upon which I rattled through my whole repository of songs, "On the Isle of Capri" foremost among them, until Eloine, about to be driven mad, could think of some reasonable alternative. "Johnny, run out to the woodpile and bring me all the sticks you can carry."

With my gutless ukulele and drum, I was busy preparing an operatic career. It was Jimmy who came up with the notion of opera singing, whatever that might mean, and passed it on to me, his wide-eyed naïf who'd believe in anything. We had, among a dozen thick records for the windup Victrola, one by Amelita Galli-Curci and another by Lily Pons. No tenors or baritones, as I recall, but no matter. I'd be a coloratura if that's what it took. By pressing your finger gently against the head of the needle arm, you could cause Amelita or Lily to hold a high F interminably, until Eloine emerged from the kitchen on the verge of breakdown. "Let that po' woman rest!"

She ranked opera singing in about the same order as glossolalia or ululation (Latin, *ululare,* to howl), a lapse of consciousness, an opinion arrived at long before she could possibly have heard, by some accidental twist of a knob, Maria Callas. She would have agreed with Plato on this aspect of mentality.

Opera singers, or even visiting trained church singers, who held their mouths in unnatural positions (she never saw Leontyne Price) drove her into uncontrollable giggles, her eyes streaming behind her hand. When introduced to overwrought singers, she was apt to say with a smile laid over a straight face, "I'm so tickled to meet you."

Billy saved his money all one summer, herding goats for old Alf Rainey, to buy a radio with a battery as big, almost, as the kind used in cars. He strung a wire from it through a window up to the windmill as an antenna, and at Eloine's insistence, a special weather rod as well, because she believed antennae attracted lightning, that pulled by the radio beams it would sizzle into the windmill and then straight down the wire into the house.

On it I heard my first opera, *Aïda,* with Milton Cross explaining as we went. I especially liked the ending, where Radames, stuck in the underground tomb, finds Aïda and screams, *"Tu—in questa tomba!"* and then together, until they run out of air, they sing, *"O terra, addio."* For some time after, I thought this was the normal end for singers in Egyptian opera, as one of my daughters, at age nine, wept—way up in the Family Circle of the old Met—for Gilda (Roberta Peters) stabbed in her gunny sack, yet bravely if limpidly singing, as her father prepares to cry, *"Ah! La maledizione!"*

Society

*A*s Eloine liked to say, "Least we have a pretty view."

Starting at the front yard, a patch of barefoot-beaten dirt but with a three-yard-long double hedge of wild yellow roses, thorny and timidly flowered, anchored in one corner by the heavenly tree—a stinky specimen in which orioles hung their sock nest each year—the view proceeded through a pair of useless posts on which hung a prolapsed gate. . . . Starting anew: Think of the overture to Donizetti's *Don Pasquale.* Let the rose hedge be represented by that luscious cello song at the beginning, Ernesto's theme. Now follow along, both visually and aurally, as the music runs across its tunes and the eye across the vista. Okay, the gate. Beyond, the turnaround, a version of the circular drive, then the gentle slope of catclaw bushes, cocklebur and foxtail, horehound and prickly pear, down to the low palisade of bluish gray scrub oak at the fence line demarcating Patterson's campestral cow field. A barn off to the right side, unpainted, stoic, barnlike. A bit below, near where our slimy pond exists, a slight rise, the midden of some long-ago Indian family, occasionally giving up shards of pottery, sometimes an arrowhead, a half-finished obsidian spearhead, a petrified fingerprint in a bit of brown clay, the source of Grandma Shoup's arrowhead collection and, possibly, the spot from which she first began communicating with Brahms. The pasture, beyond a sweep of swamp watered by the underground stream, leaps into green verdancy where white-faced red cattle ruminate in it, the bucolic equivalent to Donizetti's Moderato passage, *leggero e stacc.,* because if you were walking in it, you'd find it alive with frogs, field mice, green snakes, butterflies, grasshoppers—a whole textbook of entomological life. Farther off, at the midhorizon, cottonwoods, a stately shag of them, follow the course of the big creek, brilliant jewel-green from spring through summer, then to yellow-gold in fall, a wintry touch of Payne's gray for three months thereafter. The view is widening, as Donizetti is lifting into his *Più allegro*, funneling open to the brown hills, low and lumpy, across the railroad bed, its tar and bones, and beyond to the blue mountains, final, enclosing, and grand against a bright sky. In the hands of Carlos Fuentes, this would be a spectral sight, dark with blood, speckled with gore and the rotting hardware of passing, repassing, and finally defeated troops. In the spookery of Carlos Castaneda, there would be peyote here, sage, spirit, and joke.

Implied in Eloine's note of resignation, "Least we have a pretty view," was an accounting of all we did not have. "I do wish Sister Lena could see it." Sister Lena, along with Sister Clara, had been dead for more than thirty years, of scarlet fever, but Lena had artistic talent and could paint like the dickens. I have, god knows how it filtered down to me, a rat-chewed pressed board on which Sister Lena in the late century-before-last painted a country church scene along the order of Grandma Moses but stiffer, coldly Presbyterian. Sister Lena, one can assume, was not a relaxed young lady of Bohemian manners, but a twenty-two-year-old virgin living under the caution of a bony house-hold.

To Eloine, myopic, this scene must have looked like something the French painters were trying in about the year she was born. It evoked in her both serenity and anxiety. She was, after all, *stuck* in this scene, as she was every day forced to battle the subtle forces of discord by the name of poverty. Even while standing in a source of beauty and apparent harmony, she must have sensed it as a model of transience. The same landscape painted every day only becomes a series, however scumbled, not a new scene; you feel evolving life rushing past, sun, clouds, and shadow, night and decay and fear.

"Law," she exclaimed one morning following just such a reverie, "I've got too much to do to sit here and gaze at the stars." With a Calvinistic lurch, she rose from the porch rocker and headed back in.

"You boys bring me in some wood and I'll scratch us up something for lunch."

"Doughnuts," suggested Jimmy.

"Chocolate pudding," I said. Chocolate pudding or chocolate pie with meringue were two other causes of my vomiting at picnics.

She set out a perfect lunch: wieners boiled till they busted, then sliced lengthwise onto white bread with mayonnaise, a plop of potato salad, and hot doughnut holes. Milk (*pacem* Bossy) from a Carnation can, half diluted with water. We had, on average, two soda pops a year, treats at the store, except Jimmy when he was younger, so they told me, and had a mysterious illness and like to died. He got to drink—in fact, was begged to drink—all the soda pop he would, all colors.

"And then I want you to run up to the store and get some things. Tell Mrs. Warren she'll have to put it on the bill again."

"She always does up her mouth—like this—when I say that," Jimmy objected.

"I know. It sticks in my craw, but it won't be for long, I reckon. Just till our ship comes in. Comb your hair and put on some shoes."

"Why do *we* have to go?"

"Now, don't you chime in. Sister's coming down on the train in the morning and I don't have a crumb in the house."

"Can we buy a jawbreaker?"

"We can't afford it."

So we walked and dawdled, with many a detour, some to examine such phenomena as a newly discovered dead cow swarming with maggots, others to avoid the living ones, once to climb a cottonwood and hide from Alonzo Contreras and Hank Ramon on their horses because, being full-grown cowboys, they had threatened to cut off our ears, along the cow paths, up the creek, across a pasture, and along the big road lined with sunflowers, ditches spattered with brilliant red Indian paintbrush and Mexican bird-of-paradise, the white trumpets of milkweed, and the fat globules of locoweed that could drive a cow mad, quick across the culvert in which, sometimes, hobos lived, to the store.

There Hap waited on us as usual, Mrs. Warren herself busy gossiping with the woman who pumped gas across the road and Mrs.

Kennett Ida, who was thought by some, Eloine among them, to be losing her mind and to whom Eloine referred as Mrs. Idle. Hap had a clubfoot and walked, as I have since imagined Lord Byron doing, with a great heave and thump, but with purpose and energy. He lived in a tiny square house at the foot of the garden behind the store and had become, to our jug ears, something of a tangle lately, owing to a one-sided conversation overheard between Eloine and Billy, who was always in some "serious" trouble or other, such as neglecting to come home at night, or snitching the Dad's tobacco, or causing the father of some teenage girl to come over for a talk. The diatribe we heard had to do with Hap . . . and something, something, not clearly understood through the walls.

"Ow!" Billy began.

"I'll pull out more'n your hair, you hear me?" Eloine said. "You and that pack of ruffians—you leave that po' man alone."

"Well, he did it. He's the one asked us to come in—"

"Don't talk back to me, young man. What that fellow does is none of your business and if you can't be nice, stay away. You've got sense enough for that, haven't you? Leave him alone." Then her voice dropped and we had to almost squeeze through the cracks to hear. "Not everybody's the same in this world, you ought to know by now."

"But he—"

"Hush. And let me finish. I don't know about these things, not exactly. I do know he's a man to be pitied, and he can't help it any-more'n he can help having that crippled foot. Some people—well, not every man is the same. I won't have you and those Christoffersen boys tormenting him, you hear?"

"Yes, ma'am."

"All I've got to say. And I better not hear another word about it."

Dang. Not another word.

"What do you think it was?" I whispered.

Jimmy thought Hap had been naked.

"Nekkid?" I gasped. In his house? Walking around in his house *naked*? On his bad leg? My imagination would not stretch so far. Unlike city kids, who have opportunities galore to see each other naked—in the swimming pool dressing room, the showers, the gym—

we were as timid as convent girls about our bodies, except with each other, and even then segregated into The Two Older Boys and The Two Little Ones. An occasional glimpse of the Dad dressing, a sorrowful instance of which I am coming to anon.

"Or he was hiding his gold under the floorboards." Jimmy, reading *Silas Marner* at the time, made a logical leap.

So this day, at the store, we examined Hap openly but couldn't find any development to speak of. He seemed his normal, busy, thumping self.

Food was Eloine's way of making overtures or amends. The next time she walked to the store with us, slowly, a tedious process along accepted paths, she carried a bundle wrapped in a cloth and we paused at the wire gate leading into Mrs. Warren's garden. "Here," she said, "run put this on his stoop."

"Aw—"

"Hush now, and do as I say." She knew perfectly well we had overheard her small lesson with Billy. Teaching, not by parable, but by the glancing blow.

What was probably in Hap's basket:

ELOINE'S APPLESAUCE CAKE

½ cup butter
1 teaspoon ground cinnamon
1 teaspoon ground cloves
1 cup sugar
1 egg
1 ¼ cups cold applesauce
1 ½ cups sifted all-purpose flour
½ teaspoon baking soda
¼ teaspoon salt
½ cup raisins or dried cranberries
½ cup chopped nuts

Preheat the oven to 350°F. Lightly grease a 9 × 5 × 3-inch loaf pan.

Cream the butter with the spices, adding the sugar gradually. Beat in the egg and applesauce. Into another bowl, sift the flour, soda, and salt. Add the raisins and nuts to the flour mixture, then add all to the butter mixture. Stir until everything is well blended. Pour into the loaf pan. Bake for 1 hour or until a broomstraw comes out clean. The cake cuts better if allowed to relax a few hours.

As I have said, Eloine's sense of class distinction had much to do with how people fed their children. When in the store, she cut her eyes this way and that, quite deliberately dawdling, not only to hear the gossip but to notice what others bought. Many had no more resources than she with which to indulge cranky appetites.

But even in such a small place, society was sliced into a terrine of layers. Although from the South and therefore steeped in its traditions of race perception, and although I imagine her picture of those entering heaven to be much like Mrs. Turpin's in Flannery O'Connor's "Revelation"—accountable for good order and common sense and respectable behavior, with the darkies trailing far behind—she believed nice folks ought not make a big to-do over their prejudices. If we had ever said "nigger," we'd've been slapped and sent to bed without supper, punishment of which there was none greater. There were no black people in Skull Valley.

Careful not to teach prejudice outright, sometimes her own burst forth unwittingly. As many women might say "Shit!" when their cake falls (the boys' fault, slamming doors, pounding through the house), Eloine said "Shoot!" more completely, "Shoot a big black monkey!" an unconscious, or interiorized, racial slur.

How we learned the Dad's mother—dead leaving him but one of a passel of kids—was Jewish came about because his one surviving sister, I.T., a woman of leisure, occupied her days back in Tennessee amassing family information. By some stretch of genealogical interpretation, fiddling with data mostly hearsay, she concluded we were related to "the lovely" Jane Froman, a rather famous radio singer of the day. She also proved we were related to Meriwether Lewis and that Davy Crockett once spent a night in some long-ago relative's cabin on the edge of the wilderness. This sort of folderol set Eloine's teeth on edge, not because she cared a bit about bloodlines (as long as there was no hint of the woodpile), but because a woman of her own approximate age had nothing better to do than write letters to ragtag relations, visit county records offices and cemeteries, and amass a compendium of essentially useless information. Besides, the one time she came to visit, when the Dad was ill, she used a dozen—*twelve*—egg whites to whip up meringue for a lemon pie. And made sidelong remarks about the condition of the house, its holes above and below, as if they were the fault of Eloine's housekeeping.

Eloine's pride rose up on occasions like this, being, she believed, from a better background than her sister-in-law, better educated, but alas, much poorer. I.T., a comfortably well-off widow, lived with her son and his family in Donelson, a modern suburb of Nashville, and never had to do a lick of work, except perhaps putter in the kitchen with a Nigra to clean up after her, making sky-high meringues.

Discrimination based on food followed the fault line of racial division. Piñon nuts, prickly pear fruit, cactus paddles, foreign to her, Eloine associated with Indians, sustenance of a different degree of poverty from our own, savage, as I think she also thought of goat meat but could hardly make an issue of it considering where she lived. Squirrel and possum and catfish were Nigra foods. When it came to greens, ham hocks, and corn bread, all barriers dissolved.

Of the whites whom Eloine did not care to associate with—for the wiener-and-soda-pop reason, *supra*—the summer pickle pickers ranked first. These itinerant laborers, hired to pick cucumbers on the Christoffersen acres, pitched their tents down by the creek next to their black cars and cooked on open fires or in homemade metal barbecue contraptions and then, after a few weeks, passed from sight like smoke. But the pickle-picking women, despite their circumstances, wore their hair up in sour frozen curls and whips like Mrs. Vonda Olmstead and her daughter, who both had size 4 feet, and that made them even a bit more suspect.

Following were the berserk Christians, the fevered believers who sponsored tent revivals out in the bushes, attracting more of the same from Prescott and Wickenburg and who knew where all. Their singing and pounding drums, their shaking tambourines, their trumpeting and hollering, saving each other ten times over, their general Cain raising, Eloine found embarrassing, a poor light on our small community. She speculated they ate nothing but some dreadful stew from a communal pot, that there wasn't a woman among them could cook a decent meal.

There was another sort of outsider, epitomized by Pearl Cowry and her much younger husband, Reimoldo (I'm not sure of the spelling), who grafted a chapel in between two huge granite boulders out beyond the Kuykendahl road. A sweet, disconnected woman, she said they were looking forward to the millennium—at that time more than sixty years off—and were equally on the lookout for German flying ships hiding behind all tenderloin-shaped clouds. Besides preaching about the end of time and living the simple life in the meanwhile, Pearl told fortunes and tried to get a sect going, altogether too much for Eloine. "There's more religions than you can shake a stick at now," she said. "I don't see the point of making up another one won't put food on the table," an assessment somewhat in the spirit of Montaigne's "Man . . . cannot make a worm, and yet he will be making gods by dozens."

Pearl was, like all prophets, ahead of herself. A generation later, during the era of unwashed hair and feet, homegrown smoke, the collapse of poetry, the general drift of Eastern mysticism, she would have succeeded, her chapel humming with Ginsbergian fuzzle and canned sitar music, the boulder walls melting into phantasmagoric delusion, the clouds hiding not Nazi rockets but friendly though shy ships from beyond the ozone layer.

I wanted to have my fortune told, but Eloine said I'd find out soon enough, don't rush it.

The Reverend Mrs. Cowry's much younger husband, Reimoldo, had uncommonly blue eyes, completely unknown on anyone else in Skull Valley, and what Eloine called an "absent" face with dimples. He wore his hair ever-whichaway too, wood-shaving curls falling as they would down over the brow above those piercing eyes and into the collar of his shirt. He seemed to like everybody equally, which was dubious. He didn't know the first thing about horses or cattle or goats or mechanics, the Dad said, though he built that "modren glassy chapel." He drove their automobile, a dove-colored turtleback Plymouth, over one road and another bringing some sort of soft message, generally near lunch time, to whoever happened to be home, usually the wife. Mrs. Warren said.

Otherwise, young Reimoldo seems to have set out to clean up the countryside of its discarded machines and equipment, things he found, first on the rocky acres he and the Reverend Mrs. owned. He cut them up, hauled them to venues alongside the road, and then reassembled them into what Eloine called "Arizona gods," the thought of which, each time she said it, sent her into giggles. To get to the Cowry place, then, as everyone did at least once, you were taken along a route of startling confusion, déjà vu rampant on a field of rust. Yet yard art was not unknown to the citizens of Skull Valley. Most had some.

Jennifer Price, an L.A. freelance writer, has made a study of the plastic pink flamingo as American lawn ornament since its invention in 1957, surely a turning point in twentieth-century taste, but to my knowledge no one has given equal serious attention to the rusted farm implement as yard art. Well, someone probably has; I've missed it. There was yard art long before plastics and in places where there were no lawns. The first question is, What do you do with a ruined baler, a dead truck, a superannuated plow? The next question is, Why choose a plow over a harrow for your front yard? A John Deere tractor over a hay rick? (Annie Proulx believes, quite rationally—and I'm with her—that abandoned tractors can think, talk, and exact revenge.) Can sculpture be this casual? If David Smith were yet among us, he could cut these machines into pieces, weld them in new integrations, attach hands where ankles should be and heads beneath armpits. As it were. And that is, I guess, what Reimoldo Cowry was doing before him.

Ms. Price says, "Below a certain level of wealth, taste ceases to operate." She is wrong in this, of course. Taste runs all the way down to the ground, though in the passage may shift from "good" to "bad," depending on who's looking.

One does not suggest that these farmyard works convey, through either transcendent or subversive visual rhetoric, a comment on consumerism or deflated objects of desire. What they do say is, "Here's something used a plow or hold water or churn milk but don't no longer so we flung it out." Thrown-out things can be literally so in the country—right out the doors and windows—or figuratively, as when a truck or tractor is left where it expired to gradually slink molecularly into the landscape. On the other hand, some women in Skull Valley, those especially who had yards along the main road, used old truck tires to bed petunias in, a juxtaposition of the ugly and the beautiful with no satire intended. Or better yet, washtubs on trestles. With petunias and trailing nasturtiums, they impart height in the gardenscape. Don't tell *me* there's no taste. Thus, the placement of discarded objects becomes deliberate, not accidental, and as art the act becomes intellectual. Doesn't it?

Much farm implement art involves wheels, intrinsically perfect things either to run on or to be used somewhere in steering, in gears and ratchets, and further, there are levers, pedals, and knobs, each aesthetically challenging, and great rakes like fantastic claws or teeth fallen from monsters' mouths.

There's another, smaller level of yard art, of course, the sort that lies closer to the ground and belongs to the creatures who creep about. An arrogant plastic pink flamingo stands inflated with a sense of its own beauty, but a stamped-on galvanized milk bucket, shot through with a few .22 bullets, might seem a spectacular Bilbao Guggenheim to a colony of garden spiders, their webs, the blown-in accidents of grass stem and dandelion thistle, as engrossing as Sol Le Witt's walk-through hard spaces. A withered flower as chilling as Jim Dine's red Venuses. A silk-wrapped housefly as tremulous as Damien Hirst's shark in formaldehyde. How do we not know?

Reimoldo, the much-younger husband, out on a recruiting mission collecting iron and spreading Pearl's wisdom, ended up shot in the wrong bed by Vonda Olmstead's daughter's boyfriend, who came home at an unexpected hour with a buddy of his, both of them just fired from the Phelps Dodge mine, to share a couple of beers and maybe, who knew, his girlfriend in an afternoon romp, a surprising turn of events that I guess was not foretold in Reimoldo's own fortune. This made for a fuzzy story you had to hide behind furniture to get the gist of. According to Kenneth Kuykendahl, whose older brother knew everything, Reimoldo was caught peeing up Vonda's daughter's dress, an anatomical anomaly it took me ten years to straighten out. Jimmy, not to be outdone, cobbled together a version of his own, too lurid to understand. "They were engaged in amorous conjugation," he said.

"In what?" Conjugation had to do with verbs, didn't it?

"Like me and [a girl who shall remain nameless under the cotton-woods, whom I'll tell about later]."

That could get you killed? A scary world.

Vonda Olmstead's daughter's boyfriend was up for murder but he got off.

It was for reasons like this, not all so dramatic, that the two Olm-stead women, mother and daughter, with their curls and tiny feet, had reputations, in Eloine's mind.

You needn't try to seek out Reimoldo's sculptures today. They were all cut up (again) for scrap metal when the war broke out.

And then there were a few Mexicans, falling uncomfortably in between the keys. Some, almost like the itinerant pickle pickers but working on the railroad gangs, came and went too fast to know and were therefore generalized. These families lived in rolling boxcar houses and got to go all kinds of places. A few of the kids showed up at school for a couple of weeks, bewildered and miserable. But there were two other strata of Mexican, the servants such as employed at the Ida spread, and the bona fide cowboys who worked on the big ranches in Tonto Basin or on the Ida place at the verdant south end of the valley. Naturally handsome, swaggering, creaking in their saddles and boots, smelling of leather and horse and manure and tobacco, they caused idolatrous uprisings in the blood flow of both sexes.

Roberto Arenas was one such, though he disappeared before my memory. The story goes that he set his cap for Martha when she was seventeen and still living at home. Even took her riding a few times (Omer is now telling this fifty years down the road), with Omer riding double behind her, a humiliated chaperone. Roberto never got all the way to his goal, but sometimes when he was hiding in the bushes, waiting for Martha to sneak loose and join him, he sat back against a tree trunk, lit a cigarette, opened his Levi's, took out his dark brown prick, grinned, and let Omer and Donald Shoup play with it.

The Dad got wind of some of this. Being a member of the school board and so forth, upstanding citizen, he called a meeting at the Community Hall and gave a coolly impassioned speech having as its theme, "What about our wives and daughters?" Roberto was run out of town. A very large loss, according to Omer. Martha died at sixty-nine, a spinster.

Unknowable Parts

*T*he following reveries on Eloine's cooking are only kitchen thoughts. What one picks up, like discarded drawings, old designs, sketches from the corner of a master's workshop, stitched together even in the slippery folio of memory, become a singular mode of self-examination. Forgotten tastes, like smells, sometimes cross back over the brink of introspection and enliven a buried scene. This will come as no news to anyone who writes nor, probably, to anyone who eats.

Of those foods, besides calf brains and rice, one must occasionally eat but had rather not—or anyway, had rather not know about, including where they hung within the beast or their function—Eloine must have sneaked in not a few. No extispicy was intended, no divination; to her those parts weren't intended to excrete any smoke of augury. It was cheap meat.

Beef liver (or venison) with onions was acceptable if cooked hard as a board. Chicken innards—giblets—belonged to gravy, were in fact indispensable to it if one were facing a Christmas turkey. Sliced thin, dredged in a flavored flour, and quickly seared so the inside remains pink and the slab pliable, touched off with a dash of Madeira, laid over (not under) a bed of onions caramelized with a few raspberries, and sprinkled with leaves of sage, liver can be a refined dish, but one I wouldn't dare serve a tableload of company. There would be someone bound to pale and, by the ripple effect, cause everyone else to lay down his fork.

Henri de Toulouse-Lautrec, who apparently loved to cook as well as hang around whorehouses and paint, made a dish of liver laid out on planks of bread buttered and spattered with mashed juniper berries, bacon, cooked in a hot oven to medium-rare. He also cooked a *whole* larded calf's liver with prunes and cognac.

Beef heart, tongue, sweetbreads, the excretory kidney, euphemistically called "variety meats," would have set off a firestorm of vile sounds at Eloine's table—unless she had blanketed their basic nature under some false identity and loads of gravy, as she must have done, those cuts being cheapest of all, the most apt to be given away when somebody was butchering. Not yet familiar with Mexican cooking, she would have found succor in chiles, a serviceable mask for unknowable parts. Sliced heart with *chipotles en adobo* sauce, for example, a volcanic dish, takes the mind completely off the subject.

Tripe, however, the honeycomb stomach lining of cows, I cannot eat and hope never to face again. It is not only the revolting look of the stuff but the texture and smell that gag me, even in the Mexican soup *menudo*. Charming Elena Zelayeta has, in her book, a recipe for "Elegant Tripe," which strikes me as a confusion of terms or perhaps something lost in translation. She says, "Have you noticed how popular tripe has recently become?" Not in my neighborhood. Further, she suggests that *menudo* has "a very salubrious effect on those who have celebrated too well the night before." Facing a bowl of stomach lining with a bad hangover; that ought to do it.

In an Asian market I like to frequent, I find something called Bible tripe, pork tongue, pig tails and feet, hog maws, and though no mountain oysters, there are pork uteri and pork bung, the origins of which I believe I'll refrain from seeking.

Oxtail stew, on the other hand, a rich fabrication made from the furthermost end of the cow, or tongue from the front end, delicately handled, can pacify one's dark angels. One night during a period of bachelordom, roommate Dan P. and I laid a whole cow's tongue in a loaf pan, sunk it in, sigh, barbecue sauce, baked it for an hour, set it before ourselves on a platter, and, one at either end, sliced it toward the center, ineluctably devouring the whole thing, a little like—with a cinematic strain—that gorging scene from *Tom Jones*.

Eloine made head cheese and employed pig's feet and chicken feet for their gelatinous properties. In cool weather such additives would have come in handy to her, who knew by then, twenty years into parenthood, when to voice and when to keep her own counsel. Once only she served a platter of blood sausages that someone must have given away, surrounded by mashed potatoes, altogether a disorienting event that tends to stay in one's nightmare closet forever. *Boudin noir* are made of pig's blood, fat, maybe ears and head meat and trotters, onions and fruit and bread, all stuffed into intestine, looking like large black slugs. I have learned lately that sometimes New York chefs, a species of primate yet unclassified, like to gather in a colleague's kitchen late at night and eat these things, savoring the spurt of spicy blood into their mouths, a Dracularian moment not ordinarily observed by common man asleep.

Nothing edible was thrown away. The dog got scraps. *Leftovers* were different, not secondary food but merely something to be provoked and returned in a different temperament at a later time. Probably six out of seven meals were made up of parts of four or five previous meals coming 'round again, like the buckets on a Ferris wheel. Eloine didn't follow the Tennessee farmhand agendum of serving seven more dishes at night than could be eaten, then laying them all out again for breakfast, then dinner, then supper, until they were either devoured or gone by the wayside. Aside from hotcakes on Sunday mornings before the trek to the Community Hall to hear Grandma D'Armand sing about the roll being called up yonder and to watch the resident psychopath hold us like spiders over the flames of Hell—or the occasional pan of hot biscuits, oatmeal once in a while but not really much liked—breakfast in Eloine's kitchen was brief and snatch-as-you-can. Cornflakes or shredded wheat. Like me now, she hadn't much enthusiasm for early-morning food.

Following is Eloine's recipe for oxtail stew—or soup if she added more stock. It was never the same twice because it depended on the availability of vegetables in days before supermarkets or frozen foods. The boys called it "tail soup" or "heinie stew," but not within her hearing. I love the Italian: *coda alla vaccinara*.

ELOINE'S OXTAILS

4 pounds oxtails
salt and black pepper
1 tablespoon paprika or cayenne pepper
flour for dredging
1 tablespoon oil
1 tablespoon butter
¼ pound bacon, ham, or salt pork
1 onion, chopped
1 carrot, chopped
1 bell pepper, chopped
1 to 2 celery ribs, chopped
2 cloves garlic, whole
1 tablespoon tomato puree
3 to 4 ripe tomatoes or canned Italian tomatoes, chopped
2 bay leaves or a bouquet garni
a dash of cloves and cinnamon
2 quarts chicken stock or half stock, half water
dried orange peel, reconstituted in liquid, then sliced
1 bunch of parsley

Season the oxtails with salt, pepper, and paprika (or cayenne). Dredge each in flour, shake off the excess, and brown on all sides in hot oil and butter in a Dutch oven. Then remove the oxtails to a plate, pour off most of the oil, and cook the bacon (or ham or salt pork) and the vegetables and garlic until done, about 20 minutes.

Put the tomato puree and chopped tomatoes in the pan with the other vegetables, then return the oxtails to the pan. Add the bay leaves (or bouquet garni), cloves, cinnamon, and stock. Bring to a boil, then adjust the heat to a simmer, either on the stovetop or in the oven. Cook, tightly covered, for 2½ hours. Uncover and simmer for another half hour to let the sauce thicken. At the last, touch it up with a sprinkling of salt.

Serve in bowls with a few slivers of orange peel and some parsley.

Note: I use red wine or port in place of half the stock.

Corn on the cob, cut into two-inch pieces, she sometimes dropped into this and similar stews if it was the season, or root vegetables such as rutabaga or the silly parsnip.

Eloine's Hungarian goulash, another cabalistic meal, was probably not only continents but planets away from Budapest, yet it contained sauerkraut, caraway seeds, onions, and paprika and sour cream—real cream gone sour. In the boys' minds "goulash" meant an indescribable mixture, a generic word for "mess," the result of tossing everything into one kettle when it had lost its clarity. This solution she fell back on for mutton or goat when it came her way.

Horse meat was not, to my knowledge, ever served from Eloine's kitchen, but I'll bet if it had been, we would have thought it repulsive. We tend to forget that for a cavalry army, a wounded horse, slaughtered, makes a ready meal for a hundred men or more, though what its soldier rides the following day, assuming he survived, is anyone's guess. Giovanni Rebora says, speaking of the time of Sulieman the Magnificent of Turkey, "Donkeys yielded very good meat, and mules, which by the thousands tracked along mountain trails, provided meat intended for sausages (blended with pork and pork fat)." I wonder what that might be called in a modern charcuterie. Eating your pack animals when they've done their time seems reasonable, a benefit you'd never get from a Jeep or Humvee. A great painting, such as Il Borgognone's seventeenth-century *The Battle of Lützen* in the Pitti Gallery in Florence, gives a breathtaking idea of the horse carnage awaiting hungry survivors at the end of the day. In fact, the Pitti and Uffizi Galleries are resplendent with food paintings.

Indian novelist Kamala Markandaya somewhere says, "When the palate revolts against the insipidness of rice boiled alone, we dream of fat, salt, and spices." It is perhaps owing to the filmmaker Ismail Merchant, who loves to talk about food almost as much as himself, that we have become acquainted with garam masala. It's a rich spice blend used in Indian cooking, easy to make at home in a coffee grinder but available these days in any Mideast or Indian grocery. There seems to be no set recipe; some are sweeter than others, some hotter. Any recipe has cinnamon sticks, coriander seeds, cumin seeds, black peppercorns, perhaps several cloves, maybe some cardamom and ginger and hot red pepper flakes. They're all whirled together in a grinder until powdered, then stored in a glass jar. Eloine would have loved having it in addition to her standbys, cayenne and paprika. She understood the efficacy of a liberal smear of spices on venison or beef on the brink of going off or when a new conglomeration failed, as even hers did sometimes. Lapses of judgment or taste occur, of course, even in the best of society. For instance, I have heard James DePreist and his otherwise sensible Oregon Symphony play Ravel's *Bolero*.

When eating something slightly questionable at her own table, Eloine sat up especially rigid, chewed with exaggerated delicacy, and in general steered the subject far off. Signals like this warned us the topic of the food on our plates was not broachable.

Like any mother trying with pennies to feed persnickety kids, Eloine evolved a few dishes with entertainment value, such as her spaghetti and standing egg. In this the hot spaghetti was swirled up with some "carbonara" sauce, that is, her regular white gravy with bits of salt pork in it, and laid nestlike on the plate. In the center of each she stood a raw egg in its decapitated shell. Each diner stirred his own egg into his own spaghetti. The quicker you did this, the more likely the egg was to cook, and a contest could be invented—the quickest, the most done, the sloppiest. A long time later I ran upon this dish in a promenade café in Cannes, much improved in price.

She prepared chicken livers (and probably gizzards and hearts) with sage. The following is an adaptation of the *fegatini alla salvia* I first ate at the Trattoria Madonna in Venice, during a time I was very much in love, which may be why it reminded me of Eloine's treatment, a precarious surmise, as I really don't know her method, and fondly remembered taste is but illusion.

Fegatini alla Salvia

A simple first course for two.

½ pound chicken livers
2 tablespoons olive oil
2 tablespoons butter
1 handful of fresh sage leaves
sea or kosher salt
freshly ground black pepper
2 tablespoons Grand Marnier or cognac
a splash of balsamic vinegar

Clean the livers by removing any fat and connective tissue. Cut them in half. In a skillet over high heat, warm the oil and butter. Drop in the sage leaves, add the livers, and cook, stirring, 2 minutes. Add the Grand Marnier (or cognac) and vinegar; cook 1 minute. Season with salt and pepper. There should be sauce in the skillet to lightly coat the meat. (If you don't use enough sage, this won't work.)

Note: The livers may be lightened, Manzano style, by soaking in Italian white wine with peppercorns and 1 bay leaf for 6 to 7 hours in the refrigerator.

Socrates, on love, said our souls once had wings and even now, in exile, when we look upon beauty and fall in love, those joyous pains we feel are our wings trying to sprout again, presumably so they can carry us—and our lumpy hearts—to the beloved. If we're rejected, our innards collapse, our stumps retract, we suffer a different kind of pain. And when we are old, beyond the lunge of Eros, unable to couple in the honeyed beds even if we could find someone willing, we have only the agony of too much age.

The Dad was fifty-six when I was born. I've tried, but failed, to imagine him and Eloine locked in amorous congress, yet they continued. Our beds in Skull Valley, being fewer than there were individuals, had to do at least double service, except for the Dad's. I slept with

Eloine. Sometimes, especially if he had been long absent, she'd murmur to me, "Now, you go on to sleep. I'm going to slip over and talk to Daddy awhile." She'd move from our bed to his, and while they talked quietly about this and that, the bedsprings would begin a rhythmic squealing, a most peculiar and perplexing sound. The reason for it I could never divine.

"My Own Darling Buster," begins a letter from Omer to Eloine, dated June 27, 1916, from Bristol Mine, Canada. "I received your dear letter last night—written the 18—and you was wondering why I didnt write. Well sweet I have certainly written you every chance and I am at a loss why you havent been getting any letters from me." He runs on in this vein, with much wonder at the inefficiency of the postal system, and mentions he'd written what "I thought was a very important letter and you have never mentioned it." In any case, they were married in October.

Being country kids, we knew what the dogs and cows and horses were up to when the male climbed on the back of the female, and we understood from such laborious activity puppies or a calf or a foal would eventually result. But how people achieved this connection and made human babies, neither Jimmy nor I could figure out. The word *sex,* if ever used at all in our house, would have been reluctantly applied only as a gender designator, not as a verb of action. Like many boys, we were taught all about human reproduction through lavish silence. If it's true, as the Chinese say, that the genesis of wisdom is in calling things by their right name, parents, school, and church directed us down divagating paths of ignorance.

At age nine Jimmy could erect a prodigious announcement of his future as a man, so I assumed all human males did at that magic moment. Therefore, starting at six and a half, I began impatiently waiting, yet confirmed in the inevitability of such a certain event. And was sorely disappointed when, on the morning of May 17, 1941, I laid back the covers surreptitiously, and my underpants, to find . . . virtually nothing, certainly no change, nothing to crow about, neither a sprig of musculature nor hatch of hair.

Swallowing disappointment and shame, perhaps my first experience of the sublimation at which I became expert, silently assuming I was subhuman, I put the matter to one side, watchfully, and grew ahead two more years in the clutches of childhood.

Further humiliating, I discovered Jimmy, age eleven, and a neighbor girl—the one who shall remain nameless—engaged in sex (the verb form) every afternoon at about four-thirty as they wandered home from school, hidden among the fallen cottonwoods. This scene I was once invited to watch, though physically unable to participate in. Fortunately, and all unbeknownst to the gathered company, though naked they weren't going about it right, their activity more resembling a doctor's exam than a true coupling. The girl was delightfully into fellatio, however, and one wonders, at this far remove, where at eleven she had picked *that* up. (Latin, past participle of *fellare,* to suck.)

For reasons inscrutable, what remains most vivid for me in all this is a vision of the bony white tangle of fallen cottonwood limbs and the olfactory memory of sweet green leaves. Ever after, they mingle with sexuality and nudity in my mind, along the lines of the male pissing-in-the-woods syndrome so abhorred by feminist lesbians. The romance of pastoral sex, I am told, is strictly an invention of the male psyche.

Jimmy was not only sexually precocious but, as I've said, quite capable of setting traps for me, egging me on to do things he had better sense than to try. We had one wood-burning heat stove in the main room, set up in fall, removed to the barn in spring. At it, sometimes in cold weather, the Dad would undress, long underwear and all, while the rest of us sat around shivering, doing our homework (Eloine would have slipped out into the kitchen). One such evening when the Dad was bare, Jimmy whispered, "I dare you to go pull on it."

I did. I gave it a yank. And got slapped across the room, an injury most foul. For two reasons: (1) I was smiling and (2) it wasn't my idea.

The Dad was quick with the back of his hand.

Hunger

THE LONG SNAKES, the poisonous ones with brown diamonds, came sliding farther down from the hills, the waterless arroyos, as summer deepened, crossing our meadow toward the swamp, which never dried entirely, even in the longest drought. They said, Be careful of the snakes now that dry weather is here. They looked toward the horizon when they talked like that, and fanned themselves with handkerchiefs or dishcloths.

Sometimes I saw the snakes curled in the shade of a low bush or traveling with purpose across, never along, a path.

In the shallow pools of the swamp, small green frogs lived, splotched by darker green on their humped backs, yellow-throated, yellow-footed. They ate the skating bugs. The snakes would eat the frogs if the drought continued.

Near the origin of the swamp, where it came without reason out of the ground and made the earth suddenly green in all the brown and dying grasses, fifteen cottonwoods grew like a family, white-bodied, leaning toward one another, as if weeping for something or sharing joy.

One day, early, a hot day when a blue underside of the sky pulled me away from the house at the opening of the foothills, I went to the swamp to see if the brown poisonous snakes were feeding on the frogs and the frogs on the water skaters. Passing by the circle of trees, I glanced among them and saw her sitting here, like me early away in the morning, like me steeped and aged in seventeen summers, seventeen seasons of drought, the daughter of our only neighbors: the man who owned the thousand white chickens.

Her hair was long, her eyes bright like stones in her brown face. There seemed to me, at seventeen, exactly nothing else to do but put her down on the dusty leaves, last year's faint skeletal webs, either by agreement or force.

I sat beside her on the arch of a fallen limb. Do you come here always? I said. I hung my arms over my knees and pushed my toes under the leaves, the remains of the leaves.

She said, I've seen you here bending over the water. If you aren't careful, you'll fall into your reflection and drown.

We listened to the cicada, which would stop gradually as the morning heat rose.

Hear that? I said. Kickadees.

She said, What do you watch in the water? You don't wear shoes and you watch things in the water. She laughed. She dug designs of circles and crosses in the ground between her feet with a stick.

Did you know the snakes come down from hills, weather like this, to drink? I said.

Is that what you watch? I don't care about snakes. But everything has to survive, I guess.

Yes. Everything has the right to try.

I hummed and listened to the cicada rattle his final sound till evening, until the sun makes the hills put down their shadows and the gray doves whistle out of the oaks and go bobbing on the ground for seeds. I was overcome, as with heat, or as when standing too suddenly, by the knowledge of hunger, the *knowledge* of hunger, which is different from the instinct. There came over the family of trees something so much like a voice I jerked up my head and opened my mouth to answer.

I turned to her and spread my hand on the smooth limb beside her hip.

She cried out once, and held her lower lip with her teeth, when we joined together, finally, firmly, and I sensed in the remaining few weeks of childhood we would learn a shape to all this, to the round world, to the summer following the spring, the grate of the cicada, or the reason for trees, for drought and the rain, the care of both hunger and poison.

When we came apart, our skin, smooth and brown, was wet and reddened in blotches, like her face and breasts. We could not stop our faces or our eyes or our breaths.

One day rolled over another at a great distance. The trees put us into shadow morning after morning, sometimes with each of us running into them from opposite directions at the same moment, sometimes one, restless since white dawn, hunched there, afraid the other would not come.

Her hair was long and brown, streaked yellow by the sun, dappled from reflecting mirrors of the sun going down through the trees. She learned to lift her hips up to mine and hold with her legs over my back. The curve of her neck was salt to my tongue. We learned that hunger is insatiable, that gorging begets feasts, and that desire blinds. We wondered if others had ever discovered what we knew.

The rains came late in the month and pushed back into the hills the brown poisonous snakes. The frogs thrived. Toads came up out of the ground.

The last time we spent the day, the whole long day, in the family of trees, we did not talk much in order to say all that had to be spoken.

She said, Must you? Will you really leave?

Yes, I said. I am seventeen.

She said, When will you come back? But she sensed as well as I we had burst open the pod, not closed it, that what we knew, like the knowledge of hunger, was kindling to a longer fire.

We were talking, a few pages back, about foods or parts of animals not everyone likes. Obversely related to these are What I Like to Eat Alone. The table as metaphor for social intercourse, for union, togetherness, family bickering, and poetic flights has hung about literature since at least Homer and the Bible. You can hardly read a modern novel that does not have at least one major scene—usually a nasty one—set around the family dining table.

As befalls my lot, I've never lived alone, not even for a week, yet there are times when some private invulnerability is devoutly to be wished. José Saramago has pointed out that, strange as it may seem, some men can spend their entire life alone and enjoy solitude, especially if it is raining and their crust of bread is hard. When I have a day alone, besides dawdling as I please, going about in shabby clothes, uncombed and unwashed, I can paint or not, garden or not, write or not, read, sort out something in a box, go to a bookstore (if I clean up). Or not. No one will know. Like a brief alternate life when you get to do the other things you want to do. Also, I can indulge in edibles no one else in the house will touch or which are considered too fattening, too beneath one, or too suspect.

Oysters: Fresh—the small firm ones, not the blubbery soft kinds, bluepoint perhaps, or Kumamoto or Olys or Wallapa Bay—to slurp directly from their shells or to make into something more complex. I consult M.F.K. Fisher. Will it be soup or stew? Gumbo, fry, Rockefeller? Eating oysters requires attitude adjustment, peaceful time to lay out and approach, to arrange and reflect, anticipate. If as a first course live on a bed of crushed ice and rehydrated seaweed, why not as a second course of breaded crispy animals removed from their shells, served with Mexican salsa? Tecate beer.

Paris is replete with places in which to find oysters, no doubt, but once having located the Terminus Café, across from the main doors of the Gare du Nord, we've never needed to look elsewhere. There they build, on tiers of crushed ice, seafood plateaus of several kinds of oysters, mussels, clams, spiffed up with some cold cooked crayfish, bread, rouille, and lemon, assembled outside on the sidewalk, then brought in with a great French-waiter swoosh. These plateaus come in two sizes: reasonable for two and enormous. Muscadet, or if in autumn after the third week of November, Beaujolais Nouveau.

Macaroni and cheese: Made at home from boxed dry macaroni and a mélange of cheeses, whatever may be in the refrigerator, lots of it, melting and gooey, but run under the broiler for a minute to toast bread crumbs sprinkled over the top with butter. Pinot Grigio.

Wieners: Two only, boiled to bursting, split lengthwise, and laid with mayonnaise on white or light wheat bread or a crusty long bun. A few pickled jalapeño slices, a slice of tomato from the garden. This is white trash food, thus served with chardonnay.

Garden tomatoes in hot biscuits with butter, sardines out of a can mashed up with mayonnaise and chopped onion, etc., etc., on toast. Cold fried chicken, deviled eggs, baked eggs with bacon, leftover meat loaf sandwich (actually, anything left over, especially pot-au-feu), purchased chicken potpie. Snails in their shells with parsley-garlic butter or, à la Balzac's Cousin Pons, *escargots au gratin* or fricasseed with onions and tomatoes in butter, and I'd eat a platter of those little black snails you get, with a pin, in Bordeaux if I could buy them, laid out on fresh salty seaweed.

No one, even in kindness, likes my humble hamburgers, so I might make one of those. I might even grill it outdoors, set forth in a crusty French roll—not a doughy American bun—with everything I can think of added on, except no mustard or ketchup. Homemade mayo if there is some in the refrigerator past its shelf life. Chianti Classico.

Funeral, Feast

*A*ll households in Skull Valley were, to one degree or another, entangled with Mrs. Warren, proprietor of the grocery and general store and owner of a most beautiful meat case tiled in black, green, and white, which I coveted and still do. Above the shelves there was a frieze of stuffed animal heads all 'round the four walls, a menagerie of dead deer, elk, moose, lion, bison, bighorn sheep, coyote, a pair of Texas longhorns but without the head that originally went between them, even a horse, legacy of the late Mr. Warren, who died under a car. I don't mean the car ran over him or fell on him or crashed with him in it. He was just under it when he died.

Mrs. Warren had large dark eyes that didn't miss a wink. She did not believe she had any bad qualities, but being smack in the center of things, she knew everyone else's and how those of one person could be matched up against another's. In this she had achieved the ability to hold onto innumerable details, run them around in the machine of her mind, and send them out, laundered, into the vast world—that is, among the one hundred seventy-five local souls—to be confused with the truth. "How she manages to take in so much information and never stop talking herself is beyond me," Eloine said. Reluctant herself to broadcast anything personal Mrs. Warren might recycle, Eloine was covertly delighted by what she gathered in. In addition to the sorts of information the passing of which must needs be coded so as not to sully the waxy ears of children hanging about, Mrs. Warren was big on diseases and cures. To her credit and the boys' relief, she recommended a black goo in a tube to draw out splinters buried in bare feet.

Also postmistress, Mrs. Warren handled every piece of mail. This gave her another level of information, especially when the sack had some postcards in it and on them anything she could develop into an aberrant circumstance.

She had already gone through two husbands and was on the lookout for the next one. She had even—I can't recall how we knew this—taken a shine to the Dad. If the boys knew, then certainly Eloine did. But being in debt to Mrs. Warren in the matter of a never-caught-up account, she couldn't afford to get on her bad side. There was no other store. She didn't take Mrs. Warren cupcakes. That would not have been begging, quite, but admitting to being beholden, too much of a business deal, besides submitting her baking to a wide anonymous jury. No telling what they'd say without Eloine on the spot to declaya, "I just don't know what went wrong this time."

In December each year, Mrs. Warren special-ordered two fresh coconuts for Eloine's Christmas cake.

Christmas, celebrated in traditional style and paid for in large part by Uncle Horace's check, occupied the whole of December, a flurry of planning, though the menu never varied. The steamed pudding, in a three-pound Hills Bros coffee can, she made first, several weeks before the twenty-fifth, wrapped after cooking in cheesecloth in the outdoor cooler, and moistened regularly. But with what? As I've said, there was no liquor in the house. Probably a few spoonfuls of cider enlivened with cinnamon and cloves.

Nearer time, a couple of the boys hiked up onto Old Baldy, which wasn't quite, to cut a scraggly evergreen and drag it home, down the rocky slopes. This forlorn tree we set up in a corner and fell to decorating with stars and bursts made of colored foil, strings of cranberries, and icicles saved from previous years. Since Santa Claus was yet a factor in my beliefs, only the packages from Tennessee were laid out as they arrived, wrapped in the same paper we had sent east last December, hoarded and ironed. Santa, meantime, was entreated to concentrate on toys with wheels or instruments of noise.

Eloine made both her coconut cake and the syllabub three or four days ahead. The three-layer cake (it must be white, not yellow), stuck together and covered all over with white icing, then a thick shag of shredded coconut, she moistened twice daily with dribbles of the re-served "milk" from the fruit, harvested by poking the eyes out of two coconuts and letting them drain, balanced on the rim of glass jars. The continual moistening for three days made a dense, damp cake infused throughout with coconut flavor.

In my judgment we could have skipped the turkey, dressing, sweet potato soufflé, the cranberry sauce and cloverleaf rolls, certainly the Brussels sprouts, and gone directly to the cake and sillybub, even in the quite sure prospect of a suffering stomach. Eloine's syllabub, a "boiled custard," actually what we would call today crème anglaise, was drunk at outdoor-cooler temperature in a glass. No wonder I vomited (again). Being sick during vacation held no advantages. During school one sometimes got to stay home a day, cosseted in bed with scraped apple and a chance to read, once more, about Big Claus and Little Claus, whose relationship to the third Claus was ever confusing.

Christmas food: When you reach the point, as we all must, when you cannot bear to cook one more cornbread-stuffed fat turkey, turn southward and look to the Yucatán, in tropical Mexico, that eerie, blood-soaked area of jungle ruin. There, in Mayan country, they smear turkey (wild, if possible) with bright red *achiote* sauce and the juice of limes and oranges and mangoes, stuff it with what may seem an incon-sonant mix of vegetables, Gulf shrimp, black beans, and chiles, wrap it all up in banana leaves, and give it about three hours in the oven. The degree of elaboration you impute to the dressing is inhibited only by your own timidity.

For expert help on these things, one goes to Mark Miller's Coyote Café books. Miller is an impressionable cook who thinks, perhaps hysterically, that there is still time to develop an American cuisine apart from hand-me-down European influence or the quick boxed fix, the gastronomic equivalent of a hit of Novocain. Yet we are obliged to him for his line of bottled sauces. Miller, like other restaurant cooks— Waters, Janos, Trotter, Too Hot Tamales—with a staff and power tools, assumes you are already about as expert as he is. He understands, through educated intuition, that great food, like an alert contemporary painting, does not lie inert upon the canvas but sets up a conflict of anxieties to be resolved in the cooking and in the mouth, a de Kooning of the palate.

For many modern restaurant chefs, Ezra Pound's dictum "Make it new" means only to make it technically dazzling. In the manner of hair designers and interior designers, food designers create architectonic plates of airhead food, aimed at style and transience, to the loss of form and content. Certain of these elaborate fusions collapse in their own gastronomic fecundity, like an explorer who hacks himself deeper into a fresh jungle that grows up behind him again in the night. What good is a gorgeous hibiscus if you're lost? Such cooking is the road to cynicism, the path, of course, Hollywood has always taken. Still, Los Angeles is one of the great epicure centers of the world, if one skips over West Hollywood, Santa Monica, Beverly Hills, and Westwood and goes for the Gold (Jonathan), who's ever prepared to lead one unerringly in and out of the little-traveled byways of ethnic dining. The lighting may be bad (especially for starlets of both sexes), the plates plastic, the decor rubber geraniums, but technique will be subsumed into the cooking, not separated from it.

Among cooking teachers, as opposed to restaurant owners who write books, Julia Child remains unsurpassed for clarity, wit, and style. I knew her briefly (one week) long ago at Bread Loaf, when she was already a star and I had not yet cooked my way through the first volume of *Mastering the Art of French Cooking* and was too tongue-tied to discuss food with her. Later, at about the time Beverly Sills came into our homes as a blessed relief from Callas or Sutherland, I began on volume 1. Doing Child while listening to Sills makes a lighter quenelle.

Eloine cooked a Christmas yam dish with brown sugar and sliced almonds on top, rather than a caramel on the bottom. The version following came down to me from Margarita Padin, the Argentine comedienne.

MARGARITA'S YAM SOUFFLÉ

¼ cup sugar
2 pounds yams, peeled, sliced, and boiled soft

4 eggs
4 tablespoons butter
¼ cup liquor
freshly ground nutmeg

Preheat the oven to 350°F.

Make a caramel by melting the sugar in the bottom of a 4-cup metal mold until brown. Blend all the other ingredients in a food processor. Scoop on top of the caramel. Set the mold in a larger pan of hot water and bake for 1½ hours or less. Cool, then unmold by inverting the soufflé onto a plate.

The last Christmas the whole family spent together, in Skull Valley or elsewhere, was 1941, a few weeks after Japan bombed Pearl Harbor.

By the following spring, Omer had joined the Air Corps, Martha had been transferred to the Navy Department in Long Beach, Billy was off somewhere working in a copper mine for five dollars a day, a 1,000 percent increase over Omer's slave wages, and the Dad was dead.

At the funeral in Prescott, a vast preacher in a gray suit, whom none of us knew ("Laws a-*mercy,* I thought he'd never stop harping on the condition of this family"), eulogized a man he had never met and used the opportunity to put in some good words for God and himself. The tenor of the portion given over to the deceased seemed to be that he, the Dad, was better off in the hands of the Lord, while he, the preacher, must walk this wretched earth spreading truth, solace, and retribution to the heathen. This was my first city peddler. Sleek, pink, smooth as mascarpone, with even more grease in his hair than Billy was using at the time to hold up his wings and duck's ass, he seemed awfully taken with his exalted appointment, like Cowper's eighteenth-century parson:

> The pastor, either vain
> By nature, or by flatt'ry made so, taught
> To gaze at his own splendour, and t'exalt
> Absurdly, not his office, but himself.

It was Cowper, on a like note, who disliked poems as well "that have nothing but their oily smoothness to recommend them."

The preacher's face was made up of two large gray slabs hanging down on either side like a goat's testicles, with small eyes, a nose in the center like . . . *stop. Dear god, don't let me giggle today.* "Behave yourself, Johnny," Eloine whispered. In the natural course of days, I've attended lots of funerals since and I usually have the urge to laugh. Maybe it is only nervousness, being on edge, standing on the brink of hysteria, or maybe it is the ludicrous business we go through to dispose of lifeless bodies. Maybe crying and laughing are more closely linked in some of us, just a toggle switch apart.

However, on the brighter side, Mr. Sanderson, whom we did know, sang "In the Garden" so well I decided to include it in my repertoire. My opera career hadn't advanced noticeably yet, but I was a loud and committed singer and knew all the hymns, all the Christmas carols, and school songs by heart and would render "On the Isle of Capri" or "In the Gloaming" upon request. At about this time, Jimmy (I don't know how *he* found out) showed me how, on the Community Hall piano, the notes in the hymnals matched up with the keys on the piano. This was an epiphanic moment.

I had never before thought about how one got the marks on the page to direct one's fingers on the keyboard, despite my years studying the silent ukulele. Knowledge was piling up. Knowing how you read music sent me skittering off toward yet another career—concert pianist. There being no piano in our house or money for instruction, that part would have to come later. I've never let circumstances deter me from notable pursuits, though now I suspect I shall never replace Nureyev because of my false knee, even if I could find the time. James Baldwin moaned, much too loudly, about the gap between what one hoped to become and what one actually achieved. Adjust your sights, as the Dad tried to teach us with the .22 rifle, and you'll hit *something*.

Mr. Sanderson's wife sent us horehound candy regularly, good for all kinds of things but taste.

Well. While we were in Prescott at the funeral, our kitchen filled silently, miraculously, with more food than it would normally see in a year, chief among it chocolate pies, Jell-O salads (green with pineapple slices, red with peach halves), something Eloine explained was "German" chocolate cake, pineapple upside-down cake, brownies, apple cobbler. There must have been some ordinary dishes too, some plain loaves and fishes. While I ought to have been overcome with grief, I actually spent the rest of the day finding reasons to wander through the kitchen, nibbling and anticipating—How could anyone choose a single meal from all this?—mentally saving, holding back, delaying gratification for what appeared to be a long future of piggish delight.

Traveling Forward

WHEN HE DIED I gave my father exactly two months to come back to life, from his deathday in March to my birthday in May, or else I was determined to be finished with him once and for all. Since he had gone upward, I presumed he would return downward in a spaceship of impregnable aluminum in the shape of a v-1 but larger, and to that end I went so far as to prepare scenes he and I would begin as soon as the hatch opened and he stepped out, smiling, tanned, and looking younger than he had in his casket. He did not show up for my tenth birthday, his absolute cut-off date, and so, true to my word, I closed the lid on him.

If my father had returned in a timely manner, I anticipated his craft would land—horizontally, not on end—in the flat, weedy area out in front of the house, the circle around which cars turned, when there were any, beyond the gate hanging at the bottom of the path lined with wild yellow roses. One of his trucks, abandoned and cannibalized, was parked off at the south edge of this circle, gravely rusting. Under it is where he shot Lindy, who was dying of distemper. He claimed.

My first wife was fond of dry martinis and of saying in her operatic mezzo at faculty parties the only reason I got tenure before DeWalt and Hebersandt was that I processed my papers before the deadline. They squeaked in barely under the wire. Early papers are a sign of a rigorous mind, as I tell graduate students, one of whom I eventually married. She wrote an essay on the quantum theory of gravity. Or Heisenberg's uncertainty principle. Something. The point is, it came in three weeks early, so I had opportunity to read it and make a couple of office appointments with her. Being also a physicist, she understands the necessity of order, scale, and time, though she can drift. I could never be intimate with a woman who studied Victorian poetry, for instance. Or studio painting. I mean, I *have* been to bed with a few. It's always messy. For one thing, our timing's off. For another, they want to talk about it, find out what it meant.

Although I'm a good deal older than Dawn, I intend to impregnate her this August so the child will be born in May. Normal birth is one of those basic events, however insignificant it may seem measured against the cosmos, reassuring to the mind because it predictably follows in nine months. Scientists, we will have amniocentesis evaluation, of course, and perhaps chorionic villus sampling to make certain everything *is* normal. Being the last of five children makes me now thrillingly aware of the statistics of daily probability. Dawn murmurs about this plan, but she's dawdling over her Ph.D. and needs an absolute goal. "Finish by November, as planned," I tell her, "at the end of your first trimester. Just in case."

My father used to tell me I was an afterthought, by which he meant *accident*. Deformed children are called accidents of birth. I am an accident of fucking.

"I can still remember the peculiar look on his face when he'd say that," I tell Dawn. "Like I was supposed to say, Good for you!"

"He must've been trying to tell you he was glad."

"That I was born? Or that he got it up so late in life?" In any case, I remind her, she's nearly twenty-seven, time to get on with it, and she responds by claiming there's no such thing as absolute time, as Einstein proved. She's twenty-seven only relative to some arbitrary event. "How old I am in big bang time, that's the point," she says.

I appreciate that. But still, while we're trying to imagine the fourth dimension, we must be operative in three. Whatever life may mean, it is given us to be used. We shouldn't expect only to lie back and let it expand over us like ether. We can't all be bums and bag ladies.

My son, Eric, is mine every second Saturday, every third Sunday, and whatever Wednesday evenings he can take away from homework long enough to go to dinner. Twelve, he, too, tends to be languid. I can't blame him for not caring much for his stepfather, Randy DeWalt, an intellectual slob who skips classes to play tennis with the dean. He carries a racquet in a backpack like a sophomore and, I have heard from his students, he makes irrational marks on their papers and his lectures fairly glimmer with sexual innuendo. This is unpleasant, I tell Eric, but he must see himself not as an integral part of his mother's life, which includes Randy DeWalt, but rather as a separate force traveling through space-time somewhat in tandem for the moment. Gravity keeps us all nailed down, in a sense, but we can move horizontally. We can veer off.

Tonight over Wednesday pizza, he asks if we have a soul that flies upward when we die. What would be the point? I ask him. If space were infinite, where would it go?

"To heaven," he says belligerently.

"And where is that? Eric, listen to me, we've had this talk before. Why are you clinging to these ideas?"

He shrugs and looks away, over toward the corner where two boys are banging on an electronic game about Uzies and bombs.

"I've told you about the infinitely expanding universe. If heaven were a place, it would be moving outward constantly at incredible speed, beyond reach. Nobody's soul could get to it any longer, if they ever did. The idea's as preposterous as believing Lazarus came back from the dead. Or a virgin birth."

If my father's silver spaceship had landed in the front yard, beyond the wild roses, it would have been a huge surprise for everyone but me. The neighbors would have driven over and brought covered dishes. My mother would have frazzled and run to the kitchen to throw wood in the stove. He would have had a pilot with him because he hadn't any flying experience before this, however often he claimed he could fix or operate anything mechanical he had ever seen, the truck under which Lindy died notwithstanding.

It would have been that blond pilot who bumfuzzled my mother. She was awkward in the presence of strangers. My father was, as she said, forever and eternally bringing some guy home unannounced for supper. He was comradely with other men. On the occasion of his return by spacecraft, the problem would have been somewhat amelio-rated because of the neighbors and their covered dishes. We would have had to improvise picnic tables under the peach tree and caution everyone to watch out for snakes.

But, of course, nothing even remotely like that happened, so when his time was up, I stopped the clock.

Then Eric tells me he can't see me next Saturday because Randy DeWalt is taking him to a soccer game. He seems impassive when I point out it is our Saturday to spend together and time does not roll backward. "We can't ever make up a lost day, you know. Besides, there's a critical value at stake here. Your mother and I agreed to certain basic operational procedures. You're supposed to be with me."

"I know," he says.

"Don't I take you places? The space and science museum? Griffith Observatory? Mount Palomar—and that took pull." More than Randy DeWalt would ever have. "I didn't know you liked soccer."

"I don't know if I do or not. I've never seen it."

"Why can't it be the following Saturday?"

He shrugs and continues lining up the edges of his pizza crust around his plate. "Because it's this Saturday," he says. He lifts his eyes, brown and soft like his mother's, and says, "Okay?"

"I don't want to disappoint you." This hurts but it wouldn't be appropriate for him to know. I realize I shrug exactly the way he does. "So, how's your math?"

"All right," he says. "Average."

"Doesn't that trouble you?"

"Not much. A little. You know."

"Average gets you nowhere. Average is not in the competition at all."

"Randy helps me sometimes."

"That explains it, then. Shall we go? If you've finished playing with your food."

"You're mad. I can tell."

"How?"

"That mark on your head. It always turns red when you're pissed."

I know the place he means. Above my left eyebrow, about the size of a fingernail moon, it brightens when I'm angry or excited, turns pale when I'm frightened. I touch it and feel the faint indentation.

"Yes. Well. It'll pass. Shall we?" We leave the pizza place and head for my car. I look up, instinctively, but there's too much haze and light tonight to see anything.

Out in the country, five hundred miles from the coast, at night you could see the stars as bright as glass, the Milky Way like a whirl of sugar on a black dish. Falling stars streaked inside the bowl with blazing afterburners.

There was something important in the bucket, I can't remember what. Milk, maybe. Or in June when the well ran dry, it might have been water. Anyway, it was too heavy and I dropped it at his feet. He gave me the back of his hand, the one with the silver ring on it shaped like a saddle. Blood ran down into my eye and Mother thought I'd been blinded. He circled around the kitchen swearing while she screamed and dabbed at my face, then he went outside again and threw rocks at Geronimo until he knocked him off the roof and he ran away forever. After that, sometimes you could hear him yowling out in the brush, but he never came back.

At home I walk in to find Dawn and three other graduate students sitting on the floor drinking wine, talking, shouting to hear themselves above the music. Cross-legged, Dawn leans over from the hips like a snake charmer and turns down the CD player. She sweeps her hand toward the other three and the wine and popcorn. "Hi," she says, and flicks her long hair back from her face. The others dip their heads and grin. From the bob end of the conversation, I hear they're arguing about the anthropic principle. I should have thought of that when answering Eric about the possibility of heaven. It's hard to think of existence at all without believing we evolved expressly to be the epitome of it, its most complicated organism, and to believe we are the living proof of God. Or the living explanation for the universe, take your pick.

Tim Nyguen, sitting on my living room floor shit-faced with booze and pot, has to submit his thesis problem in three days or he's out of the program. He won't make it. He may be brilliant but lacks any concept of propriety. I drift on toward the kitchen to find something to wash out the bitter taste of pizza.

Dawn follows, impales me against the refrigerator door with the heat of her body. On her temples she has pale blue delicate veins like an older woman. She touches the scar above my eye. I don't ask whether it's red or pale. "I have to update my notes on galactic formation for tomorrow," I remind her. There are always new data, exploded theories. "Don't confuse me." Her mouth tastes rich, full of comedy.

"How did the seminar go today?" She takes the can from me and pours my beer into a glass.

"Too much theory," I answer. "It's only been worked out so far with simulation. I don't think they found it interesting."

"I like questions. They make problems."

"Problems have to be solved."

"And that's how we get the Nobel Prize." Then she says, "See you in bed in one hour. Think about that." She laughs, slips out of my hands, and goes back toward the living room. I do think about that. In the bedroom she will bloom out of her clothes like a flower, into what she calls her naked singularity. On the ceiling above our bed she has written in bold red strokes $E=mc^2$ so whoever is facing upward can see it and be inspired to greater glory.

But in my study I'm befuddled. My notes on galaxies seem so dry they're in danger of spontaneous annihilation, more dust to help choke the universe. If I aimed it out the window, the artificial light from my desk lamp would travel outward at 186,000 miles per second into infinity. So what. The voices of Dawn and the other young people float on waves of sound from the front of the house, traveling over a great distance. Tonight they all seem fragile, even though I know they're not. For now Dawn and I sing a sweet chord together. Our temperatures are compatible. I also understand I've reached my critical speed and have already begun my fall to earth, while her trajectory still rises. Chances are we'll peel away from each other in time.

It's Eric I worry about. He no longer seems capable of excitement. I talk to him about goals and frames but he doesn't hear me. His mind drifts, as if he's slipping in and out of consciousness. I wonder if he's on drugs but he says no. When he does talk, his information is hackneyed, like his arguments for an afterlife or, worse, reincarnation, stuff his mother and Randy DeWalt would dump on him because it's easier than using their minds. Even dead bodies give off energy; maybe he would accept this fact as a substitute for thinking he has a soul capable of flying up like microwaves when he dies, to be numbered among the chosen.

Standing in the afternoon sunlight at the bottom of the pneumatic stairs, my father asked what I'd been doing since he'd been gone. Anticipating the question, I was prepared to rattle off a list embroidered in my mind each day—all A's on my report card, including Attitude, four gold stars and one silver in Sunday School, seven gophers trapped, for which I was owed a nickel each, and so forth. Chores accomplished. Responsible actions. I refrained from telling him right off the bat my older brother was in trouble again for stealing and we had a new dog named Buster or how I'd found Geronimo's corpse out back in the junk pile, a mat of fur and bones, probably dead of unhealed wounds. Coyotes had raided the chicken coop and made off with my fat hen, leaving nothing but a handful of brown feathers. I would report this latest disaster because he'd have weapons with him now capable of seeking out a coyote and blowing it to smithereens.

And he might have listened had not Mother just then come to the screen door with her apron balled up in one hand and said, "Judas Priest, is that you, Oma?"

He turned away from me and said to the golden-haired pilot, "Come on in, Buck, and meet the wife."

They walked up the path between the dusty roses, side by side, with the older man's arm stretched across the shoulders of the younger. My brother stood at the corner of the house with one bare foot on top of the other, like a moron. "You boys get on around back, now, and see if you can't help your mother rustle up some wood. We're starved."

The son of a bitch.

As his two-month limit approached, just before I slammed the lid, there was something else he'd have given a pretty to learn. Mother, hysterical with poverty, unable even to pay for his funeral, sat on the porch three or four evenings every week after supper while the tree toads and the whippoorwills sang, and listened to Mr. Hugh Patterson talk. He was foreman of the big ranch in the valley, a widower with good habits. Their voices rose and fell, like the rhythms of the night.

I finish my notes on galaxies, lay down my pen, and notice how much brighter the light seems to be, how mellow. I think of those eerie white photos of Triton, supposedly the coldest thing in the universe, its oceans of slush and rime, its stark aloneness, like something that never should have been created at all. I reach for the phone and dial Eric, his personal number. He answers sleepily.

"I want to be with you on Saturday," I say.

"You mean with Randy and me?"

"No—not with you and DeWalt. Not Dawn, either. Just you."

"You do? Why?"

"Because I've got everything else in place. It just came to me, like a creative act or something. The part that's missing from my equation you've got."

"Yeah?" There's a gurgle in his voice, the way he sometimes laughs. "What's the equation?"

"We equals I times you squared."

"Talk about *my* fantasies. What do you know about soccer?"

"I'll get a book. If DeWalt understands it, it can't be too deep."

"So what'll you give me for it—the equation?"

"All the time in the world. Something like five thousand billion years, in round numbers. Until the big crunch comes. Just about long enough for us to get everything done."

"Deal," he says. "Good night."

I shut off my lamp and head for the bedroom. They say *Voyager 2* will drift on and on, past the edge of the solar winds, into the helio-pause, and pass our brightest star in three thousand centuries. Once out there, a spaceship just keeps going.

Cowboys and Chiles

*T*he scene stands still. A shack moored at the back to a capricious windmill and water tank, at its side by a spindly, bent, transplanted and unhappy cottonwood, in front by the heavenly tree, the whole set in a crumple of rocky hills with a single hawk drifting above in the thermal streams. Across it, in low relief, pass the people, a family in one year disintegrated from seven to three. The Venerable Bede quotes someone from the court of King Edwin as comparing human life to the flight of a sparrow through a lighted hall "from winter to winter."

Eloine stayed in Skull Valley one more winter, a year and a half with her two youngest sparrows. So far all her children had survived without being brought low by typhus, mauled by a mountain lion, or bitten by a snake; none had drowned in the raging floods or been electrocuted by lightning; she hadn't been stomped to death by cows; the house hadn't burned. Now she worried about the two in the war but could do nothing for them except send boxes of fig bars—cupcakes being too fragile—and socks. Innocents and mothers all, she and some other women gathered in the Community Hall kitchen to make cheerful food to send overseas, having little idea of the logistics involved with getting a shoebox of brownies to Fort Ord, much less the Marianas.

In school we were challenged to interpret, with crayons and re-cycled cardboard, quotations from government posters: "Do with less—so *they'll* have enough"; "If you tell where he's going, he may never get there"; "Save Freedom of Speech—Buy War Bonds"; "The battle-wise Infantryman . . . is careful of what he says or writes. . . . How about you?"

These we pasted to the front windows facing the road and, more earnestly, the railroad along which occasional troop trains moved, south to north, full of uniformed boys bewildered by this turn in their lives. While the engine took on water at the station, the soldiers tumbled out to piss and throw gourds at each other or passing yokels. The gourds grew all along the ditches and embankments, useless as food, as Eloine had learned, as all squashes were to us boys. In olden days, Miss Gerrish said, they were used by the Indians as drinking vessels or whatnot holders.

There was a lot of talk about not talking, and we wished we'd learn something important to the war effort so we could try not talking about it. I began my war campaign button collection, by what means I don't remember, probably whining and wheedling. I liked wearing them all at once on my shirt, like a much-decorated hero, though Eloine wouldn't let me appear in public with the one that said, "To Hell With Tojo."

For those eighteen months she tried to make ends meet by leasing out the zinc mine herself. Though the war caused a minuscule rise in the price of zinc, we didn't get any richer. A number of men called, negotiating their sedans over the wild terrain, and two or three signed contracts of intent to mine the ore for a payment of seventy-five dollars a month, which would have been enough had the offers panned out, and perhaps a couple actually did for a while. Also, clear to periscopic ears, these men came to court the widow. Another suitor, Hugh Patterson, himself recently bereaved, was a good candidate from my point of view because he was in command of several horses. Eventually Mrs. Warren got him.

Eloine was over fifty by then and on the treadle Singer still made her own housedresses—and our shirts—and tiny outfits for babies from her ragbag, out of which she could materialize enough scraps of velvet, lace, sprigged cotton for one more, and when company came, she still rushed to put on her girdle. Her black hair was never unloosed by day nor her feet left bare, and her capacious breasts displayed a proud, powdered décolletage. Yet she didn't fall for any of these men. She did not consider us to be "good country people" but something rather more progressive, in the sense that, when this Depression blew over and our ship came in, we would move on up again.

She depended on will, her reserves of educated gentility not yet quite rusted away, her ramparts of breeding shining through those same old wobbly round spectacles with the black rims and gold nosepiece, to defeat these callers, ordinary hard-working men whose appetites did not overlook the evidence of a good cook. One, an old crony of the Dad's, Jay Davis by name, she dismissed outright because his feet stank so abominably when set beneath her dining table she lost her appetite. "And he like to've talked my head off," besides.

Gradually she realized she was defeated. No grown male to move the heat stove or chop wood or haul barrels of drinking water. Two practically useless boys. Financially foundering at the store, where, despite patriotism, prices climbed. Bread went up from ten cents a loaf to eleven, a 10 percent rise in the cost of living. For reasons already given, she couldn't make a victory garden. Then one day a rattlesnake killed Buster, he who had done to pieces so many of them. Not even a watchdog left.

Blissfully asleep and unaware, protected by the night, neither Jimmy nor I could imagine the terrors Eloine must have sometimes felt, especially after Buster's death, with only herself and two boys in that shack a mile from anywhere, no light in sight except the stars and moon, the outdoors swarming with any manner of animals and, who knew, maybe tramps. Though she didn't understand how to aim them, I think she would have blasted off one of the guns if she'd been pushed far enough, just to scare the daylights out of whoever or whatever lurked in the yard. I remember once waking to see her stretched across what had been the Dad's bed, looking out across the screen porch into the moonlight, which glinted on the ten-gauge shotgun by her side. "Oma!" she said right out loud, "come here!" not that she'd forgotten he was gone but to fool any human intruder into thinking she wasn't alone. She had heard a prowler. Probably a lion.

On October 14, 1943, she conjured a local man with a truck to load us up, everything unattached, and haul us up the mountain, twenty-one miles, into Prescott to another, smaller shack, but on the good side of town. For the first time in two decades, she had electricity, a refrigerator, and an inside toilet. At eleven I had never yet turned on an electric switch.

Jimmy and I had two white cats, rescued from drowning at the Shoups'. I gave mine the perfectly sensible name of Mickey. Jimmy, however, named his Janitore, to rhyme with *Il Trovatore,* giving further evidence of a brain off wired. On moving day, terrified, they disappeared, never to be known again.

We had seen Prescott, the fabled Gomorrah, only a few times, in my case primarily on emergency trips to the doctor, such as when, at five, I fell out of the apricot tree onto a barbed wire fence and tore a gash in my arm through which my insides poked ominously, and at age six, when I flew out of the peach tree and broke the same arm. A third time was for an attack of 'pendicitus, which was caused, no doubt, by a bout of picnic gluttony. The fourth, for the Dad's funeral. Our ignorance of city life was nearly complete, even for a city of five thousand.

Migration away from our sacred trees, our swamp, our singular landscape left me unattached, like a marble in a cup, vulnerable to whatever new forces came along, large among them a school with many rooms and dozens of teachers, not one. Seventh grade was not a nightmare exactly, but a dream, a place without proper edges. Like the medieval Scandinavians, so tied to one place they lost even their religion when forced to move, I had no means for articulating this sudden wrenching of time and space. Let alone the ability to toss a football, which I had never seen before, or swing a bat or draw in what was supposed to look like three dimensions. This was a rite of passage, one of several yet to come, but uncelebrated. I carried my silent life with me, locked up like the clarinet case I hauled back and forth to school for years, a second half unseen and unannounced.

I began to live both as a cheerful extrovert who always said the wrong thing and as a somewhat more heroic secret second self, but one, I should explain, of the mind only. I did not rob old ladies or peer in windows, poison dogs or practice wiring bombs. Good at standing still, watching, I found out it was okay to touch the buildings, even the Bank and the Masonic Temple. Listening, I heard snatches of passing conversations and wondered what they attached to.

In the country there had been certainty in passing time. Watching a rabbit go about its timorous business could occupy fifteen minutes. Throwing rocks at something to terrorize it into flight provided a moment's sense of exhilarating superiority. Dropping flies down into a garden spider's tunnel-web passed an hour, especially if you imagined the scene from the spider's perspective, gazing up along that sticky white gossamer as it opened from dark to light with on it, occasionally, a quivering meal.

In town, sitting in the dusty woods far enough back not to be stumbled over, I could still wait—frittering—and watch a blue jay scratch under a scrub oak or a rhinoceros beetle of a new kind lumber over a twig, though suspecting I ought to be doing something worthwhile. Squatting there like a toadstool was my beast time in the jungle, where I was already learning to anticipate a biography elaborate as a rococo altar yet never jewel centered, never a corporeal body. Now, one must ask, did it happen? Life?

If the toadstool had been more of a psychotropic mushroom and I had chomped on it—like a purloined slice of fried baloney—some clarity might have evolved, some glint of understanding fallen onto my head.

Perhaps everyone has this subaltern, interior life. More often alone in Prescott, in the midst of a big school and town, without the apparatus of bush and stone and bug, unable to penetrate the social life I'd heard rumors of, I gradually extended my incipient kingdom. My understanding of human relationships, suddenly as complex as a dodecahedron, was refined in the crucible of loneliness. If, as some think, loneliness is the font of all knowledge, I ought to have been a genius, but missed by a mile. Something like this happened also to Jimmy, but we were no longer companions and had no more a language to express our feelings than we could jump over the moon, no longer cat and fiddle.

I was an impostor in school, going through the motions, unknown, ignorant, contributing nothing to the place or my life on earth, an orientation out of whack. Suspecting I was not alone in this, that other kids were having astonishing setbacks too, didn't help any because they had someone to explain it to.

The junior high dances were evenings of exquisite social misery. Not only had I not even the rudimentary steps, but believed I was supposed to attempt something committed with my partners along the lines of locker-room smut. One could but watch in envy Bill Tope glide lubriciously past with his girl enwrapped. Or Alfred McCoy, also smooth, as with a quick hand at your crotch, a lightning squirrel jab at your nuts when you least—well, you never—expected it, then sliding away with his partner.

The brain, to Emily Dickinson, is just the weight of God. Mine seemed dry and empty, an abandoned cocoon still connected to that scene in the draw of the hills, still suspended, abandoned in the sense of something animate, like the two white cats you've gone off and left bereft.

And I suspect something similar—an inexpressible melancholy perhaps, an impossible yearning for irretrievable youth and a surround of relatives—lay on Eloine's shoulders, like the astonishing trio of fox hides I had seen on a woman's suit. She took a job as housekeeper of The Pioneer's Home, a formidable brick structure overlooking the town, run by the state, into which dependent old people were embedded for their final years. Later she cooked for the school lunch program and lastly in a homey café featuring fried chicken, meat loaf, and mashed potatoes, right down her alley.

Eloine rented our one-bedroom cabin, formerly a summer mountain retreat for Phoenix people, from Kate Cory, a pioneer artist still famous for having lived, a lone white woman, among the Hopi Indians for seven years and for building her own house from scratch with her own hands. It was an unpainted two-story box of a place, with one large utilitarian room downstairs: living room, studio, kitchen. For food she favored not rice but an open can of beans, the 28-ounce size, set on her cylindrical stove, which also served for minimal heat. From this can she ate a mouthful whenever the thought struck her. In our house, at occasional Sunday noonday dinners, not only did she wear a black hat, black dress, black stockings and shoes, but declared it was unhealthy to drink both cold and hot liquids at the same meal. This was my first lesson in the theretofore unheard-of idea that one could modify the health of one's body by considering what one put in it.

She also politely bypassed Eloine's fried chicken, a heresy almost too shocking to record but perhaps motivated by a commitment to vegetarianism learned on the high mesa.

Now, I believe Kate Cory—who lived to ninety-seven—was sent west by her prominent eastern family because she was not only an independent cuss but an artist and a lesbian. The out-of-town solution. She had a plain, weather-beaten face, pulled-back hair, a determined, black-clothed walk with a cane, as if every trip downtown were aimed at confronting the mayor.

She painted desert flora. Not with the impacted sensuality and near-surrealism of Georgia O'Keeffe, whom she sharply resembled, but more as a naturalist trying to place within the space of a canvas as many plants as possible. Of course, the high Arizona desert floor is replete with a variety of things, set apart usually, as if giving each other some breathing room. Some drinking space. The last time I tried to run down the whereabouts of Kate Cory's paintings, I had no luck. No one knew what had become of them. Of course, *someone* knows where they are. I just haven't asked the right person yet.

I learned to read Poe beneath two of those paintings, on opposite walls of the jewel-sized, architecturally flawless public library, and also first looked up the word *homosexual,* the definition of which, entwined in "mental disorder," "rue morgue," and "orang-utan," did nothing for my enlightenment or sense of peace.

The paintings were mainly pinto-bean brown, both the raw and cooked sorts, with a good deal of violet and cream.

Slightly off the subject, one old lady of my acquaintance claimed to avoid the rooty-toot-toots (Julia Child's term), you dump in a spoonful of baking soda sometime during the boiling of beans. While the theory may be open to more rigorous testing, the result of the addition is overwhelmingly entertaining. The soda causes a maelstrom of activity in the pot, usually over the sides and down into the working parts of the stove—Pelée bitching in her volcanic meditations. In the fourteenth century, powders of ground spices were alleged to drive off wind, as well as to improve sexual output. The opposite attack was employed in *Like Water for Chocolate,* a weapon of vengeance against the sister who stole the heroine's lover, proving food can be used for militant ends.

Old Kate Cory did not recognize us boys the last time we were sent to see her with a basket containing four Miss Ruby cupcakes, and shut the door politely but firmly, like Emily Grierson when the town council called about her taxes. In the meantime, she had divested herself of all property except her own house, giving the cabins to their residents. Thus Eloine became a homeowner at last. Crammed with Skull Valley leavings, some odd bits of furniture once belonging to Kate Cory, green-flowered linoleum, yellow paint inside, brown shingles out, clothes hung on hooks on the bedroom wall, a pull-down sofa, up-swinging windows, school books and shoes and Billy's high school woodshop hat and magazine racks, a new little dog named Slippers, light bulbs screwed right into the ceiling, a listing kitchen, it must have looked like a Red Grooms construction on one of his loonier days.

Of course, I didn't have to learn a new language, as many displaced persons do, except as nuance, as slang, as a social grace at which I was maladroit. I couldn't even guess what the locker-room arcana meant: twat, pussy, come (n. & v.). Eloine, consciously or not, kept things at home as seamless as possible, learning all over again, as we were for the first time, how you live in a town. During the war many foods were rationed or unavailable, but in the general patriotic fervor, Eloine, like everyone else, made do, even without her favorite ingredient sometimes—sugar. Sliced bread was outlawed by the government, supposedly to cut down on replacement parts in bakeries. Wieners were stretched with soybean products. Macaroni and cheese grew in stature, with our certain approval. Spam replaced fried baloney in my hierarchy. Yet she was usually able to find a fryer for Sunday. On weekdays, because she had to go to work, we began in small ways to learn independence. How to get ourselves to school on time, to get home, make lunch, return again, to shop and prepare some of the preliminary steps for supper. Generally we came and went at ease. Exhausted, Eloine brushed her long hair before the stove, patted on cold cream, and went to bed with the chickens. Maybe a chapter of *The Robe* or *Green Mansions*.

The trees in the plaza lost their leaves. All down in big, ordered heaps.

There were two movie theaters, another new experience I could occasionally afford (ten cents). I preferred the Studio because it was seedier and favored more fanciful films with werewolves and recovering mummies, Transylvanian residents and merciless space visitors. I'd walk home after, late at night, blitheringly terrified.

Despite her misgivings about preachers, sensing how footloose we seemed, in one of her psychological nudges, Eloine suggested one Sunday we walk across town and try the Baptist Sunday School, "just for something to do, to see if you like it." Timidly, we approached the cold stone building and were taken in, a virtual nest for me, though Jimmy, already a gray wolf, found it less comforting. There I met not only affectionate adults but also a group of kids with whom I could relax a bit and with whom I certainly was not required to speak of prongs, dicks, or cunts.

It is one of the great pities of passing time—that is, from then to now—that Baptist adults have become so bigoted, so narrow and hate filled, so afraid, so intolerant of people who cannot fit their molded ideas of human existence and behavior. Then, though the preachers might have been witless actors, the general grown-up seemed peaceful, smiling, hugely tolerant of kids, and to my delight, perpetrators of an ongoing stream of potlucks, picnics, wedding receptions, banquets, and church suppers.

The rules severely laid down from pulpit and Sunday School, mainly negative—no fornication (*what?*), no smoking, no drinking, no dancing, no card playing, no "taking the Lord's name in vain"(?)—we were then too young to be much affected by, though with time we would test them all. These were called *sins,* italicized. The complete list, much longer for adults, which we looked forward to, formed the basis for every sermon preached in church, so far as I could tell, but Digger and I and various others became expert at ditching the eleven o'clock service in order to do something with a higher entertainment value, returning to mingle in the flock just as church was letting out. The trouble with a certain classification of sins is they can't be very clearly explained with words alone, but neither can they be illustrated or demonstrated without the consequence of disgrace or embarrassment to the teacher. Thus he or she ends up frustrated, like a baboon trying to communicate its desire for a banana, jumping up and down, making inarticulate charades sounds and gesticulations. How do you explain *no fornication* to a twelve-year-old?

Precisely how we were to expunge those sins that did befall us, on purpose or from ignorance, was equally unclear. We had no confessionals and certainly no minister who would have listened with the least particle of indifference or understanding. Anyway, as the poet Czeslaw Milosz believes—or has in any case stated as a truism—"All religions recognize that our deeds are imperishable," it wouldn't do us any good to tell adults. We'd get in dutch for nothing. All children, except the most ingenuous, begin to learn in infancy the improvement of silence over disclosure, perhaps the first lesson in life's conspicuous goal of separating children from their parents. It doesn't happen in a flash at age eighteen but has been nascent all along, an accumulative weaning. I think it's neurologists who say babies are born with far more synapses in their brains than adults have, that a lot are abandoned and left to die along the way. The signals for always confessing the truth about one's behavior are weeded out as unnecessary because all they do is get you in trouble.

Digger, an easygoing boy a year and a half older but in the same grade (because I had skipped second), the only child of one of the town's two undertakers, lived in back of the church, the "loading zone" of the mortuary facing it across the alley. We became fast friends, intimate for all the rest of our years well into college, with occasional freeze-outs, some side-drifting, as his term of endearment for me, horse's ass, makes clear.

Coddled but unspoiled, Digger had great freedom and was already allowed to drive by the time we met, the summer before ninth grade. Helping his father, he had learned all about dead bodies, which arcanum he soon taught me, an eager student. Together we knew how to make incisions, how to exchange blood for embalming fluid, to wire a mouth shut, use a trocar, dress, rouge, powder, and comb. While some kids were out throwing balls at each other (but where did they do this?), fishing, or (allegedly) fucking, we learned the exterior shapes of the body, its nooks and crannies, although on rather uncritical specimens. Then, for funerals, dressed up and solemn, we acted as ushers, the bereaved having no idea we had but a day or two before manipulated the beloved on a stainless steel table in the room just beyond the one they were sitting in, listening to Mary Ruffner play the Hammond. It was during these years I distilled a love for hothouse flowers—gladioli, carnations, chrysanthemums, and lilies.

A while later, at fifteen and sixteen, Digger's father let us in on another, much more electrifying aspect of a mortician's life. One of the military establishments of the settlers' days was Fort Whipple, in its original condition a typical log fort built in a square, with a court in the center to accommodate troops and their horses, a stronghold against Indians and a protection for new citizens, mainly miners at that time. In our time Fort Whipple was a large recuperative hospital on the edge of town, a mélange of random-looking buildings with screened porches, part sanitorium because the high, thin air was considered salubrious for tuberculosis patients, many from World War I. As a matter of routine, those who died were autopsied, one assumes for the gathering of medical knowledge or perhaps to give practice with knives to young interns.

In any case, after the pathologists got through cutting, someone had to put back together again the destroyed corpses.

Digger warned me. Still, it came as a jolt to see for the first time a human body laid open, sternum to crotch, ribs sawn out and set aside, brain trepanned, internal organs missing. . . . Well, in the interest of decorum, one must desist and say, merely, it was an experience only we two teenagers in town had, or, if one may borrow from essayist Cynthia Ozick in another context, it set up a "dim tolling of some indefinable aboriginal chime," a faint understanding of transience. It becomes clearer therefore why, through moments so binding, Digger and I developed into inseparable twins.

Arizona, "the baby state" before Hawaii and Alaska joined the union, was admitted in 1912, though of course always there geographically, the roaming grounds of thousands of Indians for ten thousand years. The lower half is a vigorous desert; the upper half, pine forest and high, windy plateaus, peaks, canyons, the Colorado River, and the Grand Canyon. Places like Skull Valley tuck into larger mountain ranges, their varied soil the product of millennia of effluvial runoff, the water heading south to spread out and disappear in the low, hot desert floor.

Food on the lower half, dominated by Indian/Mexican and Spanish tastes, has a much older indigenous culinary history. The Deep South influence fades out somewhere in east Texas. Eloine's own heritage, as should be clear by now, was southern, a rich, thick marmalade laid over a basic plantation cuisine, almost Arabian in its use of spices, raisins, and nuts, but then you could say Austrian for its uses of pork and cabbage, African in its employment of green plants and roots. Eloine claimed her heritage was "Black Dutch," whatever that might mean.

Prescott, an insular town still, founded in 1864, evolved in both philosophy and inebriation by cowboys and miners, though with more than a tremulous passing nod to eastern architecture rather than the Spanish style found down in the desert. That is, the town's founders came sideways across the nation, not upward from the Mexican border.

Yet there were many Mexican families in Prescott, mainly just south of the high school in a gentle ravine-valley and up its low slopes, along the edges of Granite Creek. They weren't recent immigrants usually, but the kids, having learned Spanish first at home, spoke English with a lilting accent. We were all in it together, not so much when away from school, yet I never thought there was prejudice, no doubt naively, as members of the majority are so often blind, deaf, and dumb. As I learned from the get-go as soon as we moved, injury can be inflicted in invidious ways.

I had a couple of crushes on Mexican schoolmates, but they never amounted to anything vaguely steamy, partly because my social life emanated from the Baptist Church and theirs from the Catholic, poles apart in matters of sin and transfiguration—the chief preoccupation of the Baptists—and idolatry. Besides which, it comes to me late in life, their moral standards were higher.

The black families, two or three or four or five, lived on the north side of town rather than the south, in a quiet neighborhood that still had dirt streets. We went to school with two boys, Robert—whom I hope life was finally good to—and Claude, for whom I've never wished much. Later Lottie, a strong, cheerful, beautiful woman, became a friend of Martha's over many decades and was the only nonwhite at her funeral, yet I don't believe she was ever invited to the house.

I don't know what happened to Ruth Mitchell, the only American Indian in our class. Ruby, the sole Chinese kid in town and part of the Baptist gang, now lives with a Siamese cat in Tucson.

There was one Mexican café on Montezuma Street, El Canerio, where I developed my sine qua non regarding enchiladas, chiles rellenos, and huevos rancheros. Going there we ranked in the domain of risk and adventure, as likewise we viewed the one Chinese café a block north along Whiskey Row, as we also did—a gang of us—when we visited other churches on Sunday, especially the really mysterious ones, like the Assembly of God and the holy rollers. We claimed this as part of our liberal education. Digger did the driving in one of the mortuary's big black DeSotos. The object was not to giggle.

One day Eloine came home with a bag full of dried New Mexico red chiles, a gift from the superintendent's wife, who got down to Phoenix often, and thus launched her quixotic deflection into Mexican cooking. She began to pick at Mexican food, trying her hand at enchiladas and tacos at home, either with the dried whole chiles or powerful boxed powders. She learned to develop the basic red chile sauce, talking whenever she had the chance with other women of more experience. Her taste buds, never damaged by smoke or drink, remained impeccable. With a little smacking at the front edge of her tongue and lips, she could tell you what was in most anything as soon as she'd been introduced to it once. Fond of strong flavors, she took to Mexican sauces right away. "*Um,* I'd give a pretty to have some venison now," she said. "Or a rabbit."

She was already hooked on paprika—*Capsicum annuum*—exported to Europe from America long ago and then to Hungary in particular, where it's the national treasure, and sent back. At Neill's Second Hand Store she found a wooden tortilla press and somehow ran down a source for *masa harina* and white Mexican cheese, *panela* probably.

Mexico, a large country, unassimilated, with remote states vastly separated by nearly impassable mountains, a largely nonmobile citizenry, with both a huge inland mass and thousands of miles of seashore, has a cuisine as varied as any country's in the world except perhaps

China's. The one constant is its indigenous pith—its use of corn products, for instance, and its hot chiles—but otherwise, local dishes depend
on district and tradition and who the conquerors were. What Eloine
learned to cook is the Sonoran style, "southwestern" in general nomenclature, including all of northern Mexico banking up to the U.S.
border—lower California, Arizona, over into New Mexico and Texas,
even so far as Louisiana, to touch upon the Cajun and Creole flavors,
though stretching the point a bit.

In Prescott, never an adventurous place, with nothing much in
the way of culinary history, "Mexican food" meant tacos, enchiladas,
chiles rellenos, beans, and alas, the ubiquitous "Spanish" rice about
which Mark Miller, in a moment of flair, has written, "the ever-
present, ever-tasteless, ever-mushy . . . pour soul . . . bastardized to the
point of having no identity, texture, taste, or character." My feelings
exactly. This slop is added for cheap volume and weight to combination plates in countless ugly cafés throughout the West, including now
the Northwest, which claim to serve authentic Mexican cuisine—the
same lifeless stuff day in and day out, unsullied by the slightest talent,
imagination, or innovation. I admit, reluctantly, that Miller's sweet
cinnamon rice overcomes many of my objections—if he makes it.
Fewer if I must.

Likewise, many American cooks think all Mexican flavors come
in cans. A sauce like the one following isn't hard to make and is incal-
culably better. Besides, you'll have a half gallon of it to keep in the
refrigerator. None of these rudimentary sauces require a precarious
plunge.

BASIC RED CHILE SAUCE

20 to 25 whole dried New Mexico red chiles
1 pound tomatoes
¾ cup chopped yellow or white onions
1 to 2 tablespoons oil, plus more for cooking sauce
2 quarts water
6 whole cloves
5 to 8 cloves garlic, chopped

1 teaspoon ground cumin, or more to taste
1 to 2 teaspoons ground Mexican oregano or a dozen leaves fresh
1 to 2 sprigs of fresh thyme if you have it
1 to 2 sprigs of fresh cilantro
½ teaspoon salt

After removing the stems and seeds from the chiles, hold them directly in the flame of a gas burner, turning to toast, for 3 to 4 minutes; or roast them in a dry heavy skillet. Don't let them blacken. Blacken the tomatoes in a dry skillet. Cook the onions in the oil over low heat until lightly browned.

Combine the chiles, vegetables, and water in a large saucepan. Add the remaining ingredients except the salt; cover and simmer for 20 minutes.

(*Note:* If you're going to be using chicken parts for tacos, perhaps, or enchiladas, poach them in 3 cups of the chile liquid at this point. Remove when done. Return the chicken-infused liquid to the main pan.)

Put all the ingredients in a food processor, including half the cooking liquid. Puree until you have a medium-thick paste, adding only a little more liquid if needed. Strain to remove any solids, saving all the chile liquid.

Pour some oil or lard into a deep skillet (so it won't splatter), heat until almost smoking, pour in the sauce and let it sizzle for a few minutes, maybe 5. Add water to the sauce if it gets too thick and ½ teaspoon salt. You might drop in some more chopped onion here.

New Mexico red chiles can usually be found, dried, in plastic bags hanging somewhere near the vegetables in western markets, expensive for what you get. If you're serious about making sauce, buy a whole *ristra,* a three- or four-foot-long dangle of chiles on a string. Produced every fall after the harvest, they can be bought by mail order. I call Josie's in Santa Fe, (505) 983-6520, and Rick Bayless contacts www. chiletoday.com. There are many other reliable purveyors of chiles, mainly in New Mexico, including Herman Valdez at (505) 852-2129. At home we use three ristras a year.

Salsas, essentially raw rather than cooked, can be kept on hand or quickly made for tacos or ceviche, to toss over an enchilada or the present-day "nachos," a kind of tavern fix meant for chomping with tequila or dark beer while watching some ball game or another on a 56-inch TV. Like the medieval artichoke, they are good for the ego.

Basic Salsa Mexicana

5 fresh serrano or jalapeño chiles
5 Roma tomatoes
1 onion
1 green bell pepper
1 red bell pepper
3 tablespoons olive oil
3 cloves garlic, chopped
some fresh cilantro leaves, chopped
1 teaspoon ground cumin
½ teaspoon salt
black pepper

Toast the chiles over a gas flame or in a dry skillet. Leave the onion and bell peppers raw. Chop them all into small pieces, mix together, and add the oil and remaining ingredients. Let stand an hour or two.

Variation (Salsa Verde): In place of the red tomatoes, use 20 tomatillos, softened in hot water, skinned of their outer papery husk, but not peeled. Use 1 cup of chopped cilantro.

Maricruz's Chicken with Peanut Sauce

From San Miguel de Allende

Fry 1 cup of raw peanuts in oil for 10 minutes. Remove and drain. Fry chicken pieces in the same oil until browned, 10 to 15 minutes. Cook 3 medium tomatoes in hot water for a minute so the skins will slip off. Peel. Add 3 dried red chiles to the same water to soften.

In a food processor, grind the peanuts, tomatoes, chiles, some raw onion, and 3 garlic cloves. Strain this sauce. Pour it over the chicken pieces and heat together. Serve the chicken on a plate with extra sauce.

Maricruz presents this with rice. I'd prefer a fresh green corn and cheese tamale.

Mexican dishes didn't overwhelm Eloine's southern style but slid into it sideways. After she changed to a more pleasant job, her spirits began to pick up. She joined the Eastern Star, patriotically stomping around in their ceremonies carrying a flag, and on the Singer made me fancy cowboy shirts with piping and pearl snaps. She looked forward to the future. The war was changing everything—not just causing a closer awareness of shortages—though maybe no one realized it quite yet. Eloine, in some unrealistic, vague yearning, expected Omer and Billy to come back and settle down nearby. Jimmy and I stretched outward, ready to fly as soon as possible. Though the older boys survived un-scathed, only Martha returned.

Historically, Prescott was a Janus town, both rowdy and sedate, the latter half represented by a stately white stone courthouse set like a cube of alabaster, a pre-Michelangelo marble chunk, in a plaza inter-sected by walkways, plots of grass, elms, green benches, shade and sun, a wrought-iron fish pond, and rococo bandstand. Ruined later by some architectural ignoramus who added an irrelevant entrance and public toilets on the west side, to say nothing of some decoration committee who attached *permanent* Christmas lights so it looked more like a confection than what it had been virginally—a splendid Greek Revival structure—it was the center of law and order. The jail occupied the top floor, with latticed views out over the town and a suicidal drop to the pavement for any who might try escape.

To the west it faced Whiskey Row, like Wyatt Earp glowering at Bonnie and Clyde, if one may be allowed to anachronize western folklore.

The town continued living with its deranged cowboy peculiarity. In their snazzy boots and flowered tight shirts and Levi's with enviable crotches, these men had but one aim in life, to get drunk on at least one night of the weekend and let it be loudly shouted. These romantic figures worked in rain and heat and manure and blood out on the ranches surrounding the town during the week, got paid a little, then drove their pickups on dirt roads like the spokes of a wagon wheel to the hub. Some brought women with them over whom it was obligatory to fight, hard-haired girls wearing pants and forward-piercing breasts. The others, it was fondly supposed, found whores to roust with, though Digger and I were never able to corroborate this.

I drank a first beer at twelve on an eighth-grade homeroom picnic at Granite Dells (playground/camping area), illicitly furnished by a boy with an older brother, but didn't think much of it. However, diligence and practice, as with all acquired tastes, gradually breached the buttress, and I became cautiously adept at fourteen and was drinking with Digger in the bars on Whiskey Row by sixteen—though as an occasional lark, not a habit, a chance for me to hear western music and for him to seek wanton women. Digger was a highly adaptive organism, altering and adjusting the energy he needed to expend according to the likelihood of reproductive success, what paleontologists call a "life history strategy."

When first we sauntered down Montezuma—"Don't lollygag on that street at night," Eloine warned us—there were only older men and their younger kids, but by the time we actually entered the saloons (some were "restaurants") the war was over, the final plangent bells had rung, and the ratio of age-to-age realigned.

The first Fourth of July celebration in Prescott occurred in order to commemorate the eighty-eighth year of the union, in 1864, and the holiday ever since has been a season of ritual—a ritual of parade, rodeo, carousing, wildness, frivolity, fornication (heightened), drinking, gambling, *la société du spectacle*—and an ongoing frustration to the Baptists, in front of whose establishment much of the above passes by, usually on Sunday. Food, extraneous at this time, drops down into the corn dog and cola category.

The parade, mostly of horses and their riders—those who could stay on following the previous night, the horses, curried and flossed, sometimes bedecked with silver trappings—tripped along Montezuma, around the plaza onto Cortez, and dispersed somewhere out in the direction of the fairgrounds, where the rodeo would be held in the afternoon. The high school band played Souza marches. Smells of horse manure rose in the heat. Cowboys who had no steed to ride in the parade and who did not intend to try staying on a bull a couple of hours later stood on the sidewalk at the entrance of The Green Frog and The Palace and The Antlers with bottles of beer, making wonderful, arcane comments full of snorts and jeers.

At the rodeo, age twelve, I had my first paying job, somehow "discovered" by Eloine. You could take a galvanized bucket and a can opener out there to the fairgrounds, a long dusty walk, buy a dollar's worth of cold drinks from the Rotary men, then walk around in the grandstand selling them for two dollars, a 100 percent profit, half of which you then reinvested for the next bucket. I wasn't allowed to sell beer but discovered Jimmy, who played tuba in the high school band, drinking one, a serendipitous detection I could use for ballast in case he had something on me, such as the time he caught me *la masturbation interrompu* with the magazine rack. Billy's handmade magazine rack with the leopard-spot burns on it. *Jesus.*

Acquaintances are not friends and, to the southern mind, friends cannot replace family. Eloine looked forward to letters from "back home," all noting the passing of someone or a visit someone had with someone else, all meaningless to us boys. One summer, when I was thirteen, she left us with Martha and took the train, alone, back to Tennessee for a month, the first time in twenty years. This spasm of time, while great for her, encouraged Martha, fourteen years my elder, to begin thinking of herself as my surrogate extra parent, not a happy conclusion. She even attempted to edit both my reading and my coming and going. But since she and Jimmy worked all day, I was let loose in the town, a situation bound to have reverberations. The days would hardly have been worth living otherwise.

Mornings I spent in the library under the peaceful Cory landscapes. Afternoons I wandered, picking up bits of information, the value or meaning of which did not click into sense for years to come, like the reason for the Dad's squealing bed frame.

To wit: One afternoon, dwelling in the marble halls of the public restroom on the ground floor of the courthouse, a young, rather scruffy man next to me at the urinals, holding onto a most peculiar-looking ridged stiff member, asked, "You know where a guy can get a job around here?" I thought he was looking for employment, so politely and helpfully said, "I hear they're hiring down at the railroad."

Such small sorties into sophistication had nothing to do with Eloine's being gone to Tennessee except insofar as I didn't have to report home for lunch so could eat whatever I could pay for, El Canerio's enchiladas, for fifteen cents a pair, high on the list.

Knowing I'd be footloose and useless while she was away, Eloine left me a packet of easy recipes I was to prepare now and then for supper for the three of us, with instructions in the Escoffier manner; that is, vague as to measurements, mixing, and temperature. Of those suggestions I can't remember making any but a single dessert. I still have the original recipe writ large in her looping style:

DOUBLE BOILER DESSERT

3 cups milk
3 eggs
⅔ cup sugar
pinch of salt, vanilla
8 marshmallows
2 envelopes gelatin
whipping cream
maraschino cherries
pineapple chunks
nuts

Cook the custard in a double boiler until it is thick enough to coat a spoon. Stir in the marshmallows and two envelopes gelatin, dissolved in cold water. Chill. Then whip the cream,

fold it into the gelatin-custard mixture with some maraschino cherries, chunks of pineapple, and nuts. Refrigerate
for several hours.

While neither exactly haute cuisine nor cowboy food, this dessert
suited me to a T.

Marriage and Family Living

As the organizing principle of Sonoran cooking is red chile sauce, the principle of cowboy is chaos. By comparison with him, the blessed, the upright, the serious, good and pale, are but shed snake skins.

The vitality of the cowboys, not only in their carousing but in their games, amounts to a destruction of order. Pitting themselves in body-to-body combat with animals much larger and heavier and faster than they are, they distort their own humanness but sharpen their individual distinction, though as a walking, talking mass they, like angels, are hard to tell apart.

Perhaps the cowboy is no more between two worlds in his initiation than the general rank of youths passing through. His dead-serious rampage with other animals (which can bring him silver buckles, money, sex), though tough to do, requiring strength, practice, agility, fearlessness, may be different only in kind from the twenty-five-year-old who still plays soccer or Telemachus protecting the honor of his father's home. World reality stretches only as far as the horizon.

The cowboy becomes not a disinterested rancher, the grower of an edible commodity, but a partner of the commodity, as if trying to meld himself with that other flesh-and-blood creature. When separated, let loose in town, in an alien environment, he gets tanked to blur the edges of this separation from the creatures he both hates and loves. In his great comic pastoral in *The Hamlet,* Faulkner and one of the Snopes boys go it a bit further. All the way, I guess you could say.

Or maybe his carousing is an alternative to the sex he deserves but hasn't been offered; it is the logical reward. Actually, logic has no part here; sex should be his mythic reward.

There is something paradoxical, if not grotesque, about a man riding a bronc or a bull, dogging a calf—which in this latter instance he may kill, butcher, and eat—just as there is beauty in his calm parading or working with his horse. It's when he attempts, even for six or eight seconds, to connect to a beast that will never love him, their synapses firing contrarily, he becomes both most man and most vulnerable boy. I'm not talking here of the professional rodeo bum driving a battered pickup with clattering pistons from town to town, sometimes hundreds of miles in a night, in order to compete in the next day's dusty arena strictly for money, but the boys who actually live on ranches and grow up like siblings with horses and cattle and along the way decide to take it one step more, to perform with animals, to compete in this act with other performers, not as a team the way town boys do, but as fearsome individuals.

Only ten miles separated the courthouse and the gate, yet the cowman and the alderman never seemed at ease with each other in Prescott, were rarely friends. Neither was it easy for us "city" kids to make friends with boys from the ranches, though I remember some exhilarating times with Digger staying over with them in a bunkhouse, to which boys were usually banished for their maturing season starting at about thirteen, as if they were too much of a menace to have in the house at night. They were neat, tidied up after themselves, washed their own breakfast dishes and their clothes, too, if they wanted something exact to wear. I never did meet any of their mothers. It was as if the boys had been knocked completely over onto the male side of things.

Getting up early on a spring morning, before dawn, frying your own thin slab of beef taken directly from the freezer and dropped in a hot skillet, an egg, and last night's extra biscuits, coffee. Saddling the horses and riding out to do chores along the fences. Rounding up calves for market. Burritos and beer for lunch. Dirty and exhausted by sundown. But you were never more than a weekend guest in that world. You could never enter it to stay. For one thing, my horsemanship was not good enough. Growing up in ranch country does not mean you got to ride much. I'd been on a horse only ten or twelve times in my life, thus struggled, during these weekends, simply to stay on with a certain degree of panache. A number of years later I did fall off a horse—actually a donkey—twice in the same day, first on the west bank of the Nile, then later while crossing over a rocky hill, in the July sun, from the Valley of the Kings to the Valley of the Queens. Jim, my longtime companion, laughed so hard he split open the seam in the crotch of his shorts and had to, for the remainder of the day, hold his hat over his saddle to avoid a debilitating sunburn, a retributive turn of events of the kind that makes you think there might be a desert god after all.

Racist, sexist, and homophobic, these ranch boys knew all the high school lingo, even I did by then, but found no reason to use much of it beyond a coarse joke or two, some serviceable swear words for a recalcitrant steer, because gabble was an unnecessary and embarrassing impediment in their fathers' houses. Specialists, they could talk shorthand to other specialists, get the job done and over with, knowing it would repeat itself the next day, while we were still standing around working on the first phrase. After you've summed up the weather and the livestock, what else is there? These silences didn't seem like need, but perchance they were. How could there be nothing worth talking about just for the fun of conversation? Maybe because they knew how to do things they'd been concentrating on since age five, while the rest of us could hardly do anything but stand at the blackboard, usually in humiliation, parsing somebody else's dead sentence.

Our school didn't have a rodeo class, as Annie Proulx says they do in parts of Wyoming, but it would have been popular. Neither did the ranch boys play team sports. First, they had chores to do at home and had to get from here to there before dark, and second, they played— that is, worked—alone, whenever there might be free time, with their animals. They hooked a girlfriend eventually, only one. Then they married, had a baby, and so on and so on. Family values.

On those working days with the ranchers' sons, if we weren't going to get back to the house for lunch, we rolled up something edible—refried beans, slices of the breakfast steak, leftover potatoes, a fried egg—into flour tortillas and stuck them in a paper sack in a saddle bag. I believe I've read somewhere that Mongolian marauders actually tenderized and more or less cooked their lunch meat by arranging it on the saddle between their butts and the leather, so as they bounced along, friction and some kind of chemical breakdown occurred, in addition to heat.

Nearly every ethnic culture in the world uses a form of folded bread in which to stuff something for lunch. It's a peasant working person's solution, a convenient way to eat on the run. Mexicans wrap meat or beans and cheese or anything else nonliquid in flour or corn tortillas, to make a one-handed meal called the burrito, at least in Americanese. Pueblo Indians, who also invented the tortilla, make a flat bread, piki. Chinese form egg rolls from rice flour wrappers to hold chopped vegetables or cook thin pancakes in which to enshroud mu-shu pork. Ethiopians dig from a communal pot with snags of flat bread. Tunisians form a *brik* of thin dough with a raw egg (or whatever) dropped in, then quickly fry it and dip it in *harissa,* one of the planet's greatest hot sauces. Anglo-Saxons make sandwiches. One could rhapsodize on the theme of lamb souvlakia in pita eaten on the hoof in the Plaka on a warm, cacophonous evening.

In San Miguel de Allende we discovered a flattened meat burrito, achieved by pounding the dickens out of a small piece of cheap cut with a round metal pounder until it was about a ten-inch circle, quickly seared, then rolled up in a large flour tortilla with whatever condiments you want, easy to carry down the street or off into the next revolution. And in Guanajuato, similarly, the flattened beef, fried, then topped with refried beans, roasted green chiles, and white cheese, run under a broiler to toast, sprinkled finally with cilantro and a couple of thin slices of purple onion. Convenient for rolling, it's called *sábanas sin historia* (sheets without history), for what reason no one claims to know.

Another Mexican carry-all is the taco, the most Americanized of all these imports and the most vulgarized by fast-food chains, *infra dignitatem.* A couple of generations of American kids have grown up lacking as much in the appreciation of a good taco as they do in the use of English. The sawdusty, dry, crumbled-ground-meat-pellet object you buy at a convenience window in no way resembles what may be done.

Most taco shells, bought already bent or fried at home, are filled with some kind of meat after they've been shaped and crisped in hot oil. In Eloine's version, a thin layer of ground meat (beef, pork, turkey) mixed with chorizo and spices is patted, pushed, molded onto one-half the circular tortilla first. The tortilla is folded, held in hot oil with the fingertips to crisp the spine, then laid down, first on one side, then on the other, to finish browning. The tacos are placed *en pointe* in a dish with paper towels to drain and served on a platter. Each eater completes his or her own from a diversity of agents: chopped green onion and cilantro, chopped raw tomatoes and lettuce, grated cheeses, both yellow and white, perhaps some cooked green peas (Tucson style), and red or green chile sauce. Guacamole. Cold Mexican beer on the side, with limes.

An enchilada, correctly made, is one of my two or three most favorite foods. "Correctly made" is the operative, if inelegant, phrase here. I have seldom been able to achieve it. As I cannot, with any certainty, boil rice or roll out dough fit for a pie pan, I rarely can make an enchilada that doesn't (a) fall apart, (b) stick to the dish, (c) taste like a frozen one. Sometimes it is the simplest plan that fails, as Robert Burns was not the only one to tell us.

An enchilada should—and will in the hands of an expert—stay convincingly rolled, exude a cataract of melted cheese, be easy to cut, and above all be wed to its red sauce, which ought to be on the fiery side. You can achieve this by adding a tablespoon or two of canned *chipotles en adobo* sauce, extremely hot, to the basic red chile sauce, creating a dark (*negra*), smoky flavor of high temperament. *Chipotle* is the dried form of jalapeño, the most common green chile used in the United States, famed for its exuberance.

While I prefer my enchiladas rolled with only melted cheese and a bit of red sauce inside, more on top, and a smack of raw chopped onion, tomatoes, and cilantro, others use cooked meats, such as chorizo, chicken, smoked duck, rabbit, brisket, even lobster or tuna, and serve the whole thing in a slough of sour cream. As I suppose everyone knows, the filling is rolled inside tortillas, available everywhere these days; we even found some in Aix-en-Provence while living there and suffering Mexican withdrawal. Mark Miller uses crepes instead, flavored with *guajillo* dried chiles, which are probably "in the hands" of any cook. Essentially, enchiladas are tortillas that've been dipped in a somewhat thinned red chile sauce, lightly fried (but not crispy), or vice versa, filled with cheese (any yellow melting type or a combination with white goat cheese), and rolled. In order to get them all to the table hot and oozing, you lay them side by side in a dish, folded edges down, pour sauce and grated cheese over the top, plus a few slices of fresh jalapeños, and pop them into a high oven or under a broiler for a minute so they come out looking like molten lava. Yet they must not cook so long that they lose identity or disintegrate when lifted, and therein lies the trick.

Eloine made a noble version of enchiladas with Anaheim green chiles, easier to assemble ahead of time.

ELOINE'S GREEN ENCHILADA CASSEROLE
Enchiladas Verdes

12 to 14 New Mexico green or Anaheim or poblano chiles
4 or 5 tomatoes
1 onion, chopped
3 cloves garlic, chopped
3 tablespoons oil, plus more for frying tortillas
½ cup heavy cream
salt and black pepper
1 teaspoon ground cumin
12 corn tortillas
½ pound cheese, grated

Blacken the chiles directly over a gas flame or under a broiler; place in cloth towels for 15 minutes to steam. Then peel, leaving bits of blackened skin, take off the stems, discard the seeds, and chop. Blacken the tomatoes in a heavy skillet or *comal,* seed, and chop; you should have about 2 cups. Sauté the onion and garlic in oil, then add the tomatoes and chiles and sauté for 5 minutes. Add the cream, salt and pepper, and cumin and cook another 2 minutes or so. Thus, the sauce.

Preheat the oven to 375°F.

In a skillet, fry the tortillas in hot oil, not too crispy. Drain on paper towels. In a baking dish that may go to the table, lay 4 tortillas side by side (you're going to build up 4 individual stacks). Spoon some chile sauce over these and some cheese. Add another layer of tortillas, sauce, and cheese, and so forth, stacking up the 4 squat towers ending with a layer of cheese.

Bake the casserole for 5 to 8 minutes, until the cheese is melted. The stacks are now ready to lift out and serve. At the last, you might top them with chopped cilantro, bits of raw onion, a blob of *crema mexicana,* or—best of all—an egg barely poached in a pan of heated *red* chile sauce. Serve guacamole on the side.

Note: The choice of cheese might be longhorn, cheddar, Monterey Jack, or the Mexican *asadero*—just so long as it's a melting kind. Try crumbled white Mexican cheese, *queso fresco,* at the last—on top of the egg.

Chiles rellenos con queso is my third most-needed food, a common Mexican border dish. *Relleno* means "stuffed," and *queso* means "cheese." I don't recall either El Canerio or Eloine using anything but cheese, but you could stuff the chiles with whatever's handy, I suppose. It wouldn't be an improvement, only an elaboration. I've heard, but have no direct evidence, of people stuffing them with rice. Wouldn't they just.

CHILES RELLENOS CON QUESO

4 fat poblano chiles
2 cups grated jack cheese
½ cup grated Fontina or Gorgonzola or blue cheese
2 to 3 teaspoons minced fresh marjoram

6 eggs, separated
oil for frying
red chile sauce
cilantro leaves

Blister the chiles over a gas flame or under a broiler, sweat
them in a towel, then peel, leaving some black bits. Leave the
stems on. Slit open just enough to get out the seeds, then stuff
the cavity with the cheeses (or whatever else you may, in your
delirium, feel inclined to use). Separate the eggs and keep the
yolks individualized by returning them, for the moment, to
one half of each shell. Beat the whites until stiff, then beat the
yolks, one at a time, into the whites. Mix in the marjoram.

 Heat deep oil in a skillet to 375°F. Dip each stuffed chile
into the egg mixture to coat generously, then lay them down
in the hot oil, spooning it over the tops as well. When half
cooked, turn the chiles over carefully and finish the other side
to an even golden brown. Serve on plates covered with warm
red sauce. Decorate with slices of avocado and cilantro leaves.

 Eloine didn't, and thus I don't, use any flour with the eggs; however, some people do. About 1¾ cups in the above recipe would create
a batter, and then you might as well go on and add ½ cup of Mexican
beer. TV chef and author Bobby Flay stuffs his poblanos with goat and
Monterey Jack cheeses, dips them in a beer batter, then cornmeal
before frying them. But he's a New Yorker.

 Though they can be somewhat restored by laying them in a
heated thinned red sauce for half a minute, chiles rellenos are best eaten
at once, meaning someone, the delegated relleno cook, has to keep
working while the others eat. Mexican food is labor- and utensil-
intensive, so one might as well make lots while at it. Chiles rellenos,
however, are not one of the choices I would make ahead in gross,
though Rick Bayless, in *Mexico One Plate at a Time,* claims you can hold
the fried chiles an hour or two at room temperature before reheating
them in a 400°F oven.

 Eloine cooked pots full of chile con carne, the omnipresent Texan national dish, always served with sweet southern cornbread or "Spanish" cornbread, but like most aggregate stews, it was never the same twice. And there are now, it seems, hundreds of thousands of chile con carne recipes, each one the best and most authentic, the sort of dish that—except for the essential meat and chili powder—wavers and wobbles according to one's ability to invent and the presence of a new animal to butcher. Originally the province of the chuck wagon cook, *el cocinero,* it would have been made with chunks of beef on the trail drive. Possibly buffalo a bit further back. Wild turkeys were plentiful on some of those ranges, and quail, though I don't think I'd disfigure quail by immersing them in pinto bean soup (purists don't add beans). Rather, I'd cut a green willow or paloverde stick, impale them, and roast them over a mesquite fire, plain. Paleolithic man making progress.

Huevos rancheros is the Mexican version of eggs Benedict and employed for the same reason—to get your mind off a hangover. For years in late winter, before our dermatologist forbade it, we went to Puerto Vallarta to lie in the sun on the beach just south of the tiny Río Quale. Because there was nothing to do but rotisserate, read, eat, and drink, it became difficult sometimes to separate day from night. Mainly the way to identify morning was to go into the great *palapa* dining room below the El Dorado and order huevos rancheros and maybe a Bloody Mary to steady the hand that held the fork. It seemed at the time, and still in memory, there was no finer food. But one understands exotic eating is often tied to a complexity of attending stimuli. The palapa was a cool respite from the blistering heat, open on all sides to views of the ocean, the tiny Indian peddlers, the fish-on-a-stick mongers, to breezes. One was rather more newly in love. The waiters were quick, young, and handsome, the same ones you'd seen dancing, in a blur, the night before downtown. Strolling mariachis sang Mexican soap operas, blissfully oblivious to tonality.

Kids sold three-foot-long iguanas for pets or food, take your pick, across the bay from where *Night of the Iguana* was filmed, when Elizabeth Taylor spent her days floating in an inner tube, it was said, to keep an eye on her husband of the moment, Richard Burton, and Ava Gardner. I have never eaten iguana. They have faces like Saul Bellow in his advanced years.

Huevos Rancheros

2 corn tortillas per person
mashed cooked black beans or refried pinto beans, heated
plenty of grated yellow cheese
some fresh or pickled jalapeño slices
Basic Red Chile Sauce (page 124): If mild, add a tablespoon
    of chipotles en adobo (OK canned) because remember,
    you are supposed to be suffering from guilt.
1 to 2 eggs per person
chopped green onions for garnish
crumbled white cheese, such as *queso añejo*

Lightly fry the tortillas, but not too crispy; keep them warm
in a cloth as you go. Lay one tortilla on each plate; cover
with a layer of beans, then cheese, jalapeño slices, and red
chile sauce. Lay on a second tortilla; top with cheese and red
sauce.

Soft-fry the eggs in red sauce, then lay one or two on
each pile. Pour' more heated red sauce over everything
swimmingly. Toss on some green onions and white cheese.

This may be, to some, indistinguishable from the *huevos motuleños*
of the Yucatán. In any case, it is a pragmatic dish, not rich in psychological detail. A *mole* sauce made with Mexican chocolate, Oaxacan
style, is brilliant on huevos rancheros.

Because at Puerto Vallarta one has moved from the more inward,
arid desert of Sonoran cooking to the seaside, fish are given attention in
the better cafés, such as The Bistro on a spit of land below the bridge
over the river. Typically, the style is Veracruzana, however, from the
opposite side of the country, on the Yucatán peninsula.

Nowadays the fish—preferably *huachinango,* the red snapper of the
Sea of Cortez—is wrapped with its sauce and vegetables in tin foil. Foil,
a utilitarian but quite ugly wrap, tasteless in both senses of the word,
can easily be replaced with something else: large nontoxic green leaves,
such as banana, ti, plantain, taro, which even grows in Oregon in late

summer, rehydrated seaweed sheets, green corn husks, fig leaves, grape leaves, or parchment paper—the French *en papillote*. Banana leaves, though pretty, tend to split and leak. The world is replete with cloaks more attractive and natural than tin foil, unless one is a pack rat or magpie.

There was always something lacking, to my taste, in these packets of fish and tomatoes, onions, lime juice, olives, peppers, and herbs; something did not weave together but left an acidic cruelty. In one of those culinary cross-continental leaps the imagination can give birth to, and thanks again to Ismail Merchant, I now add a bold smattering of garam masala to fish Veracruzana and everything comes together, a simple tapestry. Inauthentic, of course. So add a dollop of guacamole or beans to the plate if it makes you feel better, a handful of tortilla chips. Some salsa cooked in the Texan style.

You can do essentially the same with a half breast of chicken, pounded thin or sliced. Caramelize the onions first to further recipro-cate the flavors. Or, you want to really blow them out of the bay? Cook down a sauce made of Grand Marnier, cream, pear nectar (2 table-spoons each per serving), ½ Anjou pear per person, peeled, cored, cut in thick slices, and tossed with a sprinkling of sugar (caramelize if you want to). Add all this to the chicken packet, lay in some herb branches —marjoram, purple basil, thyme—and bake awhile. Serve it with *crema mexicana aguacates* (blend 1 avocado, 1 cup *crema,* a pinch of salt, juice of 1 lime) and raw salsa.

Some of these basics I began cooking in high school but only just, despite the idiosyncrasy of a required course called "Marriage and Family Living" or something as silly, one half taught by the home ec teacher, who, a maiden, was so embarrassed she liked to died when any inkling of human compatibility arose, and the other half taught by a fatherly male whose deepest lecture on the subject, to a segregated passel of mostly horny boys, concluded that we should not stand on the street corner whistling at girls, which, so far as I saw, no one ever did anyway.

And he read from a morocco-bound quarto an impenetrable pas-sage, the source of which, quite accidentally, I stumbled onto years later while reading about the James family. It warned, "The development of puberty may lead indirectly to insanity by becoming the occasion of a vicious habit of self-abuse in men" (Maudsley, *Body and Mind,* 1870). So both whistling at girls and self-abuse were out. No one raised a hand to ask what "self-abuse" meant, which is just as well, as knowing might have seriously curtailed one of the intense and only pleasures of being a heterosexually celibate teenager. I think self-abuse was what the Victorian doctor William Acton was edging up to when he warned, in 1857, "that an awful risk attends abnormal substitutes for sexual intercourse" and that, to summarize, you could kill yourself through prolonged indulgence.

As David Friedman has emphasized in *A Mind of Its Own,* speaking of the penis in the hand, as it were, of Augustine, "[it] was the most perilous part of the body," and self-pollution one of the several more destructive preoccupations a male teenager could succumb to in this, the most dangerous of all possible worlds. According to Friedman, to curb self-pollution one German writer, S. G. Vogel, "urged an updated version of infibulation, a practice invented by the ancient Greeks in which the foreskin is pulled forward and sewed, tied, or pinned shut." There were worse "cures" than this, invented by sadistic doctors who must have been ashamed of what they did as boys, but surely nothing like this was being practiced by doctors in the days of which I speak, though the aura, the scent of condemnation, remained in the air, floating just beyond identification like a rancid perfume, a quarter-spoken threat.

The *idea* of the penis, as Freud would have contemplated it, and its counterpart, the vagina, the entire reproductive activity, lay still in the stygian realm of the supernatural, something essentially inexplicable, rendering it beyond question or explanation. Any adjunct information, such as of eunuchs or castrati (Could eunuchs really fuck the women in the Arabian harems or not? Would castration make you queer automatically?) being unthinkable, would never be broached at all, a minor but luminous illustration of the power of darkness. The less they know the less they need to know.

The physical contrarieties between males and females, largely figured out already along the cheery byways of trial and error, they illustrated (again in segregation) with slide shows or jerky films that ran off their tracks, jammed, or burned up regularly. These educational marvels, supposed to show the operational equivalents of procreation in cross section, radiated a darkness more profound than algebra, as if to say, Now that you've seen a bit of light, let's show you how really dense you are. I knew *my* penis didn't look like that innocuous hemisection, and I'd seen enough dead women by then to understand at least their outward physiology, and felt up enough living ones to get the idea in my fingertips, as it were. These films created such a narcoleptic state you ended up feeling the gum blobs under your desk to stay awake.

However, there was one gripping commercial "educational" film circulating left over from the war, when its intent was to horrify the troops, which as juniors and seniors, with parental permission, we could view at the Elks Theatre on one of two successive nights in honor of gender separation. On the subject of venereal disease, it was surely one of the most ghastly films ever concocted by the mind of man, in this case some Hollywood producer reduced to making patriotic works. I survived it all until the caesarian birth, at which point I was compelled to turn around in my chair in, fortunately, the topmost row of the balcony, and vomit—I who had by then restored numerous chopped-up dead bodies. *Dead* must have been the difference. The point of the film was to scare you into a lifetime of celibacy. It made you wonder how all these healthy-looking adults busily reproducing, including Mr. Miller, our handsome coach, survived from generation to generation. The effect of the opposing arguments annulled both, so we floated back on the tide of misty ignorance.

To our credit, we did know, theoretically, what caused babies, unlike anthropologist Bronislaw Malinowski's famous Trobriand Islanders, who as late as 1915 hadn't made the connection between the sex act and the children. Apparently they thought a woman filled up and delivered a child every now and then, as randomly as rainstorms came or blew away.

Another of Malinowski's observations, that even in preliterate societies it was the custom for the male to ply the female with pre-copulatory gifts in order to smooth the path to his goal, still held in Prescott High. Lockets, class rings, pins, anklets, sodas, movies, corsages, all fell into waiting hands but of course did not always bring the hoped-for result. Human relations seemed inexplicable and arbitrary, and fortunately often irrelevant, as one labored beneath the ominous cloud of Marriage as the prerequisite to unbridled licentiousness, "the blessed state," I believe the Victorians called it.

Something we *were* learning, by example and observation, was the art of deception. Everyone knew that everyone (including oneself) danced a ballet of lies, moral short leaps, of splendid but hollow entrechat. You were supposed to say what you didn't mean. And certainly you weren't expected to say what you really felt, although unconsciously, from time to time, we must have slipped into the evolutionary temper of gratitude and compassion. "Personality" dominated "character." The more one had of the former, the less one had need of the latter. In girls, personality seems to have been expressed in bright tessellations of shriek-and-giggle illustrated with Edenic bodily slitherings. In boys, it was the opposite. A democratic if self-interested friendliness motivated both. Any recognizable trend toward seriousness or integrity worked against personality and thus against popularity.

But we were urged to cook, boys as well as girls, and there with Marvin H.—who over time fathered nine children, possibly more—I helped make a first cake, which, whatever its faults, was greedily consumed by the class next morning, a session of great comfort to Miss Pipes, who felt at home critiquing pastry.

We all had to come up with topics on maturing, the dangers thereof. And how to run a household. The only one sticking in my mind still was a girl's rather giddy report on se-Phyllis, over before any of us knew what word she was mispronouncing.

This was all a gentle far cry, a dove's song, from the classes I helped teach after the seriousness of AIDS hit home, about 1984, when we instructed college freshmen, including the shy, nearly silent Asian girls, in the intricacies of putting a condom on a banana in a useless exercise of self-preservation. The boys, who should have been listening, were elsewhere, choosing to find out for themselves, just as, I guess one could through extrapolation say, the boys of my high school class preferred to find out about sex firsthand, despite the slides, the cutaway drawings, and the serious intonations of voice-over.

While in many courses—music, art, PE, English—you were allowed to practice, not merely theorize, with any topic having to do with normal (or aberrant) human sexuality, it was all theory or, *vide*, incomprehensible "visual aids." In the biology lab there stood, year after year, a gallon jar on a shelf for all to see of a fetus aborted, floating in a grave of formaldehyde like one of shock artist Damien Hirst's installations, but with no one to talk about it. To illustrate the lengths to which this topic was kept mystic, my biology project was one of the most gamic (from the Greek, *gamos*, or "marriage"). I was to attempt crossing red-eyed fruit flies with white-eyed fruit flies in the assumption of creating mutants with eyes that did not match their bodies or ones that behaved in ways unnatural to the received truths of some drosophilic moral majority. I had to take them home over Christmas vacation and keep them in their test tubes behind the stove so my subjects would not freeze to death. Their culinary requirement consisted of an ugly sludge cooked in one of Eloine's pots, though they would have preferred a ripe banana. "Crossing" flies is what I was expected to do. "Copulation," "coitus," "fucking" were terms unmentioned by Mr. Schumaker. I knew at the time how to tell a male from a female, though couldn't now, yet it never occurred to me to wonder how they actually got it on. What, I now ask, did I think "crossing" really meant and how was it done? A fly the size of a pinhead with a penis? Come on.

As I recall, nothing conclusive resulted, but perhaps the teacher showed a degree of confidence in me. Everyone else worked on dead or inanimate matter. Maybe he felt sorry for me because I could never see anything reportable in a microscope. No cells ever divided or reunited on my slides. They say the cells of one living thing resemble the cells of any other living thing—grass or horse. You couldn't have proved it by me.

The eminent biologist Edward Wilson has gone so far as to claim that research on the fruit fly, *Drosophila melanogaster,* forms much of the foundation of modern genetics. Seymour Benzer, who would have been a graduate student at the time of my experiment, has succeeded over the years in taking fruit fly research much further than I, even into the controversy of how much our genes may determine who we are and what paths we take in life, as opposed to shape-by-culture. Which gives pause. I struggle with the question. If I behaved according to my cultural embedding of the first eleven years, I ought to be living now in some materially marginalized trailer camp on the edge of a nearly uncivilized and fetid slough, rather than pressing my nose against Fauchon's glass on the Place de la Madeleine.

To circle all the way back to those calf brains in Eloine's skillet, this same biologist, Benzer, ate the brains of his experiments after dissecting them in the laboratory late at night, so as, I assume, not to waste good food, or rather more abstractly, in order to know his subjects intimately, as we have heard of soldiers devouring the liver of a slain enemy so that they might take on the additional genetic ferocity. A doctor I once knew in Heidelberg injected his patients, mostly wealthy Americans, with the cells of recently living sheep according to the order of their complaint: liver cells for cirrhosis, testicle cells for male sexual dysfunction (pre-Viagra), gallbladder for stones, and so forth—on the theory that the body is its own best defense. It needs only to be jerked awake now and then.

My work with fruit fly mutation predated, but no doubt helped pave the way for, François Jacob's renowned discoveries in genetic engineering and thus evolution in general. Jacob has written that his insights into genetic sequences "underscored the degree, until then unsuspected, of kinship between living creatures." I don't know where, exactly, he grew up, but if he'd spent half his life before ten lying in the weeds with his eyes open, he'd have known this before he ever put on a lab coat or plugged in his famous Waring blender. Like reading poetry, you probably know what you're hearing or you probably don't.

Our high school textbooks in the late 1940s still did not mention the word *evolution*, much less teach anything about the probability of human origins in subhuman species. Darwin's work on natural selection, of which we may have picked up intimations from the inverse clouds, was treated with silence at school and hysteria in the Baptist Church. Barbara, one of the BYPU gang, would burst into tears on cue if she heard "evolution," as if you'd announced "Your grandmother just turned back into a bonobo." Barbara and her creationist allies admitted the world was about six thousand years old but no older, that the universe and everything in it appeared during a one-week-long creative frenzy, and further adopted the seventeenth-century idea that no species could be extinct because God in glorious perfection wouldn't do that to one of his creations.

To Eloine, from Tennessee, the state in which the Scopes trial took place only seven years before I was born, the argument amounted to conundrum. She distrusted fundamentalist know-all tactics, as I've said, but had a hard time dealing with the concept of those oozing millions of years of Jurassic slime out of which we slithered, eventually, to this perfectible ideal. She was no intellectual, her domestic choices— poverty, children, a wanderlust husband—leaving her little time for lofty thinking, yet she was leery of too much government and believed reason and individual liberty ought to be given a chance over "jerky" revelation, that is, the cut-and-dried hardtack of podium-pounding preachers who might, furthermore, represent the majority. Or of teachers who threw textbooks at stupid kids—as they were still doing in my day—as if a good strike to the temple would generate osmosis.

In art class we were required to draw, though without instruction, as if by merely assigning the task the teacher was teaching us some-thing. Given to cartoons, like my ungrounded understanding of real life, I never took these tasks seriously, except for a set of renderings of the alley behind our house, done with black crayon on rough, creamy paper in the style (I'd like now to think) of Georges Seurat. I chose the alley because of its unimpeachable ugliness in what might be called my grisaille period, having no understanding then that any subject, any scene, any moment crossing the eyes' beam may be impassioned by giving it attention. This is what poets know intuitively, the rest of us by an occasional knock on the head.

Though these drawings, like my short stories of the time, have disappeared, one or two won ribbons at the Yavapai County Fair, an achievement upon which not too much grandeur attends, in competi-tion with the fat pink pigs, the lowing, box-shaped steers shown by the 4-H boys, the alert chickens, tumbler pigeons shown by men who hadn't anything better to do, the pies, cakes, jams, and embroidered dresser scarves entered by the ladies. Eloine wouldn't place her Miss Ruby cupcakes into competition, though they would surely have taken the dessert division, encumbered as she was by grave doubts about putting oneself forward. If you were good at something and satisfied by it, outsiders need not pass judgment.

Books: In our two-room, usually one-teacher, Skull Valley schoolhouse we had what was called the County Circulating Library, meaning once a month a van pulled into the school yard, through the gate, over the cattle guard, and a woman commenced to exchange the twenty or thirty books on the shelves for twenty or thirty others, ranging in difficulty from easy to not so. By fourth grade, the same ones had recirculated several times, of course, and I had read them all, bottom to top. I'd actually learned to read in the old Grimms, un-diluted and full of horrors, illustrated, its pages thick and musty, hard-back as all books then were, but cheap, and the Tarzan books, so most county-approved literature was soft stuff. In Prescott, in junior high, there wasn't much on the school shelves I hadn't already had a look at except the fresh issues of *The Saturday Evening Post,* but in the city library there were many, and in high school I found Stephenson, Poe, and Hawthorne. Whitman may have been mentioned on the list of great American writers, but never a poem of his crossed our desks. I was a college sophomore before being assigned "When Lilacs Last in the Dooryard Bloom'd," which I seemed to think was about lilacs, but never even then such a piece as "Song of Myself" or "Spontaneous Me," both of which I'd already stumbled through in the hometown library and couldn't believe I was reading right, any more than I be-lieved my eyes in that not altogether pleasant scene with Ishmael squashing whale sperm all morning long, squeezing "those soft, gentle globules of infiltrated tissue" that smelled of violets.

Balls: The kind you throw, kick, bounce, toss, hit, whack, lob— why are they so important? Why in the world do otherwise sane and reasonable persons spend so much time, effort, and mental distress over these spherical or ellipsoidal toys? Calculating, even regulating, their size, weight, cohesion, roundness, the stuff that makes them? The ways in which they may or may not be legally employed? The rules, the gatherings, the songs and cheers, the decorum, the expense, the *se-riousness?* How have they come to be the measure of man? *What the hell's going on?* I asked myself (anyone else would've turned me in) in high school and got no answer, other than the reassurance I was out of step, born in the wrong society in the wrong epoch.

Ludens in orbe terrarum.

So balls roll. So you chase them. So you throw them somewhere. So what?

Sitting in Miss Savage's class, tremulous with the cognition I could actually read Shakespeare, more or less, that name as important as God, I connected in a perverse way to the back of the room where the ranch boys sat, in an arch over the middle ground of athletes and pretty girls whom nothing written could touch or needed to. The ranch boys, sprawled and glowering, were the living epitome of Hamlet's actor friend's question, "What's Hecuba to him or he to Hecuba?" and pissed off for having to sit there an irrelevant hour while horses' asses like me read trippingly, and the athletes did nothing—but would be rewarded anyway because they could throw or hit or kick the appropriate ball in the right direction at the right season. This was known by the name of heroism, alas, Hector, Odysseus, Aeneas. My golden retriever dearly loves to chase—and retrieve—a ball. He even knows how to discharge it at the top of a flight of garden steps when playing alone so he can then pursue it down the hill. Sounds about right.

High school demanded little of us and we gave back even less. We were so juvenile we hadn't even developed unconscious motives yet. As naive as salamanders, we thought we were speaking what we meant to say. Still inseparable off campus, Digger and I plowed different furrows in school. A dilettante and a joiner, I had a thumb in every pie. He worked harder at seducing girls or, one might say, on the theory of seduction and even played on the football team one year, a sport he was too kind for, too easygoing. I made high grades in the arts and literature, he in math and shop. Marvin H.—he who fathered nine children or possibly more—beat me out by one point for the gold cup at graduation because football was weighted heavier than band. As Vonnegut has said so often, So it goes. You never know who's going to get the big dick.

Breaking and Entering

From my experience of it, I'd have to conclude that high school—
by which I mean not only the school part, but the age—is mainly
a mistake, a landscape of moderate heights, precipitous drops, a meat
loaf of disconnected information, amply wrong or so edited as to be
false. So much is withheld you can't even guess it might exist, and you
end up with, besides a worthless diploma, a brain so full of vapor it
would appear in an MRI like a foggy marsh in early morning.

"You don't want to grow up too soon," Eloine said repeatedly.

"Yes, I do."

"Now, don't dispute my word. And do your homework."

"There's too much I don't know."

"Go to the library, then."

"Hah. Until you're sixteen there's a lot you can't check out. Most
of it."

"Well, the time will come."

I went on with my exterior life and my hidden one and the third
tier somewhere in between, the one I spent the most effort on building. It, the middle tier, seemed to work at keeping the other two from
each other's throats. Marching through horse dung with my B-flat
clarinet in the Fourth of July parade was an example of the exterior,
community-minded, well-behaved boy. Hiding all afternoon in pine-
woods alone, except for Poe or Defoe sometimes, making up an elaborate other life, was an example of the extreme interior. Chasing around
with Digger, a mindless, testosterone-driven cruise, malingering, an

example of the third. Nights and days with no narrative direction, these vignettes required a degree of intellectual strategy on the one hand, and a large dose of fairy dust on the other.

One knew just enough to intuit there was something colossal missing, that no matter how busy, bold or bored, active or supine, there were gaps, canyons of meaningless space. Like taffy, life stretched and wrapped, came back together in a lump, silken, insubstantial, devourable. Maybe I was reading the texts wrong. Maybe I was unconscious. Maybe someday the carapace would split open with the sound of ringing brass and all knowledge would stand before me like a phosphorescent stele—like the glowing eye in the pyramid. Assigned *Beowulf*, I found myself in Grendel, shivering outside the mead hall. I didn't know what they were doing in there, but I knew I wasn't included. "Snap out of it, horse's ass. Let's drive to the Dells."

"Why?"

"To look for carnal relationships. Your turn to get beer."

Life seemed to have no back story, despite the length of days. Fellow travelers at school went about their daily sight gags, their sadistic cadenzas, their vigorous pursuits of popularity, unwavering in their belief the glamorized life was most worth living.

It takes the camera of distance to crosscut these scenes, to change the angles, manipulate distance and actor, to crop and edit, overlay with special effects, to magnify the inconsequential. Any other kid of my era, now old, would picture the *tableau vivant* of his life in Prescott with quite different furniture and companions and purpose.

My personal lacunae, forced or chosen respite from this breathless chase, turned into *noir* episodes of my own imagination. In creative assignments, being fond of blood and large staircases, I wrote of murder and revenge, what John Gardner might have called moral fiction. The two scenic elements, blood and staircases, functioned best when the latter was made of marble so the former could trickle all the way down from the corpse to the foyer, being the first thing the unsuspecting lover stepped in when he arrived too late. Knowing corpses intimately gave me, I believed, a considerable advantage, though mine were cold and bloodless. Also under the spell of Maupassant and O'Henry, I was able to attach tricky endings to Poe's overwritten style. While to my knowledge there are no extant copies, two successful fictions were entitled, indelibly, "The Fate of Fanny Philpot" and "Dear Avenger, 'Tis of Thee."

I became a breaker-and-enterer. In order to get at the pianos and organ in the church, I devised a number of ways, like a rat chewing through walls to get at a sack of grain. When inside legitimately, I'd sneak about, leaving a window on the bottom floor, way at the back, unlatched, hoping the janitor wouldn't catch it. I figured out how, with a blade, to open the big wooden front doors if no one remembered to set the bolt. Inside were a half-dozen pianos to choose from, scattered within the warren of rooms, including the formidable square grand, black as a coffin, in the sanctuary. The Hammond I could unlock with a straightened paper clip. I became an addict.

And was caught by the minister, time and again. In a righteous puff he'd demand to know how I got in *this* time but would never give me a key. He was the same vast presence who had preached the Dad's funeral, though he retained no recollection of having done so. Furious, barely Protestant in the face of my constant outwittery, he expended useless energy he could have turned to a better cause, namely teaching me how to do some of those runs and filigrees and arpeggios on the piano that he could. His fingers, like Vienna sausages, were amazingly agile. With any four-part hymn he could embellish up and down the keyboard in sixteenths, thirty-seconds, even sixty-fourths, performing lightning chromatic scales, always coming back to the tonic at the proper moment, like a hummingbird out of a fit. I have imagined him later losing his mind in anger, like Jonathan Swift in old age, but without irony. I tried incoherently to explain to the good Reverend Mr. Hyde that he was piling on himself more agony than the situation, solvable with a key, deserved. He couldn't have me arrested, exactly, without a scandal and loss of face, nor had he any proof of burglary other than the cherubic company he found before him diligently clomping along on the keys.

Sometimes, frustrated, he'd make me bow down while he improvised a prayer, a predilection of his, an absolute need. Prayer, when pointed in two directions at once, heavenward and toward a particular miscreant (individual or congregational), was yet another way of inducing guilt, by calling God's direct attention, the tattletale method. There was no stained glass in that chilling gray church—only some opaque panels sufficient to discourage gazing—but the reverend spoke *like* stained glass: colorful, overexcited, unctuous, much given to elevating parables.

I began to see him as artifact, a curiosity to be observed, to sometimes hear, but with no specific effect for my life. All preachers, I was learning, are exhibitionists, and some actually believe they can cause what they consider good by displaying themselves like African gray parrots. I wish I had known then Nicolas-Claude Fabri de Peiresc's seventeenth-century observation that "true Christianity had nothing to fear from erudition or the application of reason," though he doubtless said so without irony. As I grew taller, Rev. Hyde's vastness shrank. In those days men of the cloth and their ovine flocks didn't dabble in scabrous political issues and were unable to reach conclusions about a corrupt world except as it showed itself in their simple litany—no smoking, no adultery, etc. Generalizing from an observed or suspected infraction, *id est* dancing, they blotted out the evildoer like an ink stain, not a partial loss with other redeeming points. It made you wonder what was the use, you were bound to get caught in one web or another, like a housefly that wanders in the garden.

Autodidact, I practiced with the hymnals and purloined copies of *Etude* magazine, in which, each issue, some middling-easy and some harder pieces appeared. Completely oblivious to fingering or subtlety, which I realized even as I was pounding got me caught, I had no technique or true suppleness in my fingers. I worked all the way up to Mozart's "Alla Turca," at about three-quarters speed *fortissimo.*

Of course, with each session I moved backward, wilder into the woods I ran. No one, surely not the preacher, understood this compulsion to play the piano, how I was drawn to it like masturbation, that nothing could stop me, how the getting in, cold as could be, removing only my gloves, sitting down before the day's chosen instrument, lifting up the keyboard cover, laying open a page of music, and beginning to thump at it was as great a thrill as anything I had the chance to do. There was no one to talk to about it. Digger, no help at all with deep problems, advised, "You're being a horse's ass. Give up."

The boys at the Catholic school, we believed, had it all figured out (though who would have taught them, the nuns?), and being unencumbered with morals, were free to enact their lust and desire. Later we got to know a couple of those guys well. Our earlier suspicions were borne out. Their gliding manners, their matter-of-fact obscenities, their *use* of the terms we only spoke, their more disciplined —if equally skewed—education, gave us surer evidence that there is, indeed, inequality in upbringing, a conclusion we might have earlier reached by talking with, even thinking about, Robert and Claude, our two Negro classmates, who at the end of the school day simply disappeared.

Rorschach blots, not exactly the same but close enough, Digger and I reached effortlessly the point of nuance only close friends ever achieve, disintegrated eventually by the circumstances of life, the pressures of education, work, marriage. We knew each other intimately in both action and rest yet were much different in temperament, accomplishment, and plans. Dark-featured and steady, never quick to anger or judge, ever questing and brave and curious, he understood the goal of life was life itself, the very antithesis of those for whom some unforeseeable future after death is the end all and be all. Perhaps his ardent view of life was due to his long acquaintance with the dead. José Saramago's words, describing the patience of Franciscan friars in the early eighteenth century—"A hundred years of waiting is not great sacrifice for those who count on living for all eternity"—did not apply to Digger, eager for the living moment and too well acquainted with the humility of being dead to wish it for himself in virginal ignorance. Though I have said we were inseparable, that wasn't really true except in a metaphoric sense. We both had to work, we had different extracurricular activities, we'd each go chasing after other attractions, but then in a while, fold back together again. "Don't worry about it," he would tell me. "We got more important things to do."

"Like what?"

"Find some trouble. Or make it."

"Shouldn't be too tough. Some goal."

"Wouldn't need laws if there weren't outlaws. I think I'm about to get into Streeter, but don't tell anybody yet."

"Dixie? She only likes horses."

"Just hasn't met the right handler."

"And you're him? You're out of your fuckin' mind."

"Don't swear, dude, it hurts my ears. And you'll go to hell."

"I'll save you a spot."

Digger, like Darwin himself, knew that females are aggravatingly coy but failed to understand why. Unconsciously, they save their genes for a better mix, and the prettier they are, the less apt to be promiscuous because their chances for a superior match are high, much better than for the plain girl—though, in the general melee the plain girl will end up matched too, with the plain boy. The pretty girls can hold out for the handsome stud and the rich, as the female mountain lion prefers a virile male who can perform coitus fifty or sixty times in a day over the cat who does it only once, yawns, and walks away. So the evolutionary psychologists now tell us, too late.

Again, fruit flies could have helped. At almost the exact same time of my experiments, it turns out that A. J. Bateman, a British geneticist, was fooling around with the little bugs too and concluded, before I got to the point, that natural selection encourages an undiscriminating eagerness in the males and a discriminating inertia in the females, which amounts to the same thing: males will mate with most anything that's warm, damp, and moving; females wait for the guy with the better genes, particularly the one who tends to show he will invest in the long-run family. This helps us understand how Marvin H., so stuffed with sperm, could pause to bake a cake, a glimmer of his genetic potential for high MPI—male parental investment. He will not only make many babies but likely stick around and help care for them.

It's hard to believe that having a better scald on human sexual biology might have deflected Digger from his appointed rounds, yet it would have been enlightening, and an idea worthy of defeat, to know that females, with so much greater a burden to carry in reproductive matters, are *naturally,* not socially, coy about whom they copulate with. They want their sons to carry forth as many gorilla traits as possible. Though it is of no comfort to the less endowed to know this, we understand, subliminally, that females at the basic level are attracted by show-off males, particularly when brawn can be delivered in a Ford convertible. Arriving in a black mortuary DeSoto limousine hadn't quite the same effect.

Digger's ideal marriage being decidedly polygamous, he dreamed of a kind of Oriental seraglio, of lying back among sumptuous pillows and assorted flesh, but because he enjoyed company, he would have welcomed a couple of eunuchs to attend the braziers and the fan.

Somewhere in this time capsule, The Palace Saloon reopened and served barbecue mountain lion sandwiches and cold beer.

One began to hear ominous singing, Gregorian chants about Future Plans, College Prep, Career Choices. Required to write career papers, the what-do-you-want-to-do-in-real-life assignment, we searched frantically in current magazines for some clue. Because at that moment I believed Juilliard or the Chicago Academy of Fine Arts just right for me, though dolefully unprepared for either, I wrote on the nonexistent career of interior design for orchestral auditoriums, which, had it materialized, might have actually made me unique, the lone practitioner. As I preferred the strongest tremolo setting on the Hammond, I leaned toward the Baroque in costume and design, exactly at the wrong turn of the road, just as architecture was stripped of its glitter and folderol, just as Bauhaus, Mies, Schindler were finally catching on in America, a generation late, just as Copland was composing *Appalachian Spring*.

Just as the young men who survived came trickling home, their recent education stripped of any useless frippery. If you carry your whole life on your back and your only defense for it in your hands, month after month in conditions unspeakable, filthy and terror filled, or sitting like a carnival duck in a ship or B-29, you wouldn't have much use for curlicues, Corinthian capitals, or Opéra Comique.

At great distance one can begin to understand the frenetic busyness of priest and parson trying with what they knew were insupportable assertions and not enough hands or fingers, a worn-out broom, to sweep the stray bits together, to get them all in the urn before they, like beads of loose mercury, ran away, became forever too slippery to control. Returning servicemen, malcontent, disillusioned, behind in their lives—and sadistic to peach-fuzz boys who had been too young to go— alarmed the moralists. How could they tell these men they ought to believe in God at the risk of the designs of hell? To save their bodies for the marriage bed? To remain sober and understand their situation was laid out for them ineluctably as far back as Genesis? That the cruelties they were ordered to inflict on other human beings were okay because American? That narrow community values were more to be admired than a life vividly lived?

The summer I was fourteen and Digger close enough to sixteen to have his own car, a 1937 Plymouth coupe, we shifted our attention for two weeks to the Arizona Baptist Estates Summer Camp. The Estates belonged to all the Baptists of Kingdom Come but were located just six or eight miles from Prescott, up in a pine forest. Instead of registering and erecting a tent in the properly outlined spaces, Digger and I pitched ours off at the edge, hidden, near a back road the counselors didn't know about, thus giving us—with his car—illegitimate freedoms. I earned my tuition by working in the dining hall, my job being to carry big bowls full of green beans, green peas, and white potatoes, the only vegetables known at that time, and platters of roasted meat to the trestle tables, place them at the ends, and let the hungry kids from Prescott, Phoenix, Tucson, Bisbee, Yuma, pitch in. The cooks provided no hamburgers, hot dogs, or fried chicken, in the interests of health or holiness, though to be fair, macaroni and cheese sometimes made up the main course at lunch, and Harvard beets— those slimy, sweet-sour reminders of the hilarity of God when he has time to be amused at the expense of his own creatures. Parenthetically, I note this vile dish has dropped out of modern cookbooks; thus ours may be the last generation to suffer it, and with our deaths all memory of it will cease.

By day we had to attend religious sessions and do craftlike things and play softball. And lay plans for late-night clandestine meetings. In the evenings, after supper was cleared away, various preachers from around the state took turns sermonizing.

Solving the mystery of how gluten develops from flour and liquid to become a bun is no more complicated than unraveling the thread of these nightly sermons in which, with so little of substance to talk about but needing the work, the preachers got themselves into all sorts of theological pickles, making it hard to remember what we were supposed to believe and what not. That we may all be the children of the same god wasn't an idea as yet fallen on fertile imaginations. Living at a time far too late for scourge and whip, the pastors bopped along the dais, railing about what little they did understand with the self-confidence of full professors, who often, I have seen, don't know what they're talking about either but do so with more obscure syntax. The preachers could fall back on getting "saved" or "born again," those ever-dismal motifs, whenever they ran out of mental breath. Examples of the psychologically selfish gene, these missionaries worked to enlarge the Christian population, holding to the dream that someday the whole world would be converted to the Baptist doctrine and overrun the pearly gates, completely overlooking the fact they'd then be out of a job. All of this confused coaching only went to show how difficult it is to teach or attain perfection and makes you wonder why, when you're older and have time for thinking, anyone bothers to try.

It should be remembered, as we've said elsewhere, the ministers—some actual products of specialized schools like Moody Bible Institute or BIOLA—unlike the next two generations of religious fundamentalists, meant well and weren't deliberately mean-spirited. How their successors became not only more ignorant but more philosophically squinted ought to be some aspiring biosociologist's dissertation topic. However, the more young people they could reduce to tears and shame by evening's close, the more puffed up in humility they went about the next day.

Even in such a sylvan setting among majestic pines, Satan was in constant attendance (a note that pricked up Digger's ears), an instance being the day he caused Dorothy, a dwarf from Bisbee, to play "Ritual Fire Dance" on the chapel piano. Though no taller than a six-year-old and required to stand in order to reach the keys and the pedals simultaneously, and with tiny fingers, she could play the devil out of—well, there's the proof, isn't it. Threatened with expulsion, she refused to play another note, causing our communal singing to fall back into a cappella mode, and became, instead, editor of the camp paper, a mimeographed gossip sheet for which I drew a daily cartoon, sometimes hinting at scenes from the Inquisition, such as autos-da-fé.

Other adults at the camp weren't ordained ministers but lay persons who liked to preach now and then, such as Judge Harrold from Tucson, a handsome figure of a man held before us like a flaming sword. Though well formed, with wide shoulders and narrow hips, white haired, energetically suntanned on the Southern Arizona golf links, he was unfortunately repressed, owing to his exalted position on the bench, and couldn't bring himself to say anything in a clear, outright style. He must have suffered terribly when forced to make decisions, as his mind seemed to us to make no distinctions between categories of information—legal, moral, scientific, or spiritual.

One morning in religion class, he took as his theme a popular magazine that, he had concluded, he—and therefore we—could no longer subscribe to, despite its national importance, because it depicted in photography certain things that ought not be seen. But he couldn't come forward and tell us the name, a ploy, possibly, to keep us from rushing out at the first chance to buy it. His lesson was not particularly productive, inasmuch as it resulted in a muddle muddier than had existed before he began, but it gave us something to speculate on for an hour until lunchtime. Mycharles believed it to be *Life,* one of the most harmless publications, along with *Post,* ever invented, easily available to us in any library. Or maybe it was *National Geographic,* with its pacific photos of naked aborigines with scarred brown boobs or penis guards.

I can't guess how the mind of a judge addresses the thought of the Last One, at which moment the earth will be consumed in fire, a great scorching for all except Baptists and a bright gathering in paradise for them alone, when the heavenly bodies, lurching to a standstill, will shine forth, a monument to God's temper, in something like a Busby Berkeley dance routine.

At lunch Judge Harrold liked to join his pupils, though they were now mixed in with others, and pursue his line of thought, perhaps with the idea of making a straight highway in the desert of hopelessly contorted paths. Much of this I didn't follow, of course, catching only snatches as I set down my steaming bowls at the table ends, or my pitchers of plain water, as this was no Cana wedding.

An unavoidable problem with these talks, whether chats or sermons, was their inevitable banality. The causes or lists of evils, whether specific or metaphoric, repeated over and over and over without charm, poetry, or electricity, are bound, like a knife against wood, to result in a dull edge. Both wickedness and the formulas for goodness become dreary to hear about day after day, and the flowers of the Bible get mired in sludge. Anyway, to steal from Austrian novelist Robert Musil, morality was not undermined but proved to be hollow.

One of the duties of the adult minister-counselors or their wives was to check the beds after lights-out in the various tents to see each was occupied by the appropriate, and one only, body. This occurring at ten o'clock meant nighttime activities couldn't commence until ten-thirty, at which time canvas flaps began to rise and certain vague shapes began to emerge, running from shadow to shadow deeper into the woods.

When we didn't drive by our back road into town to check on the progress of civilization, Digger and I participated in these late- and sometimes all-night bush hazards, the major events being getting lost in the dark, sharing horror stories about wolves and bears, and eating a watermelon purloined from the kitchen, out a side window, into waiting arms—my assignment while cleaning up after supper. No one, I think, made any progress with his or her soul, either to lose or regain it, but remained in a state of stasis.

I always went along for the ride, having apparently no mind of my own or strength enough of character to prefer a long night's rest to possible—though not overly likely—adventure, and usually fell into the role Digger needed me for, namely, helping to cajole girls with the promise of watermelon, or whatever, into the forest. In this I might have been called a biological altruist, that is, an organism that contributes to the reproductive success of others at reproductive cost to itself. Mine was hedonistic, in that it gave me pleasure to help him, rather than purely altruistic, believing it would be good for him.

My unbuttoned lip kept me in trouble, in school, where information was as cut and dried as venison jerky, and in church, where doctrine was cast in concrete, though in neither case having anything to do with understanding. We were sometimes allowed to ask questions in civics class if the purpose was for clarification but not *to question,* a process of a whole different order. Mr. Spooner would lapse into barely controlled rage if, for instance, you suggested the settling of the West amounted to genocide (a new word then) for the Indians who were here first. You could actually be sent from the room for such a thought. Likewise in Sunday School or summer camp.

We weren't taught anything about mythology in either school or church, the intent being to keep us unconfused with possibilities, but I struggled with Jesse Weston in the library and with Edith Hamilton. Those were pagan beliefs, I was told, and long ago proved wrong, mere superstitions of unenlightened people. But, I said, isn't drinking blood and eating flesh in communion the same thing, superstitiously speaking? And getting dunked in a tank of water? Praying and howling to an unseen god? The way we carry on over dead people?

This blasphemy, like my curiosity about evolution, gave birth to nothing but tribulation, even a visit to Eloine by the preacher. He sat primly on one of the two chairs, the one with the big pink peonies embracing it, sipping coffee and nibbling applesauce cake, instructing her on her shortcomings so manifest in me, her son. She remained duskily quiet, a mood I knew bode no good.

And sure enough, after he left, convinced of his mission, she turned to me, gave my forelock a yank—"Ow!"—and declared, "If you can't behave, you can just pack up a suitcase and move someplace else."

"I was only asking."

"I've got too much on my mind trying to make ends meet to waste an hour like that one."

"I thought the point was to figure out stuff."

"Just keep it to yourself, then. Read all you want to, lord knows I can't stop you, but you have to learn when to keep quiet about it."

"There's just two parts to my life [skipping Digger]—school and church—and I'm not allowed to say anything either place without somebody having a cow. It's such shit."

"Don't you ever let me hear you say that word in my house again, you hear me?"

"Yes, ma'm."

"If Daddy was still here he'd give you a licking you wouldn't forget. I have half a mind to take a switch to you myself."

Well, he's not here. And hasn't been for six years. "So," I said, getting in the last word, "I don't see the difference between all those other gods and this one—but, like you say, time will tell. I guess."

Eloine regained her equilibrium working with other women in the school lunch program, cooking first in the morning, then riding in the truck to deliver mostly macaroni and cheese or "Tuna Delight" or "Fiesta Bake" to the junior high, and enjoying the kids on whose trays she plopped the stuff, quietly teaching them some etiquette, whether they knew it or not. And emanating from the same central kitchen on vacation days, until the war ended, came fruitcakes, steamed brown bread, and puddings destined for the boys overseas, sealed in real tin cans.

She wasn't as lonesome for company as she'd been in Skull Valley, where hardly anyone braved the road over. But once in a while she felt like dressing up in her navy blue, let out at the waist and well mended, and a small but rakish J.C. Penney hat and beads—usually a touch of bright red—a frilly dickey to fill in her cleavage, and striking out for church halfway to the other side of town. This trip was not made for religious reification but to get out and see people, to pick up an idea or two.

By sophomore year I was sitting in the choir, aimed toward the congregation, and so I could watch expressions cross her face. Mainly she was able to control herself, reserved and pious, but—as ever—if there appeared an overtrained soloist, someone's daughter or cousin in town for a visit, maybe even someone who once sang in the chorus of the Metropolitan Opera, she began to collapse. I watched these Byzantine transformations with horror, hoping no one else was. First her eyes would go round (she now had new rimless glasses), then her mouth, either in astonishment or mimicry, she slipped a hand up to cover her lips, then up under her glasses, her head began to lower, and you could see her shoulders shake. Out came a lace handkerchief from her pocketbook, which helped to hide the whole of her face from eyebrows down. When it was all over, when "Jerusalem!" had ended on a high sustained note and resolution, she gradually lowered the hankie and subsided, her eyes once more dabbed, then she made a big fuss of dusting her bosom. I mentally dared her to look at me. She wouldn't.

In congregational singing, on the other hand, as once represented in Skull Valley by Grandma D'Armand, here there were, in addition to the more comfortable Ionian and Aeolian modes, throw-backs to the Phrygian and Mixo-Lydian. These were caused by the Russell sisters, two middle European ladies who believed sheer noise drew us all nearer the immortal rafters where the trumpet of the Lord shall sound and time shall be no more. Together, like two band saws slicing hickory, they sang a quarter tone apart and held every final note of a verse four beats longer than it was written. This invariably caused shock and consternation to a visiting choral master attempting to lead the singing along at his chosen tempi and impart some solemnity to the proceedings. At one time, before she went mad, we had an organist who swept into the next verse without waiting for the sisters to finish the previous one, then they entered and we had a kind of round version of "What a Friend We Have in Jesus," leaving the sisters to finish the last refrain alone, forlornly wailing after the rest of the congregation had quit.

At home on Sundays, even if there was no company, Eloine still laid out an elaborate noon dinner for the three of us, and by the end of the war, four, as Martha returned from the coast and squeezed in, entering her forty-year tenure in that little house. Eloine's cooking, still based on southern farm, continued evolving, sometimes with an enthusiastic if not convincing leap, as on the occasion of her first, and perhaps only, *b'steeya,* a chicken pie with distinctly Moroccan overtones, something doubtless brought back by a returning vet, then passed around at Eastern Star. She was always strong on cinnamon, cloves, and nutmeg—but never before with meat and crust. It's a great dish, made these days with phyllo pastry, and would have been the best possible solution to those pigeons of Skull Valley.

Never one for green salads, ruffled, torn and ripped, chemically enhanced piles of roughage so many people stuff into their mouths like fodder, Eloine rooted around in her cupboard and from what she found composed gentle salads, often with gelatin, now that she had a refrigerator, still called an icebox. But one she made of fresher ingredients, laid out individually on plates, was of tomato slices, onion slices, cucumber slices, black olives, and white farmer's cheese, with only salt, pepper, and oil. Though ignorant of its credentials then, I learned it was, of course, one of the centerpieces of Western civilization—the common Greek salad, with a few adjustments: the original has feta cheese instead of farmer's, Kalamata instead of canned olives, a toss of capers or basil, and olive instead of vegetable oil.

A salad of this character, plus a plate of quick-fried sardines (of which we've spoken earlier), a glass of Demestica, the shade of a tree, a view into the harbor over bobbing boats, beats out nearly any other possibility. Certain things, being simple and therefore unimprovable, last for centuries because they're perfect in their austerity. The island of Hydra, for example, is itself like this. With rocky shores and only a couple of harbors, no discos, few bars and cafés, donkeys for transportation (or your feet), it doesn't attract too many tourists or find excuses to gentrify itself. Stepping through a blue gate set in a pure white wall, into a garden, you may come upon a lemon tree in full hallelujah. That's enough for one day.

Two Ways of Leaving Athens
ONE

WE DROVE FROM Athens to Delphi through vegetable country with magpies flashing in the trees while he read from his tattered book about Pentelic marble and the Plain of Marathon, his translation almost without modifiers, his voice without inflection. Inland Greece, hilly and brown, domed by a vivid hot sky and the sounds of insects and birds, left me with the sense our footsteps walked on blood.

His mood had lifted because a French girl recognized him the night before in the Plaka. She sidled up to our table with the feline litheness of a dancer. Apparently she had seen him work in Paris. Whatever it was she said brightened him. He reached across the table to touch her hand.

On the island of Hydra, where he sat all day beside a display case of handmade gold jewelry and racks of woven bags and seamen's shirts, it was seldom necessary for him to move. All most people saw was his straight-backed, muscular torso, his face, his head of black hair brushed at the temples with white.

The effort of walking up the terraces of the Plaka brought lines to his face; still, people who had probably never heard of him, as I had not, turned to watch, not that his face was handsome—it was theatrical, made up of exaggerated angles and planes—but he seemed to bring with him a knowledge of life from having participated at a special level of sacrifice.

Anyway, we seemed more at peace after the girl came to the table, and I felt warmed in the Greek night under the supper club orchestras competing over our heads from rooftop to rooftop, watching the promenade of tourists, the club entertainers rushing to work, jingling like lepers with bracelets and sequins, the hustlers and hawkers.

"Let us take a car and drive out of the city tomorrow," he said. "I will show you the mountain."

We stopped along the road near the Plain of Thebes to watch a caravan of gypsies pass, colorless, surly, with their dogs standing atop the bedding, a cow hobbling along behind. Farther up we waited for a herd of goats to cross. And higher still we stopped to look down upon the roads where Oedipus killed his father. We argued.

"Then it is settled," he said.

"Yes."

"For you only. You talk always of freedom. You take it too far."

"You must not depend on me," I said.

"You do not know me as well as you think. I do not depend on anyone. What I am talking about it is not dependence."

We slipped into periods of silence, like streaks of paint. The car wound up into Parnassus, past stone goat shelters and stone pens. Empty now, I imagined they would be occupied in the hard winter, goats and goatherds alike in reeking conviviality. At Arahova, a tiny village suspended from the mountain edge over a deep view, we watched the swallows for a time, then I went across the road and bought feta and a bottle of Demestica from a storekeeper with dark hands and dark brown teeth. Beside the road brightly dyed sheepskins hung on lines to alert the tourists.

"You call them swallows?" he said when I returned.

"Yes."

"Like *to eat?* The same? How funny. See how they go so about it."

In the afternoon, after the buses had turned back toward the city, we climbed up to the ruins, slowly because of his legs, taken back in time as we went up, past the white marble, past the inscribed walls—

know thyself—the ruined temple, into the theater. We sat high on the warm stones and watched the sky soften.

"You know," he said, "what it smells like back of the stage after a performance? Imagine here. Hundreds of people. The sun. Goat cheese, wine, fruit, bodies. . . . " His laugh was a tone deeper than mine and reverberated in the stones.

After a while he said, "You go on up to the stadium. I will wait."

"You don't want to see it?"

"I have seen it." He touched my knee with his, then pulled his arms together across his chest. He wore a black shirt, the color of his hair. "I want only to sit here a moment," he said.

And dream of dancing again. Down there in the orchestra circle, and smell the crowd, hear them murmur and roar.

The next afternoon we rode in gloomy silence on the little train out to the port. "I wonder which of us is the more crippled," he said.

We ate lunch in Piraeus, fried squid and beer, across the street from the docks, in a hot quiet café with dirty windows. Against the wall old men in dark clothes, with wide gnarled hands, smoked, dropped their voices and watched us.

"In any case," he said, "*my* disease is arrested."

"I'm healthy."

"Not knowing who you are is death."

He walked up the ramp slowly, entered the mail packet that would, in a couple of hours, drop him back on his island of houses like picked bones.

TWO

ANY OF IT is chance. On the sultry taut ship built for a more northern sea, plunging from Piraeus to Alexandria, I was seated at a small corner table in the dining room near a square window where I could watch the spray blow white when the bow dipped. Everyone else but the crew seemed to be Egyptian, large loud seasick people returning home from a cruise to Marseilles.

In his uniform, tight black pants and a white jacket with gold buttons and a greenish braid, he moved about the room like an athlete, self-conscious, proud, quick. A flashing smile, an appraising look.

"You are feeling well?" he asked, standing across from me, one hand placed lightly on the empty chair. His eyes were tawny, like a cat's.

"Fine, thanks. So far."

He smiled. "Good. I am tired of sick people. You are American."

"Yes."

"Then I will bring you wine you will like."

"Not retsina, please."

"Of course not. And fresh fish in a very light sauce. You should not eat more until the sea dies."

"When will that be?"

"Who can know?" He stood near my arm and rearranged the silverware. "Perhaps tonight." His face, although handsome in shape, was deeply pocked and battered.

The sea did grow calm after sunset, and the air turned hot. "Come," he said, standing at my cabin door with a blanket folded under his arm. "I know a place where there is breezes."

"Is it safe?"

"Safe?" His forehead knotted. "What an American question."

Even naked he arranged his body carefully, trained and fluid, as if conscious that the undiscovered perfect movement might occur at any time and he should be ready for it. We lay on his blanket somewhere far forward on the ship under a great black looming piece of machinery. The stars turned sharp in the sky. Planetary music.

"I read you can no longer see the stars in America," he said. "Is it true?"

I laughed. The sound of it hummed off the steel machinery. "In Los Angeles, yes. The only stars you see are on the sidewalks."

"So far away. . . . "

I didn't know whether he meant L.A. or the stars. "Some of them already burned out a long time ago, but their light keeps coming."

The wharf at Alexandria smelled of tar and fresh paint and salt, although the water was ripe with oil and the city beyond was smeared with heat. He wore a polo shirt of wide green and yellow bands and carried a wicker valise. In the strong morning light his face seemed more dented and abused than ever, like a sponge. Everywhere else his skin was smooth.

"What about your job?" I said.

He looked at me with a glance full of both anger and dismay. Turning away deliberately, he stared into the city.

In Cairo he refused the condescension of the big hotels by the river, so we chose a room in the heart of the furnace of noise and traffic overlooking a vegetable market, high-ceilinged, preposterously big, with hot water once a day. No matter how early I awoke, he was already up, sitting by the window with his elbows on the sill.

"Jesus," I said, "don't they ever sleep?"

"Some have been up all night, I think. The wagons came at dawn and old women to gather lettuce off the street. Come and look." He turned back, soft against the light, his skin golden. "Look how the sun falls already half into the market."

"This has to be the noisiest goddam city in the world. Why do they bang on things so much? And honk?"

He smiled and sat back. "They have sent coffee. And the water in the pipes is hot. Get up."

He liked the bazaar even more than the market. We spent hours twining in it, touching the ripe colored skeins of yarn hanging like fabulous hair, smelling the spices and henna in burlap bags rolled open like foreskins, listening to the pleas of moist-eyed merchants. We drank warm glasses of attar of roses laced with greasy perfumes, supposedly good for virility.

"How did you know I was an American?"

"At first I was confused. But not long. It's a way of acting, not a look. They all recognize you here in the market, despite your eyes."

I bought him a bright shirt the color of garnets.

It was all I could do to get him out into the desert to see the pyramids. He had some spooky bias against them. But at Luxor he responded to the ruins happily, not because they had existed for so long but because they had held living people. Living bodies moving as he moved, in and out among the brown columns, the shadows, the streaks of limitless sunlight. "Imagine," he said, flying from stone to stone in his bright plumage.

At the Karnak temple we watched the last light leave, bronze like the river, bleeding upward onto the tips of the pillars and the obelisk. Then in the dusk we walked through the village streets. Black fellahin women lay supine, like Henry Moore statues, on the grass with their babies, or glided barefoot and straight as if still carrying jugs on their heads. The men played what looked like backgammon in dim café gardens and the teenage boys roamed hopelessly. Unlike Cairo, here the voices were melodious, softer than the Nile.

After dark we sat in the hotel's shabby gardens by the swimming pool and watched the young Europeans dancing. "I can live anywhere," he said. "I am as free as you."

"You must go back to Greece. Back home."

"I know what I must do."

"Your family will disown you."

"Who will take care of you if I do not?" he said. "You cannot buy a train ticket, I think, without a big incidents. Or read the menus." His attention drifted to a couple dancing close to our chairs, speaking French. "If it were merely another man, I could kill him."

"I'm not able to lose myself," I said.

"That is meaning nothing to me."

"I'm sorry you gave up your job over this."

"*Merde*. Shit. You have not been asked to feel sorry for me. A job!" He banged his hand on the table. In our glasses the wine trembled.

"Do you need money to get back?"

He stood from his chair and leaned across the table, his face a few inches from mine. In the false light the craters of his skin were honey-colored like his eyes, and black. "Listen to me. I am not—what is your word? Hustler? I came on my own choice. For reasons." He straightened proudly. I thought of his long legs, the deep ravine of his spine, the fine black hairs that brushed into a triangle above his butt. "Tomorrow morning I will take the train."

"It goes the wrong way. To Aswan."

His eyes glistened. "Then damn you. I will go to Aswan!"

A Lion in the Palace

Our kind and bewildered parent(s) punctuated freedom with occasional, obligatory accountings. For her views of the best path for her boys to walk along, Eloine in the previous century would have been cited as a critic of the so-called Enlightenment in her suspicion, quite unconsciously, of the tepid, soapy wash of uniform human nature and of the idea that leading a good life might be dictated from on high. The Dad had been, while not deep, an independent man and she admired him for it. Yet she, as parents must, passed me through a gauntlet of term exams.

"Johnny, have you been smoking?"

"No ma'am." *Yes.*

"Now, don't tell me a story."

"No ma'am." *Yes.*

"And you boys aren't drinking, are you?"

"No ma'am." *Yes.*

"And you're behaving?"

"No—uh, yes, ma'am."

"I'd give a pretty to know what you do out so late."

"Nothing. Much."

"Well, I don't want to hear about you getting in trouble. If you end up in jail, we can't afford to get you out, and I'd never be able to walk down this street again." *Oh what'll the neighbors say . . .*

"Everything's okay. I never get in trouble, so you can stop picking on me."

"You needn't take that tone of voice. Where are you going to-night?"

"I'm going to choir practice and sing among the angels."

"You'll be sorry when I'm gone," closing the discussion with a universalism of motherhood.

Part of her alarm about what the neighbors might think grew from, as I've noted, the curious twist that we lived in the only bungalow on an otherwise tony street, Park Avenue by name. Across the avenue lived the judge of the Yavapai County Superior Court, and next door to us, the county attorney. Next the other side, Mr. Crawford, Esq. Yet our house, for the sake of appearances, was set as far back from the sidewalk as possible, smash against the alley, and camouflaged by pines and gray-blue bushes. How this zoning mishmash occurred in the first place must be buried in some crumbling city file dating far back, before the substantial houses were built or the street paved, when ours was one of three summer cabins tucked in among the pines. The solid homes arose around ours but never absorbed it, leaving us a slice of territory twenty-five feet by a hundred fifty.

In this front yard, Eloine scratched around in decomposed granite to grow a cutting from the Skull Valley yellow roses and some nasturtiums, her perennial favorite. She never tried vegetables again as she had before, as if the mythic association, harking back to Isis and beyond, between females and cyclic nature had, with menopause, passed away and with it the urge to grow practical foods. From a screen of scraggly plum trees growing between her yard and the county attorney's, she yearly harvested enough to make about six pints of jam.

Jimmy and I mainly disagreed in those years, often violently. Our fracases customarily culminated in his throwing a gigantic shoe, which, while not necessarily hitting its intended target, in that tiny space resulted in the destruction of something. Whether he got talking-to's, as I did, I don't know. Probably not. He was steadier than I, a better student, better wage earner—at fifteen manager of the vegetable section of Piggly Wiggly—and parsimonious, still in thrall to Silas Marner. His personal life was a secret, a tabula rasa as far as I knew. Other than playing tuba in the band and bass viol in the orchestra, he seemed never to participate in anything, though from his vegetable bins opening directly onto the sidewalk of the busiest block of downtown, he gleaned news of all types and delighted Eloine in the telling. She was so curious about people, her favorite pastime was sitting in a parked car and watching folks pass by, as if desperately making up for those fifteen years spent in near isolation in Skull Valley. There the road did not pass by, it ended, and hardly ever did anyone attempt it unnecessarily.

Anyway, Jimmy led the life of a lone wolf. Twenty years later he told me a most amazing tale. I've mentioned elsewhere his allometric sexual growth, his macrophallism, at least to the eyes of a younger sibling. Well, it turns out he was, all those high school years, a very active member of a homosexual underground, a thing we hadn't the faintest hint of. Before the stupidities of McCarthyism, and burgeoned by returning veterans with some experience of the world, the fraternity, comprising both married and single men, operated enthusiastically, if clandestinely, until one of its own members, running for public office, a Benedict Arnold, blew the whistle on all his friends and bed partners. He got elected, as traitors sometimes do. Jimmy escaped the purge by having just gone away to college.

Prescott lies, generally, in a gentle dip of land with upcropping granite boils here and there, inconsequential trees. East of Granite Creek, it was laid out primarily in foursquare blocks; toward the west, less rigidly, as if the surveyors, in passing Whiskey Row on their return from lunch break, had stopped for a convivial hour. The engineering was done by men, of course, as in every human town or village. I don't know how different it might have turned out had the women been in charge. For one thing, probably, there would have been no stairs inside or out, and kitchens would have faced the street with big windows like eyes. Outside this lumpy platter, the hills rise up more earnestly, crisped with green-black pines, but with passageways through them, the various tracks on which miners, ranchers, and cowboys find their way to town and, more often than not, back out again. You don't come into Prescott after dark the way you do a lot of cowboy towns—slung out flat in the night, at the same time bone lonesome and exciting—because it's in a bowl with hills up close all around, so you can't see it far away. Before you know it, you're right in the heart of things.

Being actually only the county seat, Prescott is the sun around which the worlds of tiny hamlets like Skull Valley whirl. A number of these are sprinkled outward ten, twenty, thirty miles, some tucked into mountain valleys, others on the grassy plains. Over another mountain is the sizable town of Jerome, where "white" kids did not pause. Built for mine workers, it was a completely Mexican town, with stores and houses hanging like Greek monasteries on the steep edges of switch-back streets. Sometimes, below them, a section of a mined-out shaft collapsed, sending the people above into panic and their houses into pieces, their sidewalks jackhammered into chunks. Known for their hostility to whites, the boys from Jerome were ferocious ball players and would, it was thought, attack you on their streets without provoca-tion. Those boys, like miners' kids everywhere, had only one pos-sibility to face, descending into the tunnels with their dads and uncles.

A few headlong miles farther down the other side of the moun-tain comes Clarkdale, also a company town but for the managers, the white-collar workers. Then, seven miles more, at the Verde River, the quiet rural town of Cottonwood, holding no interest for us whatever, but through which we passed toward Oak Creek and the red cliffs of Sedona, at that time a nearly unspoiled wilderness, though Max Ernst was living nearby creating gargoÿles and friezes out of cement. This was our bailiwick after we reached the age when somebody had use of a car, usually Digger with the mortuary's seven-passenger limousine into which we could crowd eleven. Broad travel, like learning, was not a feature of our social development.

Yet those who had traveled, such as certain teachers who'd been away in the war, taught us nothing about it. What we knew came from newsreels, *The Eyes and Ears of the World,* featuring tanks, planes, ships, and explosions. No teacher offered any comment *about* the war. In civics class it was glossed over as a clean, smooth, victorious glitch in the manifest destiny of America. Up to then the war was the bloodiest event of a bloody century, but the undiluted truth about it was consid-ered too radical or wicked to be offered; instead we got "Marriage and Family Living."

Speaking of family living, George Booth, cartoonist, is a master not only of English pit bulls and psychotic cats but of glimpses into kitchens where electrical appliances, such as irons, are plugged into ceiling sockets. Eloine's kitchen, listing toward the south ever more each year, was a tangle of electric cords, a fire marshal's delight, due to having only two sources—the ceiling and an outlet on the stove itself. Cooking a meal while trying to iron, say, or run the portable washing machine resulted in a kind of stork dance like that on an old-fashioned telephone switchboard with overlapping wires and plugs.

Nevertheless, her experimental upheavals continued, incited by social intercourse with other women and the wider availability, after 1945, of foodstuffs in the markets, including shortcuts like Aunt Penny's White Sauce, as good, she admitted, as she could make from scratch, so why bother. Still of necessity frugal, she manipulated ground beef into an amazing repertoire, including a dish I liked called "tagliarini," a flying fortress meal of pasta—the tagliarini—olives, tomatoes, onions, and corn, the kind of dinner she could make for a song and feed, if not a multitude, a dozen, not exactly something you'd see in the movie *Big Night*. She also made chipped beef with white sauce on toast, a *universal* dish known by servicemen the country over as S.O.S., shit on a shingle. I still like it.

From the pervasive ranch cuisine, she picked up rodeo pie, allegedly Mexican in origin, made of meat and corn pudding, which I'd forgotten about until finding it, or what memory thinks it is, in *Saveur* magazine, attributed to cowboy—*huasos*—life in Chile, of all places, where the staples of Mapuche Indian vegetables mix with European introductions of meat. Eloine probably liked it because at the end it's sprinkled with sugar. I never actually observed a cowboy eating this, but it's sensational with guitar music.

Rodeo Pie
Pastel de Choclo

1½ pounds chicken pieces
4 onions, peeled; 1 quartered, 3 chopped
2 bay leaves
salt and black pepper
5 cups fresh corn kernels, cut from about 8 ears
1 cup milk

6 tablespoons vegetable oil
1 clove garlic, peeled and crushed, or more
¾ pound ground beef
¼ teaspoon ground cumin
2 teaspoons dried oregano
2 teaspoons sweet paprika or Spanish *pimentón*
3 tablespoons roughly chopped raisins
2 hard-cooked eggs, cut into wedges
6 black olives, pitted and chopped
2 teaspoons sugar

Place the chicken, quartered onion, and 1 bay leaf in a pot. Season with salt and pepper, add water to cover, and bring to a simmer over medium-high heat. Reduce the heat to medium-low, cover, and cook until the chicken is done, 20 to 25 minutes. Remove the chicken and, when cool, remove the skin, pull the meat from the bones, and tear into large pieces.

Transfer the quartered onion to a food processor (discard the cooking liquid and bay leaf). Add the corn and milk and puree until smooth. Heat 2 tablespoons oil in a skillet over medium-high heat, add the corn purée, and cook, stirring, until it is thick, about 5 minutes. Season with salt and pepper.

Preheat the oven to 350°F.

Heat the remaining 4 tablespoons oil in a skillet over medium heat. Add the garlic and cook until it's golden, 5 to 7 minutes. Discard the garlic. Add the chopped onions and 1¼ cups water and cook over medium-high heat until the liquid evaporates and the onions are soft, 5 to 8 minutes. Add the beef, breaking it up, and cook, stirring, until it is browned. Add the cumin, oregano, remaining bay leaf, paprika, and raisins; season with salt and pepper. Stir in ¾ cup water, reduce the heat to medium, and simmer until the mixture is almost dry, about 5 minutes. Remove from the heat and discard the bay leaf.

Spread the beef mixture in the bottom of a 2-quart casserole or in 4 smaller ovenproof dishes. Add the chicken, eggs, and olives, spread the corn puree on top, and sprinkle with sugar. Bake for 30 minutes. Remove from the oven and preheat the broiler. Brown the casserole under the broiler for about 5 minutes. Serve hot.

Rodeo pie would not, I think, be called gourmet cooking but rustic, yet I am confused. Can a dish be both rustic and gourmet in the same life? "Rustic," most often applied to rather sloppy-looking crusts, similar to a child's clay ashtray, is a God-sent idea for me, making allowances as it does for one who can't roll out dough into whatever perfect shape may be required. Rustic releases one to concentrate on flavors over mere appearance; however, it may be advisable to announce this fact in some sly manner before serving so guests will understand. Frances Mayes, author of *Under the Tuscan Sun,* is headmistress of rustic recipes, a woman of my own tastes.

Gourmet cook. *Gourmet* kitchen. I've yet to find a clear definition of either, though I seek repeatedly of those who fling the terms about —the first usually self-employed, the second usually employed by semi-literate real estate agents whose two other words are "fabulous" and "fantastic."

Does *gourmet cook* mean a person who can read a recipe? Or owns over ten cookbooks and a card box? Has memorized all the basic French sauces from *aigre-doux* to *zingara?* Has attended at least one six-week course at an approved culinary school? Does *gourmet kitchen* mean you own a Wolf stove plus a grill, in addition to a set of Zwilling J.A. Henckels knives?

When does a naturally—or forcibly—talented cook become a gourmet cook? What, exactly, is the crossing line? Must you own the stove and the knives before you can claim the title? Or, conversely, can only a gourmet cook operate in a gourmet kitchen? If you are not the one, then you can't have the other?

Pretension in home cooks tends to manifest outwardly first in a peacock's tail of crystal, silver, and linen; in restaurants, for which one pays dearly, an aura of faintly amused stuffiness in which, it is assumed, one would never admit to having a bad or innocuous meal or dare suggest the service was both condescending and incorrect. If you are forking out so much in such surroundings, nothing could possibly be the matter—after all, the interior of the room was designed by one of L.A.'s most famous firms. Two of the owners are industry stars, don't you watch TV? The chef's great-grandfather studied under a student of Carême.

However, it must be said, in L.A., whatever your judgment on the food, the "waitpersons" are the most beautiful in the world, all actors, dancers, or models awaiting their break or next gig; the guys look like Ethan Stiefel and the women like Cameron Diaz.

As with these youngsters, so much of the restaurants' effort goes into design at the expense of taste. A Molièresque comedy in action on both sides of the Atlantic at the moment, maybe also in Tokyo and Hong Kong, is the contest among immature chefs to see who can make the highest Watts Tower on the plate, welding the tiniest and most fragile comestibles, all of which both fools and debilitates because in order to be tasted it must first be deconstructed. The story gives way to text.

One understands competition in a capitalistic world, as well as the dire truth there are only so many edible things in it. Hedgehogs and swans and seagulls, locusts, ants and rattlesnakes, grackles, have long been out of fashion. We have devoured whole species and are repulsed by others. We've learned to protect rather than eat certain animals— the mountain lion, for example. This shrinking of possibilities drives the new competitors into paroxysms of creativity, fourteen ways of looking at a crow.

For many years I taught at university with the poet Henri Coulette. Urbane, witty, highly respected among writers, he left only a small oeuvre, considering all he wrote. It became clear to me why. On a Monday, say, he'd come into my office with a new poem of sixteen lines to get a reaction. While difficult to grasp on a quick reading, his poems always seemed remarkable to me. We'd talk about the work, he'd go away and return on Wednesday with the poem, now twelve lines. On Thursday eight, the next Tuesday four, and by Friday week, completely gone. He edited himself out of existence, as if to say the point is in the process.

Something like this happened, I think, to the chef/owner of the late, aesthetically austere Manhattan Beach restaurant, St. Estephe. One time there for lunch, our companion Elaine O. ordered a special of the day, ravioli stuffed with, as I remember, salmon mousse. Whether the chef used the plural *ravioli* or the singular *raviolo,* her French-sized plate arrived with one single pasta pillow centered in a light chile sauce. And that was all. This for a lady who, though slender, is always starved for a childhood of noodle puddings. You could only laugh. And offer to share.

To counteract this barren look, the bright knights pile on tiny ovate root vegetables, something crunchy, like four fried baby calamari tentacles, three Chinese peapods, two colors of sauce with blips of green olive oil done in a Pollock drip, but much lighter, prettier, and less substantial. The Wonderful Shrinking Meal.

There's nothing essentially or morally wrong with any of this. It's merely a variable approach and must be consumingly entertaining to the master in the kitchen, a man or woman on the verge of a nervous breakdown. As Digger and I, fed a full meal at six o'clock, were starving again at ten—thence to El Canerio—diners in minimalist restaurants can stop by the local pizzeria after the late movie and stoke up. The purpose, anyway, is for conversation and companionship, another glass of wine, and who knows, the renaissance of hormonal mobility. Never, I think, should one overlook the sensual nature of, in Henry James's words, a "profanely well-cooked dinner" if you're left alone by sensitive waiters to let it come to life in the eyes and molecules of your partner. This is the candlelight, red checkered tablecloth, and Chianti scenario.

And I don't mean to imply we should sit down every night, Kansas City or Buenos Aires style, facing a sixteen-ounce steak and stuffed potato. Most of us eat too much and work too hard to erase the consequences without taking much pleasure from either. A good sauce and good company will go a long way toward filling the gaps left by *minceur* cuisine. One has but to look around, in the Midwest or the Northwest, to see packs of gargantuan eaters barely waddling along from one candy bar to the next full meal to be shocked into the perception that many people, like smokers and alcoholics and drug addicts, are killing themselves with the very substances they crave most, not unlike the Fore tribe of Papua New Guinea, who passed along the disease kuru by eating the brains of their fellow man.

I suppose it may be argued that the plate of wee food with twinkling ornamentation is a countermove against conspicuous waste, yet to see such a plate before a gentleman dressed in a Giorgio Armani suit, Ermenegildo Zegna shirt, Gianfranco Ferre tie, and Ferragamo shoes, is at least a piquant juxtaposition. This man, who probably appears quite pasty and soft nude, has adorned himself as an expression of power and seduction. Gay men, who have on the other hand reconstructed their nude bodies into Greco-Roman perfection, wear as little as possible on dates for the same reason, though they are kept out of the haute establishments on grounds of dress code. The Armani suit, if challenged by a body resembling a leather cuirass set on hairy pillars, with who knows what in between, cannot compete. The gentleman's date's attention will waver. He has one other weapon, however, a slim case of soft Spanish leather containing a depthless plastic card.

Whatever one's persuasion, it's hard to seem important with only one raviolo—from start to finish—on the plate.

Supposing that, indeed, one ought to know what is good for one and what is not, reading about it is a dolorous experience. There seem to be three styles: (1) the gee-whiz jumping jack enthusiasm of people who wear spandex in public; (2) the contralto intonations of persons with initials following their names; (3) the home economics prune-whip scold who, in addition to figuring out (how do they do this?) the fat and caloric and vitamin, carbohydrate, fiber, protein, and calcium content of every mouthful we might contemplate eating, invent precious names—such as "Fiesta Bake" or "Tuna Delight"—and have no inkling of what a misplaced modifier might be. Grammatically, recipes as written by these professionals fall to the bottom of the drink, dramatically so at the *Los Angeles Times*.

In their addiction to farinaceous meals, low-fat content, and something generically known as "comfort" food, as if one were asked to eat a duvet cover, they forget dining, for people whose circumstances allow them a step above subsistence, is or ought to be a sensuous pleasure akin to one or more of the seven deadly sins.

The Darwinist Paul Ekman claims love is not an emotion (and therefore has no universal facial expression) but "an affective commitment in which many emotions are felt." Next to the sexual fun (if it's involved at all), one of the emotions couples in love, even friends in love, quickly resort to is dining together, not necessarily to the extent of Tom Jones and his girlfriend. Perhaps we enjoy this activity because we're usually face to face and can watch each other's mouth, lips, tongue, and teeth, the ingestion. If one has also prepared the meal, this—the voyeurism—becomes an erotic act, almost sacramental. It may be instructive, then, to think, as you prepare a dish, how it's going to look going down the tubes. Long, slick strands of spaghetti alla marinara might be evocative (though it's not likely), leaving orange-red streaks on chin, cheek, or nose as they go.

With one's children, the effect must be different, yet why do we teach them eating manners? Why would Eloine say to us, her ruffians attacking lustily her standing egg in pasta, "Eat quietly, please. Don't slurp and don't talk with your mouth full." As my imagination would not stretch so far at nine to picture Hap naked in his hut hobbling, neither will it stretch so far now as to say, with any certainty, that Eloine's admonishments relative to our eating style were subliminally attached to her extreme embarrassment about the public expressions of man, the sexual creature.

A Lion in the Palace

PETER MACKEY sits at the curve of the Palace bar near the open door with his back to the blaze of afternoon sun. Built eighty years ago, when there were thirty-two bars in a row on this street, the room is deep and narrow, the drinking area beginning immediately inside, continuing on back into the gloom, ending after forty feet in a wide space for dancing.

For a time when Peter Mackey was growing up, there was a Chinese café you had to reach either by going through the bar to a door at the back or along a thin corridor from the sidewalk outside. Partway along that hall a staircase rose up darkly to a whorehouse on the second story. He washed dishes in the café for a year. Then the Chinese owner died and the place became an art gallery, of all incongruous things. He does not know what it is now.

He turns and looks out the front door. Across Montezuma Street he sees part of the plaza, and through the elms, a chunk of the white stone courthouse, the most edified building in northern Arizona.

There are four other men in the saloon, spaced down the length of the bar as if they were alone and liking it. The bartender seems ghostly familiar. But then, about half the people he has seen on the streets since morning seem familiar. Old acquaintances grown older, like himself? Or their parents? Their kids? They pass on the sidewalk and you can't think what to say. It's like strolling through a town of carnival mirrors; every distorted face tells you the story of your own.

Green and cool, the plaza is a better-looking place than the cemetery he has come to visit. In the plaza he can rove around still with only his mind's eye and place every porcelain drinking fountain, each walk, the fish pond, the equestrian statue, the delicate, ornate bandstand, and the green benches where at this time of day old men and a few old women will be cooling off in the shade before disappearing to wherever they go at dark.

"Spoiled it by adding on," the bartender says, standing with his hands on his hips, looking out on the view of the courthouse. "It used to be the same on all four sides."

"I know. What did they add?"

"Public toilets. Just couldn't leave it alone."

"What did they do with the old ones?"

The bartender's blue eyes twinkle. "Made them into judges' chambers, I guess."

You can't help picturing the marble and granite men's room on the lowest level of the courthouse if you've ever been in it. Cold and gray, as functional as a dungeon, it was where Peter had his first sexual adventure, complete in two minutes, with a recently returned veteran, a town hero because of his wounds.

His next came along soon after in the tiny kitchen of the Chinese café with Joy Ling, a giggly girl with a merry disk face. The two of them, left to clean up, got to messing around in the suds and then on the meat block, then the floor. This memory, like a relish, sweet and sour, blends with the others. How could you know when you were a kid that the next moment wasn't necessarily going to be an improvement over this one and you could miss the whole point by being in such a hurry? For a long time after, the smell of soy sauce made his blood rush.

The sunlit doorway darkens. A woman enters, chooses a stool just inside, across the turn of the bar from Peter. She leans forward on her arms, at ease. She looks familiar. Of course. But he doesn't recall anybody he's known with that much red hair.

He ought to be driving on out to the cemetery if he is ever going to. It's what he's come to do, participate in the custom, put some guilt to rest, as if they're still watching and passing judgment. Maybe you just hope someone will do it for you, think to stick some real flowers in the jar once in a while, pull a few weeds. He wonders if it is still the place where kids go to park at night, along the road on the back side where you get a view of the town, like a display of jewelry on black velvet. "Going to the graveyard" meant a steaming, groping, beer-drinking hour or two in the backseat of a car if it was winter, or outside on a blanket under the runty junipers when the weather warmed. By day the detritus beneath the trees was churned and rumpled, trashed with cans and spent Trojans. Twenty-five yards away, down the slope, the first headstone stood, facing the other way.

Mackey pushes his bottle aside and it is replaced in a deft movement by the bartender, who then makes some comment to the red-haired woman. She laughs and picks up her shot glass, holding it out before her face as if toasting. Mackey follows her gaze. High above the center of the bar, above the bottles and glasses, above the mirrors and pillars, the Victorian scrolls and niches, there stands a stuffed mountain lion, its head inches from the pressed-tin ceiling. Dusty, mangy, brown, its pink mouth snarling, it lords over the bar.

She catches him watching and smiles. "Older'n the hills," she says. "I'd forgotten him."

"Actually, it's a female," the woman says. "Sometimes she brings me luck. Or so I say."

They begin talking then, the ice broken. She is friendly and forward, as if they met every day of the week. She's not bad looking. His own age, probably, maybe a little self-conscious about her appearance. He can't tell if she is making some kind of play or whether he's interested in trying to catch the ball.

"You don't remember me, either," she says.

"Should I?"

"Janet Kincaid. I was in your class."

"Jesus." Jesus Christ. This is—was—the girl uppermost in his, and probably every boy's, mind when he kicked the covers down on a summer night or even that time he was wrestling Joy Ling to the mat with soapy arms.

A deep sadness scoops through Mackey's insides. We're more than halfway there. Homecoming Queen, Spring Princess, Head Cheerleader, and all.

"You didn't have red hair," he says.

"Silver threads among the gold. It'd be pure white without some serious help." She lights a fresh cigarette from the butt of the previous one and taps the edge of her shot glass on the bar. The bartender, smooth as a cat, replaces it with a full one. "You broke hearts, you know," Janet Kincaid says.

"First I've heard of it."

"I believe you. You were too cool to touch. Aloof."

Others have begun coming into the saloon, guys stopping by for a beer after work, a couple of office women. Not the carousers who will drift in after dark.

"Call it shyness," Mackey says.

"I forget what we called it then. Some of us thought you were queer."

"I sometimes thought so myself."

"You weren't, then?"

"It doesn't matter now." Just say desperate. And lonely.

Beautiful, followed around like the bell goat by every athlete in school, to Mackey's knowledge Janet Kincaid never gave him the first glance, much less a second one. It didn't take a bucket of brains to figure out his poverty was partly to blame. In the afternoon when school let out, the parking lot became a circus of flashy colors, mag wheels, straight pipes, squealing tires, like a motorized daily rape of the Sabines. Janet Kincaid would have been one of the first swept away in a fast car. Mackey could look forward to trekking across the football field toward town and six hours of work.

"How's your brother?"

"Rolly?" Janet taps her cigarette in an ashtray advertising A-1 beer. "He died at thirty. Still with the brain of a five-year-old."

"Sorry."

"Don't be. He was the happiest person I ever knew. Because he couldn't remember from one day to the next. And of course had no idea how he'd been fucked."

"He was about the last person I talked to before I ran away," Mackey says.

She smiles fully for the first time, a stunning remnant, a torn rag. "Nobody runs away from home at eighteen, Peter. But I always appreciated you taking up for him like you did when those other bastards picked on him. And I was, like, too occupied, you could say. See? I did notice you."

The night before he left, out walking his thoughts, Peter came upon Rolly Kincaid near the ball park, on the east side where the highway swerves in. Rolly carried a length of rope, which he twirled and ran through his hands and tripped over on his ceaseless unabashed maundering through town, one edge to the other. Sweet and harmless unless teased too much, he stopped in at the firehouse for a piece of candy, chewing it like a squirrel with his tiny wide-spaced teeth. Or the drugstore for a cone. Woolworth's for popcorn. The Studio for a show. All freely given, in charity or atonement, as if the whole town felt responsible for this, its idiot. One time he wandered in the alley door of the Chinese café and helped Peter wash dishes, carefully transporting one plate at a time across the kitchen with his rolling, wide-hipped walk.

This night, Peter turned Rolly toward home. On the back side of the ball park, they passed by the Indian graveyard, a weedy, unkempt place full of leaning gray wooden crosses. Rolly nodded, seeming to listen, running his rope through his hands, as Peter talked. "I'm going away tomorrow, Rolly," he said. "I'm going to Phoenix and I'm not coming back till I'm fucking rich."

"King-rich," Rolly said, happily turning up his blasted face, nodding, pulling at the rope, his present and future.

No one seeing them together would have been surprised, although as Peter's mother reported to him, everyone *she* knew thought it strange for a perfectly normal boy to spend so much time in the company of someone who wasn't all there. Peter couldn't explain it, either. Did he befriend Rolly because he was Janet Kincaid's brother? Maybe. Or because Rolly didn't judge, just listened, burbling and eager, to whatever Peter said, his ideas and his anger? Or because somebody ought to look after the helpless. The only fights Peter had were with guys mistreating Rolly, turning impotently on the brother of the girl they all wanted but couldn't all have.

They walked past the mass of square gray stones that was the Baptist Church, dark tomb of sins, and on up the hill to the Kincaids' white house. Peter watched Rolly enter the gate, quietly babbling over some inexplicable knot in his rope, and stood a while looking toward the lighted windows on the second floor where he guessed Janet's room would be, where she might be lying on her bed or exercising before her mirror.

But there seemed to be no life in the windows. They said Rolly and Janet's mother never left the house after it became clear her baby was an idiot, never venturing farther than the clothesline, gradually hedging in the house with tall bushes. They said she blamed her husband, who'd worked on a CCC gang, for bringing home microbes.

Janet, even in junior high, had begun to throw herself like a dervish into the idea of being popular and pretty. There was no sign of her this night, as Peter rubbed himself like a farm animal against the Kincaids' gate. He could imagine her in somebody's blocked and lowered Chevy, imagine the bright sphincter of her mouth now drawing up to sip a chocolate malt through a straw, now bursting open like a flower, her laugh itself a hard brilliance.

Only two weeks before, on a shimmering August day, the town had celebrated the completion of a new pipeline bringing plenty of water in from artesian wells fifteen miles away in Chino Valley to end the two-year drought, the summer rationing, and baked lawns. On the courthouse steps, in an iridescent green bathing suit, Janet Kincaid accepted another title while fire hydrants shot geysers of wasted water into the air: Queen of the Big Splash. The mayor talked, the band played, a Hollywood starlet judged the beauty contest.

That night the katydids grew delirious in the elms on the plaza. Across Montezuma Street the cowboys, never missing a chance to howl, continued the Big Splash on into the night, making up new variations on their joke, that they'd been conserving water all along.

Peter shouldered his way into the Palace, where the mountain lion stood above the old bar, and bought two bottles of beer. He intended to drink them both and go back for more, but after the first he lost his will and gave the other to Rolly, who was engrossed in pulling his rope and a crepe paper banner around and around the equestrian statue, wearing farmer's overalls and a straw hat. Peter imagined Janet in a pale dress at the country club, and out on the fairway boys fighting, horny animals bloodying their white jackets. When they'd get that out of their systems, they'd strip and swim in the pool, replenished with fresh Chino Valley water.

"You still have family here?" Janet Kincaid asks. "You look sort of lost."

"In a manner of speaking."

"Dead, you mean. Me, too. Mom gave up the ghost not long after Rolly did, like she'd done her time and was ready for whatever punishment comes next. The old man's around. He has a pension. Look, will you watch my things for a second?"

She indicates a fat wallet, a purse, money lying beside her glass. She walks away toward the back, where the restrooms are.

Mackey reaches across and lifts the top of the wallet. From the first plastic window a boy dressed in jacket and tie grins back, as if he's been waiting for just this exposure. Something's familiar about him but old-fashioned. Mackey takes up the wallet and out of it a long tail of connected plastic windows suddenly unfolds onto his lap. With two pictures back to back in each slot, he figures there must be thirty. About half girls, half boys. Idly, Mackey looks for his own picture, certain it won't be there. Neither is Rolly's.

Caught this way, arrested at seventeen or eighteen, most of them are recognizable, even if on the street this morning he could only vaguely suspect he was passing someone who'd once sat across the aisle from him in algebra or with whom he'd exchanged a dirty joke in the locker room or acted in a play.

"You found my exhibition, I see," Janet Kincaid says over his shoulder. She moves on around the corner of the bar and slips up on the stool with a quick undulation of her hips, giving Mackey a straight, defiant look—like the stuffed mountain lion.

"I didn't mean to snoop."

"They didn't jump out all by themselves. But it doesn't matter. Look to your heart's content."

"Did you marry one of these guys?"

She takes a long time answering, seeming to search for words the length of the bar. Beyond her, outside, Mackey sees the sun has moved from the street up onto the top of the courthouse.

Janet looks at him then and lifts her chin. "When the dust settled, I looked around and you know what? Everybody was gone. You, too."

"I wasn't in the running. Why?"

"It finally dawned on me. Who would marry someone who's got a congenital idiot for a brother?"

I would have, Peter Mackey almost says. "It isn't fair. I mean, after all the promises you must've had."

Janet's eyes, with a little anger to light them, turn almost as blue and clear as he remembers. "What's fair?" she says. "Fair. Shit." She taps her glass and waits while the bartender comes to fill it, then she shrugs and turns toward the door. "Sunset," she says. "Again. Where are you staying?"

"The St. Michael."

"You won't get much sleep. The cowboys still carry on like tom-cats, that much hasn't changed."

"I can sleep in tomorrow. Look—Janet, you want to take a ride out to the graveyard?"

"Going to the graveyard. Boy, you bring back memories."

"All in a kind of blur. Let's buy a six-pack."

Janet raises her glass to the mountain lion above the bar. "You should have been this direct years ago, Peter. Now you'd be disappointed. There've been some radical alterations."

"Well," he says, "I'm not supposed to forget my blood-pressure medication."

"Wouldn't we be loads of fun."

"I need to stop and get some flowers."

"For the living or the dead?"

"Both. And we could go to dinner?"

"Remember how after dark, when the lights came on down in town, it made you think you were someone else? Someplace else? It was like the night was waking up all excited after another ordinary day. I always imagined it was Paris. Or New York. Places I still haven't got to. And never will. The Isle of Capri. Some guy grunting and panting, and I saw Notre Dame."

Janet Kincaid digs a fresh pack of cigarettes out of her bag and tears at the cellophane. She lets him strike the match for her. "This is the first time you got up nerve to ask for a date."

"Well, it's the first time you've turned me down."

"So—you understand?"

"I understand I've been refused. Not why. But we can skip the graveyard, go someplace else. Give me a tour of the old town. I hear they've built a new high school."

"You can do that by yourself. I haven't the heart." Janet Kincaid lifts her glass again, catches the bartender's eye. He's busy now with the gathering crowd, but he sees her. Their signals are quick and accurate.

The Innocent Heart

*I*n certain metaphysical categories, Eloine was enlightened, whether she wanted to be or not so late in life, by Mrs. Going appearing in her postwar blue Oldsmobile from across town, Baptist pillaress delivering an impassioned monsoon of words, a rain of divine understanding like a medieval evangelical, in neurotic disagreement with any, especially the young, who did not see reason within her high-minded opinions. Fair-haired like Isolde, firm and rosy, she sat upright and faced Eloine, who chose a lower chair if one was handy after setting out the cups of coffee and homemade cakes.

When Eloine could get a word in edgewise, she rubbed her right-hand fingers down over her left and replied, in a voice so quiet it could not conceivably be contentious, "Well, I reckon not everyone's the same—"

"But they ought to act like it—"

"—and you have to make allowances for more ways than one."

"More ways? Why?"

"Of going about things."

"Have you taken this question to the Lord? What would the world come to if everybody could just do things their own way? The Bible is clear every man under his own fig tree is not the way God wants it, and speaking of Eula Parches, it's plain as the nose on your face, if she'd of joined in our Golden Prayer Circle instead of hiding out at home occupying her time with who knows what, she'd of stayed with us longer, but she's better off with Jesus Our Savior, praise His name."

"Well, now, we don't know that."

"Don't know what—that's she better off or with the Lord?"

"And law, the way I feel some days, I don't know whether ripe old age is the best answer."

"Of course it is, we've all been sent to light the path and the longer we keep our lamp burning the more we please Him these cupcakes are nice I wish I could cook like you do."

"I don't think they're—"

"But like I teach my Charles, some were sent to enrich the spirit and some the stomach."

Mrs. Going had a gangling son, perpetual president of the Baptist Young People's Union, whom we referred to at home as Mycharles. No matter what another mother might mention of her own offspring, Mrs. Going would say, "Oh, but Mycharles" does it better or longer or greater or more regularly. Actually, Mycharles, among the undergifted, wasn't talented either artistically or intellectually or athletically and took seven years in college to get a bachelor's degree, but he grew up tall and handsome and lived in Sausalito. He majored in religion, apparently exhausting its full possibilities in those seven fat years, and seeing no further need of it afterward became, instead of a minister, a greeting card salesman, a fitting alternative of like substance.

I knew Mycharles better than anyone, in certain ways that would have electrified his mother, yet not in a warm friendship, as he was cold and arrogant, attributes Mrs. Going failed to recognize.

She did not endear herself to me by judging the piano I bought in my senior year, a serious-looking, enormously heavy upright of obscure lineage, to be not good enough for Mycharles, who didn't know middle C from his ass. We had to jettison a desk and Billy's leopard-spotted magazine rack to get the piano in, and it thereafter dominated the house, both in size and sonority. Despite age, it was quite loud, and even silent couldn't be ignored. "Mycharles," Mrs. G. dizzily declared, "will become a leading missionary so will of course play all the music when the time comes but he'll have to be provided a better piano than this." She reached over and gave mine a single-fingered jab. "Out of tune," she said, in the same tone one might use after poking a poisoned cat. "Dead." At the time I still had not heard the disheartening news, long ago proclaimed by François Couperin in the eighteenth century and corroborated by scientists of the twentieth, that if you don't get started playing by eight, your brain will have already gone off to other adventures and you'll never catch up.

Mrs. Going held to the conventional opinion that because Mycharles was both beyond moral improvement and so little understood by his contemporaries he was marked out for greatness. Sometimes God, she claimed, in His infinite wisdom withheld a person's gifts to save wear and tear, as it were, until his time came.

Eloine, sixty by then, in some cases twenty years older than the mothers of my acquaintances, polite with Mrs. Going to her face, stormed around the house after she had gone, clattering coffee cups, murmuring tenebrously. "Lord, that woman could drive a saint to drink."

She tried not to resent other women whose circumstances made life easier than hers, women with productive husbands, three-bedroom houses set on lawns, and a car in the garage. Women who, unemployed outside the home, had time to pussyfoot about town doing good works. If they just wouldn't be so insincere about it—"For the life of me, I don't know why she thinks I need praying over"—but sit down and talk about sewing, for example, or cooking—"as if that's going to put food on the table"—or even, if necessary, Harry Truman—"or make ends meet. It's a come-off."

Where Mycharles excelled was in decorating Sunday School rooms in what I suspect was a subconscious expiation for knowing already he'd never survive in darkest Africa bringing truth to the savages or bedding down in a grass hut with centipedes and fire ants. He began in each room with a saccharine head of Christ looking beatitudinously Anglo-Saxon. Then radiating from this centerpiece, cutouts from magazines reflecting a theme or vision, perhaps African heathens (*National Geographic*) in need of grace, or the aurora borealis (*Life*) as a symbol of God's awesome power, or a loving family (*Saturday Evening Post*) surrounding their new RCA, emblem of the spreading word. Handmade artifacts found their way into these collages, such as leaves exposed on blueprint paper, bookmarks with verses on them, and overhead, crepe paper streamers in Easter colors, of which he was inordinately fond.

He had an acute sense of little kids, kindergarten and first-grade size, and left them plenty of space below his displays on which to pin their own creative trash. And for the Christmas pageant he was in charge of their robes and crowns, their frankincense and myrrh, and for getting them on and off with a minimum of tears.

Digger, usually a font of patience, had little to spare for Mycharles, but then Digger had no artistic pretensions and certainly no religious ones. And since Mycharles adhered to Baptist principles of the unexplored life, he wasn't much fun. We held him responsible for balancing out our own operative agenda.

Every man under his own fig tree was not a workable idea for us, though for a different reason than Mycharles's mother's. We had no contract to do God's labor, being overwhelmed with our own, and the more people under the trees the better, particularly in Digger's view; he was still working on a mathematical theory of probability. Not *every* girl would say no if he could only approach enough of them in some private dell. In Prescott there was not, however, an infinite supply.

While the idle ladies like the county attorney's wife played bridge at the country club and the do-good ones like Mrs. Going steered purposefully up and down the hills spreading their communicable nonsense, Eloine walked to the center of town to begin her ten-hour shift at the Home Café. As at age ten she was thrust into a farm kitchen to cook for a dozen, now at sixty she cooked for a hundred, lunch and dinner, then walked home again.

Her *mise en place* was forthright in the Home Café, with a menu of fried chicken, meat loaf, chicken-fried steak, greens and potatoes, rice pudding. Working by rote, expected to produce uniformly day by day, rubbed her the wrong way, yet she was able over time to stamp those everyday requirements with her own distinction and took some pride in their being sold out at every meal. With desserts she had some leeway to surprise the regulars with a pineapple upside-down cake or fresh doughnuts or Miss Ruby cupcakes, chocolate pudding. She disdained, and gradually overcame, catsup and the creamed-soup fixes popular then, the trend toward quick gratification a more nervous and mobile population insisted on.

Intuitively, built on years of practice with no ingredients that could be called rare or elegant—there was no caviar in her kitchen, no saffron or lobster or truffles, no virgin olive oil or balsamic vinegar—she understood the process of eating food is like hearing music. Both are ephemeral and unreplicatable, precisely. They aren't laboratory experiments, and talking about them does nothing to reproduce the sensations of taste or sound. One eats, not to hear or read about it, but to taste what can't be told with words. Eloine, though too bumfuzzled by bureaucracies of all sorts to be truly emancipated in life, had a flair, an edge to her frugal domestic creations—the shiny button over the dull—and with more money might have had a better scald on it, overall.

As is the case for virtuosi of all sorts, even with her limited repertoire, cooking for her was performance, not in the flashy way of Japanese sushi chefs, but in the food itself, whether served on a cracked plate or silver. A person who reads music well can, as Schumann observed, understand it without hearing it. Eloine could read a recipe and both taste and smell the final product. Curiously, she might say, "Hmm, that smells good," then *rip* went the hairpin. Her memory bank I imagined as a great white cookbook with ragged slips of paper sticking out of it in disarray, the whole growing fatter and messier year by year, but containing a hierarchy of memory and performance. She had what might be called gustatory imagery, "seeing" the taste of a dish on the mind's palate before making it.

And by the way, it evolved at last that Eloine could play a tune on the piano, in the pentatonic scale, as Chopin had done with his "black-key étude." Hers went as follows: "Sally in a shimmy-tail, Sally in a gown, Sally in a shimmy-tail strutting down town." (Key of F-sharp major.)

On Saturday or Sunday afternoons at home, she still longed for visitors, unless they were messengers from the Messiah. Especially, she delighted in a visit from Skull Valley, some woman with whom she had struggled in tandem, perhaps, but especially of the kind who knew how to gather and sort information. It dawns on me, late, those fifteen years in Skull Valley were the longest residence she had anywhere up to then after leaving Tennessee. As flimsy as they may have been, how planted in sandy soil, these were her roots after all, the place where her kids did most of their growing, where the days were both bright and bleak, full and destitute, rich and terrifying.

Robert Jourdain, writing of the brain and music, has said of a performing pianist, "lines blur between motion and perception, expectation and experience." Likewise, our final days "at home" quickly came and as quickly went. Some of us had left the year before, others would a year later, but we were all leaving home, and it would never again be but a place to visit. We began to split apart into individuals, cells divided, turning our backs on El Canerio, The Palace, western music, which I alone among them loved. Betty, who could beat the pants off anybody on the tennis court. Shirley, quietly beautiful, whom Digger—now David—asked to marry him, later (she didn't). Doug, who became a state senator. Beth, ethereal flutist. The three sisters, Vanora, Wanda, and Zoellen, who married Archie. Red-haired Barbara, so frightened of Darwin. Ruby, voted most likely to succeed. Mycharles. Me.

These were crystalline days. As soon as one passed into twilight, night, and sleep, it was discarded for the next, a commotion of hours hammered together like a pasticcio sculpture of found objects. We had no wish for anything to be the same again, as, of course, it wasn't. Growing older bit by bit, we stretched our muscles, looked outward toward scenes we had only rumors of, dragging our mounting ignorance, ticking off the list of sins as we found the chance. We were on the move.

The next two summers I rode the Greyhound up into the Kaibab Forest, near the Utah border, and worked at the lodge on the north rim of the Grand Canyon, living a life of alternate drudgery and dormitory dementia, long hikes during hours off, camping out on the canyon's plateaus, devising ways to bribe the truckers to bring us beer, a tricky business in Mormon territory.

I started at the bottom in the kitchen as dishwasher and floor mopper. But being essentially a cheerful person wherever placed, with a calamitous eagerness to please, I soon moved—if not always upward, at least laterally—through a number of jobs nearer the food: vegetable peeler, assistant baker, salad compositor, parfait maker extraordinaire, but was never let near the stove. Perhaps I lost any chance the afternoon I poured down the drain twenty gallons of stock. Top, the chef, a resigned and inarticulate man, held much in awe by us, mumbled terribly. What he actually said to me, "Pour off the stock," I heard as "Pour *out* the stock." Thus, an hour before he had to begin feeding dinner to three hundred guests, he was caught stockless, *le cuisinier sans fond blanc.* Top didn't swear, shout, or bawl me out but—a tall man—his shoulders drooped, he shook his head, turned and walked away, back to his burners. Somehow, like the chef/father in *Eat, Drink, Man, Woman* or *Tortilla Soup,* he resuscitated the evening.

I considered suicide by leaping into the abyss, which I could have engineered on a promontory within view of the great dining room windows at sunset. Wouldn't *that* put a damper on dinner hour.

From these summers I learned several lessons. (1) A competent chef must rise to emergencies. (2) Second cooks are hateful, being themselves lowly sociopaths. (3) Some tricks of the kitchen, to wit: Say the roast beef is sent back because it's too bloody. Just take it in your hands and wring it out like a dishrag, lay it back on the plate, rearrange the parsley, and off it goes again. (4) I never wanted to work in a professional kitchen again and have not, though neither have I been asked. No doubt Jean-Georges Vongerichten loves his work and, like any artist, is humbled that others will pay outrageous prices for the privilege of eating his food, and is serene in his fame. The cooks under whom we slaved must have been of another order. Except for Top, they were self-loathing, dirty, sloppy, foul-mouthed, and untalented.

My opinion of those cooks has been recently mirrored in writings by New York chef Anthony Bourdain, who points out what I suspected all along: there are more former cooks among the criminal classes than other professionals, and vice versa—more criminals among cooks.

As for Eloine, she was holding her breath, ready to let out a long, rejuvenatory sigh. *Nearly over at last.* Three or four more years of cooking in the café, then she'd be able to sit in the sun before her cabin, drying her long, black hair for which she still collected rainwater, awaiting news. Stir around in the nasturtium patch. Coax the tough roses back to life, cuttings from the yellow hedge in the country, a final connection.

The Innocent Heart

MY SISTER LEONA, a spinster, long retired from her civil service desk, occupies herself with dietary ideas for my longevity clipped from maturity magazines and obituaries clipped from the old hometown *Courier*. Between the two kinds of printed information there hangs a delicate span, Leona's view of my life as having been distilled to two choices. The same age as Robb, she believes this gives her privileged knowledge. This week she sent a notice of the death of Margrite Ranko, aged ninety-four. Lord, I had no idea she lived all those years.

Everybody called her a Bohemian. Actually, her family emigrated from Latvia when she was a little girl, leaving in her English a trace of the exotic, like sachet in an old drawer. But Latvia . . . Bohemia . . . both were too far removed from an Arizona cowboy town to be discernible at the tail end of a long war and its daily news encrusted with the sad, exciting names of places few Prescott citizens had ever heard of before 1942 or could locate on a map.

Margrite Ranko lived solely to organize patriotic divertissements, little musicals structured around her daughter, Nadia. She provided all the accompaniment herself on a zither, instrument of baffling Old World complexity. The performers, besides Nadia, were innocents whom she corralled about town, children with talent or with parents who believed they had. She would have preferred entertaining the troops in Europe or the South Pacific, as Prescott, being near nothing strategic to the war effort, had no servicemen in it and no USO. Once in a while you'd see a lonely soldier or sailor home on furlough, maybe two, but never enough to make up an audience.

The other person who did most for the spirit of the war effort was Robin Duncan, the soldier who embodied *patriot* the way crystal embodies light. No boy could speak of him without a crack in his voice, a hysteric hoarseness. Who knows what went on in the minds of girls and women.

Duncan: black-haired athlete, so handsome in his khaki outfit a whole vestibule full of lesser beings would fall silent when he entered, embarrassed by their own insignificance and piping voices, their shapeless bodies. Of course, he was soon shipped overseas but we still saw him, his smiling face, and the left half of his chest armored with service bars, fighting the Japanese dragons.

This was years and years ago, when I, Jed Matthew, was fourteen and wondering whether to add another *d* to my first name.

Robb comes into the kitchen, where I am reading Leona's clipping, to investigate the possibility of a Bloody Mary before lunch, his rubber tires and his power pack singing their duet. I can locate him anywhere in the house when he's moving because each room has a different acoustic response. He doesn't teach anymore, hasn't for a long time, so he travels a lot, from bedroom to library to kitchen to front porch, or down the ramp into the garden, where he specializes in zucchini. "Message from Garcia?" he asks. I hand him the obit. He never knew Margrite Ranko but remembers the Community Sing. He laughs about all those yokels who used to get up and perform.

It was because of her mother's musicals I came to know Nadia, beardless Don Juan bedazzled by her footwork. A year ahead of me in school, pale, cool, aloof, and mystic, she—alternately with Robin Duncan—came to occupy what any psychologist would have called an unhealthy proportion of my thoughts awake or asleep, or in that third state, the ecstatic ether world of nocturnal or diurnal masturbation.

At school one didn't think of Nadia in the erotic mode, dressed as she was in drab, her dark hair unfaddishly straight and not always clean. But on stage, costumed in a skimpy outfit of red sequins, blue top hat, cane, tap shoes, all her musty, flat-chested, inherited Bohemianism transformed into a brilliance, a thing of light and heat, as if each tiny flashing tessellation sent out electrical charges.

Nadia had a younger brother in my grade. Jannis (pronounced Yaw-nis), thin and timid, was a genius, everyone said, and therefore not at all interesting, but on the pretext of desiring his company, I wandered across town on July 5 to the Ranko house.

Jannis, being a genius, had evaded violin lessons, dancing, or any other involvement in his mother's entertainments, and by only barely employing his brain could figure out my sudden friendship was bogus the day I arrived at their door. Nibbling a piece of white cheese like a polite mouse, Jannis listened to my greeting, returned it, then excused himself and left the room. He was teaching himself Serbo-Croatian that summer, as I remember, as if Spanish verbs weren't enough. Jannis was always learning something with Cyrillic characters or astronautical symbols no one in Prescott could teach. Or test.

But Margrite Ranko rose from her zither with an excited gleam in her eye. She clapped her hands twice. The five or six little boys and girls relaxed and began to jabber. "Sit, sit," Margrite said, her hands fluttering out of control without the instrument beneath them. "We're about to take refreshment."

I sat on the sofa, the texture and shape of a manatee, and Nadia straddled a wooden chair, facing the back, over which she regarded me as she wiped her face with a cloth. She seemed, except for her hair, to be pink all over—her strange shoes, her bare legs, her worn and patched jersey, her arms and neck and face.

"Uh," I began. "I saw you dance last night. At the courthouse steps."

"Oh?" Her eyebrows arched and a faint expectant smile spread over her pink mouth. She stayed the cloth for a moment on the half-moon of flesh above her breasts. I told her how terrific she'd been, all that footwork, the hat and cane.

Margrite Ranko returned from the kitchen with a tray of cookies and tiny paper cups of lemonade. The kids squatted on the floor among scraps of costume materials and fell to, like hummingbirds in the throat of some Hawaiian flower.

"My, you're nice and tall," Margrite said, although I was still seated on the lumpy sofa. "You must be about sixteen."

I executed my nonchalant shrug and glanced at Nadia. She gave back a brown-eyed arcane look with the tiniest hint of a smile. "Almost," I said.

"You look like a person who'd have musical talents."

"Me? Uh—no." I thought I heard a warning *ping* above my head.

"He plays in the band," Nadia the traitress said.

Margrite, short and cylindrical—in fact, everywhere made of

tubes and circles—skipped into a brief modern dance right there before our eyes. "Isn't it wonderful?" she asked, meaning, I think, life. Or music. Or her choreography. "What instrument do you perform on?"

"Bass clarinet."

You could see the hope drain away. Outside a band, there's not much demand for a bass clarinet. It's not one of your great solo instruments. "Maybe you sing?"

"No," I said, giving a pretty good imitation of a laugh while checking out Nadia to see if she'd betray me again. She'd probably seen me in glee club too. But she only wore her cat smile.

Margrite Ranko reminded me that her troupe would be performing the next night on Community Sing. Nadia, of course, would be featured. She swept away to gather her chickadees while I tried to make a quick bit of progress.

"Will you be there?" Nadia asked.

"Well, you know," I said, climbing out of the sofa. "I don't go in for that kind of corn too much."

Which was the worst thing I could have said, but emblematic, as it turned out, of my way with women. Nadia flounced off in pink contempt.

The Community Sing, pre-TV phenomenon, probably no longer exists anywhere in the world. In Prescott it was held every Thursday night, June through August, unless rained out, at the ball park on the east side near the armory and the Indian cemetery. A free talent show, it was a chance to belt out popular—and for the most part—patriotic—songs with one's neighbors. A portable stage, something like a medieval morality wagon with one of the long sides removed, was wheeled over to about first base. Above it, a screen was mounted on which words to the songs appeared, although everyone knew them already, and a cheerful MC and a pianist got the evening started with the national anthem and war tunes like "Over There" and "The Halls of Montezuma," which made people think of the boys in uniform, not only Robin Duncan.

Sitting on the top tier that night of July 6, I tried to be both present and absent. All day I'd continued my interior debate even after I knew I'd lost. Yes. Corny or not, I'd go to the goddamned thing and watch her do whatever it was she did, which turned out to be *Swan Lake,* as the MC announced, but a mercifully shortened version, not at the time many there would've known the original. Margrite understood something about consciousness drift and the limitations of Tchaikovsky rendered on the zither. First, the little kids appeared dressed all in white and did a sort of military-looking routine, afterward falling down into poses around the stage like a circle of wild mushrooms.

Then she entered, the Maria Tallchief of my adolescence, a-flutter in white, her hair done up under a white bathing cap with feathers on it, and a silly short net skirt, and white tights—and I finally understood what those strange shoes were for: she could walk on her toes. At fourteen still functioning almost entirely on the level of intuition and impression and hardly at all on knowledge, I wondered how many of those grown men hunched over their knees in the stadium were committing mental violence. Or did they just see Nadia as a childlike artist? Should art be sexy? I knew no one who could answer important questions.

Backstage after the show, with a modicum of foot tangling, I got Nadia to agree to let me stand us to shakes at the Eagle Drug and to walk her home, during which hour I learned the following: she had dedicated her life to Art, although not necessarily exclusively to The Dance; her chances were severely limited in this provincial town, but without money the opportunities to escape appeared nil, short of the desperate act of marriage to an older man who would never touch her body but send her to New York; and her father was dying of angina pectoris. The effect all this gloomy news had on me was temporarily dispiriting, inasmuch as, I like to think, at even so young an age I was not completely soulless.

We walked down her street, the cracked sidewalk reticular with light from the old lamps and the elm trees, the night a balmy companion. "In Russia, at my age I could be dancing in the *corps de ballet,* and if it weren't for this awful war, I might be there. Did you know the ballerinas practice so hard their toes bleed?"

I admitted that theretofore I hadn't this piece of information while trying not to expose my ignorance of ballet, which was complete except for what I'd learned that night.

"Mine never have, but that's probably because I am more of an electric dancer. I do all kinds—ballet, tap, *moderne,* which you have to be prepared for in this day and age." Nadia talked on about her protean talent, the discipline required, Isadora Duncan (a distant relative to Robin, she claimed), the moral necessity of consecrating her life to the larger principles, and her misfortune of being reared in the sticks, where there was little hope of ever finding a *danseur,* while I, though confused as usual by the mention of Robin Duncan, thought of worming around with her elastic body, kissing her bleeding toes if necessary.

"Why did you tell Mother you couldn't sing?" she asked.

"It just blurted out."

"Would you be ashamed to perform with us? Oh, I know," Nadia said, about the time we reached her front porch, "I know how people talk about her. A crazy nonconformist or something. Communist. I don't even know what a Communist is."

"Neither do I."

"Jannis tried to explain it to me, but what I think is, people, especially artistic people, shouldn't belong to any kind of fraction but rather the world. Music, art, The Dance, they all trans . . . transmute hateful boundaries—"

"Transcend."

"Even Germany. Or Japan, though I don't think they dance. You must feel this way too, Jed." She came up so close I could sense her heat, smell her dancer's body, then slipped away before I could react.

From beyond the screened door she reminded me of the long, arduous hours of rehearsal lying before her the next day. I suggested a werewolf movie at the Studio for the following night. That got her started again on the subject of artistic loneliness, the difficulty of finding a partner with sensitivity, although she was sure I had it because she'd observed me being sensitive at school.

"You have?"

"Lots of times."

"When, for instance?"

"Oh," she said. "I know."

This was more depressing information, on the one hand, for me to learn I possessed such transparent inner qualities, but I couldn't ignore the bright pleasure her saying so gave me.

"I couldn't ever feel deeply for any man who didn't share my beliefs in art."

"Come on back out here and let's talk some more about it."

But "Good night," she said, in a voice both strong and soft as flannel.

I lift down a fresh bottle of vodka for Robb, who has set up his drink-building equipment on the kitchen counter, iced glasses, silver stirrer, tomato juice, Worcestershire sauce, Tabasco, celery ribs. He believes vodka can be bruised by careless handling. Over the years I've watched him gradually substitute finesse and infinitely patient preparation for athletic speed and bravado. When he cooks Chinese, he can spend two hours chopping vegetables all into the same-sized pieces, laying them out according to density and color, even though they're all going to end up in the same wok. He *trims* his zucchini vines. For a long time he got around on prostheses, back when I called him Stone-Hinge, but for the past five years his balance has given way.

"Funny to think of dancing," he says, measuring his juices. "The last one I ever did was the jitterbug."

"With whom?"

"A sailor on the beach at Guadalcanal. So what did you tell her? About life and art."

"I decided to let the project rest. I gave her two and a half days to come to her senses."

On Friday, with Timmy, Sam, and Jo-Jo, I hiked up to Seven Falls and spent the afternoon swimming and goofing off, the gloaming charring hot dogs over a pine fire, and the early starry night listening to Jo-Jo make up lies from his sleeping bag about the sexual encounters he engaged in daily. He was advancing toward manhood at an awe-inspiring rate. Sam was famous for his scatological jokes, an unending repertoire. Gentle Timmy Hyde, the Baptist preacher's son, afraid even of saying the word *sex,* concentrated on amassing merit badges. That night he practiced tying knots in the dark.

And I? As the fire died and the others slept, I gazed at the stars, sequins on the skirt of night, and determined to keep both hands out of my bedroll, thinking alternately of black-haired Robin Duncan, whose face appeared solemn and unreachably older in the firelight, and Nadia Ranko, the two tumbled and confused. I wondered if this melancholy presentiment of loss was a part of love.

On Sunday morning I listened to the fat-lipped preacher drone on about, of all things, fornication and felt he knew my innermost thoughts. "Thou Shall Not Lie Carnally," was with Brother Hyde a leitmotif and Leviticus his favorite book. He expended a lot of energy in the pulpit emphasizing guilt, and I felt bad about not having any yet.

"God will not destroy the innocent at heart," the preacher said, trying—as I understood him—to both stamp on the head of sin and bolster the morale of those with boys in the war. The pronouncement did nothing for my peace of mind about the condition of my own corrupting insides, but maybe Robin Duncan would be protected by such a truth, as if he marched under an invisible, impregnable bell jar.

By two o'clock, on the Ranko porch again, I watched Nadia contort her limbs in the pink leotard and listened to her explain how hers was not a mere body but more of an organ, a mechanism meaningless without expression.

I was saved from having to untangle that biophysics problem by the appearance of Margrite, her entries (or in this case, exit) always like a flock of startled birds. "Isn't she beautiful," she trilled. "And you will say you knew her when." Margrite did one of her brief expressive dances down the length of the porch, only slightly encumbered by the zither under one arm. Whirling to a standstill in an old wicker settee and placing the instrument across her knees, she strummed it in a dark minor key. "Did you hear about the poor Duncan boy?" she said, beginning to pick out a dirge.

"No," I said. All my insides leapt. "Robin?"

"They just got word. Wounded in action."

"He's okay, though? He's not dead?"

"That's all they know. Wounded in action. You have a brother in the service, don't you?"

"Yeah, two of them." But *not Robin*.

Margrite Ranko played on two instruments at once, the zither and my heart. "Do you know this old song?" she said. "It was a favorite in the other war. When I was your age."

Of course I knew it. Everybody did.

Robb laughs when I tell him that part, how Margrite suckered me into singing for her. While she played the tune from World War One, I eased into the first verse. Then seeing the misty effect it caused, I slid right on into verses two, three, and four. "That was so touching," Nadia said in a vulnerable choked voice. She ran her light hand up and down the back of my arm where I hoped someday triceps would appear.

"Margrite told me I had a lovely singing voice."

"Fortunately," Robb says, "I don't know fuck about music. But I make a great drink. Here." He spins his chair around with one hand and offers me his concoction.

"Actually, I had two voices that year—high and low. I was considered invaluable in glee club."

"What did she make you wear—a tutu?"

"My specialty was 'Comin' in on a Wing and a Prayer,' ingrate. For guys like you. My Boy Scout uniform sufficed."

And I resisted another of Margrite's dreams—becoming a dancing foil for Nadia, despite the proximity into which such a role would have placed me, legitimately, with her body. I don't know, maybe I'd have taken up the challenge had not two explosions occurred on the other side of the world just then, on August 6 and 9, 1945, blowing out of perspective for a long time any idea of life as entertainment.

The war was over. And I had other intimations, barely forming, that my singing on Margrite's programs for a month with two d's in my name, sharing top billing with the star, was not so much for Nadia's attentions as it was a way of thinking of Robb Duncan, fallen, yes, still of course unattainable, about whom it was impossible to believe, as the rumors said, he would never again chase a ball.

"But I make a hell of a Bloody Mary," he says, spinning in his chair. "Now knock off the melancholy shit and let's go out in the garden."

While the victory ash settled, another school year began with new diversions, the boys coming home—those who survived—gradually, Nadia fading again into her rapt gray silence. I faced the likelihood of a long continuing struggle against virginity and second-year Spanish verbs, the limitations of a small cowboy town, but most of all, the insoluble mystery of the innocent heart.

In Skull Valley, out in back of the house about twenty-five yards, along a different path than the one leading to the toilet, the junk pile gathered, decade by decade, the place where my beautiful iridescent fish cans finally ended, and broken plates, Eloine's milk-of-magnesia and Pond's cold cream jars, iodine bottles with skull and crossbones, inedible garbage, wrecked toys, an irredeemable mattress in which mice flourished with such merriment you could almost imagine them smiling. Did you know mother mice will kill their babies if you bother them too much?—for reasons I must leave to Stephen Jay Gould. The shack was torn down soon after Eloine fled with her two younger boys, after the Dad died, but the junkyard remained, a midden to a family life only a hundred yards from the Indian midden, down by the pond, where Grandma Shoup collected arrowheads and communed with Brahms. Not long ago, but sixty years later, Billy and I hiked back to the old place (the road has almost disappeared but not quite) and contemplatively turned over rusty shards of this and that with our boot toes, still able to identify nearly every bottle unbroken, each rusted pan discarded when it could no longer be soldered, or curiously bent piece of metal.

The pack rat's nest is still there, a few yards up the rocky hill. You might not know that they—biological naturalists—have learned through carbon-14 dating that a single pack rat's nest may be occupied (presumably by a succession of generations) continually for as long as ten thousand years. Probably no human dwelling anywhere on earth can compare with that. The nest interior, furthermore, is divided into a three- or four-room apartment, one space for nursery, one for pantry, one for toilet, and another for general get-togethers. The house is run by the female, the male having fled—yawn—after working his will with her, so while the exterior may seem male in its disordered appearance, it is not. One presumes he, unencumbered, flits from place to place as suits the moment. The nests, above ground, are made of sticks, cactus parts, other discouraging stickery building materials making them virtually unassailable, and shiny things like foil from cigarette packs and the fork forgotten at the picnic.

Although the heavenly tree has proliferated into a small forest, and the yellow rose hedge has finally given up—though it lived on for years and years as my periodic visits proved, as if waiting for some sort of explanation—the view remains, a bucolic landscape, a painter's dream. From the place where the house stood, snugged against a rocky hill, the scrubby slope still eases down to Patterson's pasture, green with underground water, speckled with white-faced cows and a horse or two, as if nothing has changed in half a century, then beyond, the gray hills back up to the big peak beyond which the town of Prescott lies. And Arizona skies. There's nothing so cerulean blue, no clouds so stately white.

And as for cottonwoods needing a creek bank to shelter, there's no better tree for memory, just turning their leaves to Fall. But, as Robin Duncan would say, or Janet Kincaid, cut the sentiment. Let's go to The Palace and salute the lion.

Remnant (Old French *remanoir,* to remain)

About the Author

JOHN WESTON grew up in Skull Valley and Prescott, Arizona, about which he writes in *Dining at the Lineman's Shack*. He attended Arizona State University in Tempe, where he majored in music, and later the University of Arizona in Tucson, where he became a teacher of creative writing in the English Department and Director of the Poetry Center, before moving on to California State University, Los Angeles, from which he retired as Professor of English.

He is the author of six books of fiction, two produced plays, a book of poetry, and numerous short works of fiction, reviews, and criticism.

Among his distinctions over a long career have been Scholar at Bread Loaf Writers Conference; Andrew Mellon Visiting Professor of Creative Writing, California Polytechnic University; John Hay Fellow at Yale University; John Hay Fellow at Williams College; John Hay Fellow at the University of Oregon; Visiting Professor, Université de Clermont-Ferrand; and Visiting Professor, Université de Marseille at Aix-en-Provence. He was named Outstanding Professor at the University of Arizona and later at California State University. He has appeared at numerous writers' conferences, including those at Indiana University, Cal Tech, and Pima College (Arizona).

Since retirement, he has continued his devotion to music, writing, the visual arts, cooking, and travel. The city of Lake Oswego, Oregon, where he lived for a time, named him Outstanding Citizen of the Year (1999) for his work in public art in that town. He now lives in Palm Desert, California, with his longtime companion, Jim, where he actively pursues his several interests in the arts.